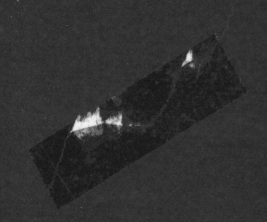

CRICKET'S STRANGEST MATCHES

Other titles in the STRANGEST series

CRICKET'S STRANGEST MATCHES

Extraordinary but true stories from
over a century of cricket

ANDREW WARD

PORTICO

This edition published in 2018 by
Portico, an imprint of Pavilion Books Company Ltd
43 Great Ormond Street
London
WC1N 3HZ

First published in the United Kingdom in 2016

ISBN 978-1-91162-201-7

A CIP catalogue record for this book is available from the British Library.

10 9 8 7 6 5 4 3 2 1

Reproduction by Colourdepth UK
Printed and bound by 1010 Printing International Ltd, China

This book can be ordered direct from the publisher at
www.pavilionbooks.com, or try your local bookshop

CONTENTS

Things never turn out in Cricket as one expects.

(Talbot Baines Reed, English writer, 1852–93)

A GREAT
SINGLE-WICKET GAME
LEEDS, OCTOBER 1857

Single-wicket games were exceptionally popular in the nineteenth century, when transport systems were undeveloped and getting 22 players in one place was not easy. Also, they offered ample opportunities for betting on specific individuals. It was cricket's answer to boxing.

Like boxing, however, not all the matches went the distance. A two-innings match in Tasmania, between Babington and Newbury in October 1896, lasted only four balls, a wicket falling on each ball. Other single-wicket games were totally one-sided. In 1820, Budd (70 and 30) beat Brande (0 and 0) after tactically knocking down his own wicket in each innings so as to prevent the possibility of too much stiffness when bowling. The big-publicity match in May 1838, played at Town Mailing between Alfred Mynn and James Dearman for a purse of 100 guineas, attracted 5,000 spectators, who were largely disappointed by the spectacle if not the betting. Mynn scored 34 and 89, Dearman managed 0 and very few. Double-wicket or treble-wicket competitions, that is, two or three a side, were generally reckoned to be more entertaining. One of the most unusual double-wicket games was played near Rickmansford in May 1827, when a man and his thoroughbred sheepdog beat two Middlesex gentlemen.

There were no complaints about the excitement generated by the match at Kirkstall, Leeds, in October 1857, when

John Grange of Dacre Banks played against James Sadler of Leeds. Each player was allowed one fielder. Grange chose William Swain, the Richmond professional, who coached him before the event. Sadler chose George Atkinson, but Joseph Appleyard had to deputise for the latter when the game went into a second and third day.

The game started at 11.45a.m. on Tuesday 15 October. Grange, batting first, lasted two and a half hours. In that time he faced 159 balls, made 80 hits, scored 17 runs off the bat and collected ten more for wides. The dearth of runs was caused by the rules of the day, which compelled a batsman to cover a distance of 40 yards (36.6m) to complete a run. Grange was out when Atkinson caught him at mid-off.

When Sadler went in, Swain fielded like two men. On one occasion he ran flat out in an attempt to catch a skier, avoiding a spectator on the way before lunging desperately at the ball, and tearing off a nail from his little finger in the process of not quite making the catch.

As news of the game spread around the district, hundreds left work at Kirkstall Forge and made their way to the Victoria Ground, Woodhouse Moor, where, with blackened faces, they stood watching with interest and money at stake. 'This match (it was stated) caused more excitement in Leeds and its neighbourhood than any other contest for the last 20 years,' documented *MCC Cricket Scores and Biographies*. Sadler amassed 24 runs off 93 balls, and was three behind on first innings. The stakes were £50 per side.

The game resumed the next morning, and Sadler began with underhand daisy-cutters, soon switching to overarm. Rain stopped play when Grange reached 21, and play was held over until the third day.

On the Saturday, the weather fine, Grange took his score to 24, made off 96 balls, setting Sadler 28 to win. On the fourteenth ball a huge shout for leg-before-wicket went up, and tension ran high. The appeal was turned down. On the eighteenth ball, Sadler hit the ball high and far. The ball hung in the air for a long time. Grange's coach and fielder, William Swain, tore after the ball once again, running a long, long way – 40 yards (36.6m) according to *Bell's Life* – before catching it with his left hand and landing with his back resting against the fence. He had won the game for his student.

GRANGE

John Grange c Atkinson b Sadler	17	c and b Sadler	22
Wides	10		227
	<u>27</u>		<u>24</u>

SADLER

James Sadler b Grange	20	c Swain b Granger	3
Wides	4		0
	<u>24</u>		<u>3</u>

CRICKET ON ICE
CAMBRIDGE, DECEMBER 1878

The fields of the Fens were full of water, and the water froze. People took to skating and races were organised across the smooth fields.

But there was one other sport, which generated interest during the cold winter of 1878–9, a sport that automatically comes to mind when looking out of frosty windows on to a field of perfect ice in the midst of a harsh winter. Yes, it was, of course, cricket.

The Cambridge University term had ended, so Charles Pigg challenged a team from the town to a game on an ideal icy field at Grantchester Meadows, scene of Chaucer's 'The Reeve's Tale' and close to the residence (in different eras) of Rupert Brooke and Jeffrey Archer. The Town–Gown game was played over three days on a wicket, which didn't show the slightest sign of wearing badly. No fast bowling was allowed. The umpires were severe on anything other than lobs.

The Town batted first and the scoring was heavy. The renowned Robert Carpenter opened the innings and helped himself to the first 50 of the match. Charles Pigg, the Gown captain, gave his team two overs each in order to assess what they could do. He eventually settled on Lilley and Boucher as his mainstream lob attack. Boucher, writing to *The Times* 50 years later, recalled a sweet moment when he lobbed up a full toss to Dan Hayward when the crack batsman was going strong. Hayward, forming strong images of how the ball would look in the next county, swung heartily and overbalanced on the ice. The ball bowled him, and the 12-man Town team were all out for 328. I should think the Gown captain would have opted for a light roller if he had had a choice.

The Gown batted and were 61 for one at close of play on the second day. Fielders chased and slid across the ice in exhilarating fashion as they tried to keep down the Gown score. Three of the first five batsmen raced to fifties, and the two Piggs put together a solid fifth-wicket stand. Time ran out when the Gown team needed another 55 runs for victory with seven wickets standing. The game was an honourable draw.

That was only one of a number of games on ice that winter. Cricket on ice has occasionally been revived since, such as the game between Broadwater Park and Charterhouse in 1895 (see *The Carthusian* for March, 1895), but conditions abroad are often more favourable than in Britain. Cricket in a frozen fiord, or on a Swiss lake, would really be something, but a word of caution. It needs specially qualified umpires to test the thickness of the ice.

CAMBRIDGE TOWN	
R. Carpenter c Scott b Boucher	89
W. Thurston run out	37
F. Pryor c Scott b Boucher	13
J. Warrington b Lilley	1
G. Hoppett b Lilley	3
J. Fordham b Wawn	42
H. Mason c Wawn b Lilley	9
W. Newman run out	65
A. Fromant lbw b Lilley	19
W. Richardson b Lilley	0
D. Hayward b Boucher	41
J. Cain not out	9
	328

CAMBRIDGE GOWN	
von E. Scott run out	88
Lilley b Newman	6
W. Deedes b Newman	56
A. D. Wawn c and b Carpenter	7
H. Pigg not out	69
C. Pigg not out	34
Extras	14
	274–4

SMOKERS AGAINST NON-SMOKERS

MELBOURNE, AUSTRALIA, MARCH 1887

The 1886–7 England touring party divided neatly into smokers and non-smokers. Rather than end the tour with a game against a Combined Australia team, who would be without key players from New South Wales, it was decided to repeat the final game of 1884, between Smokers and Non-Smokers, supplementing the touring players with local Victorians. In 1884, the Non-Smokers had won by nine wickets; W.G. Grace, E.M. Grace and Charlie Bannerman were all non-smokers, whereas Spofforth, Lord Harris and Charlie Thornton all dabbled in the weed.

This time, at the East Melbourne ground, the outcome was a record-breaking game, which was also an early example of sponsorship. Four companies put up prizes. Saqui offered 500 cigars for the highest batting score on the Smokers' team. Jacobs, Hart & Co. offered 500 cigars for the best bowling on the Smokers' team. Kronheimer and Co. offered 250 cigars for the highest aggregate batting score among the Smokers and another 250 for the highest individual score in the match. White & Co. put up 200 cigars and a trophy for the best bowling in the Non-Smokers' team. You might say that the game had a lot of ashes at stake.

Harry Boyle, captaining the Smokers, lost the toss. He led on to the field a collection of Australian and English players who were all smoking cigars. They stubbed them out before the game started.

The Smokers were reckoned to have the better bowling team, and there were no better than George Lohmann and Johnny Briggs, but the wicket was so good that all bowling became mediocre as the Non-Smokers piled up the runs. Halfway through the afternoon, Briggs, the Smokers' chief workhorse, is reported as saying 'I believe one ball in my last over nearly broke a quarter of an inch [0.6cm].' Bruce hit his way to 131 out of 191, scoring the only six of the innings, Bates scored four, and Shrewsbury and Gunn settled into their mammoth third-wicket stand. The day ended with the Non-Smokers on 422 for two. Amazingly, there were no extras.

The next day, Shrewsbury (236) and Gunn (150) took their stand to 310 before the third wicket fell at 514 – a good start. There was a chance of not only exceeding the record first-class score for an innings but also the highest in any match, believed to be Orleans' 920 against Rickling Green in August 1882, and this against some of the best bowling in the world. With the help of good knocks from the later-order Australians, the score reached 792 for eight by the close of the second day, the halfway stage of the game. The innings was closed, however, early the next morning, at 803 for nine, made from 1,209 balls, the first score of over 800 in first-class cricket. The score might have been higher had it not been for Bates suffering from a heavy cold, Barlow limping with an injured foot and Billy Barnes, a very capable batsman who averaged 23.38 in his Test career and was third in the averages in this tour, being unable to bat with an injured hand. Two days in the field had tired the Smokers, who were described in one report as 'puffed out'.

Yet, at the end of the third day, when the Smokers were 302 for three, the match was destined for a draw. Even when the Smokers collapsed on the final morning – the last seven wickets made only 54 runs – there was little hope of a tangible result, and attendance at the game, which had been around 500 on the first day, was down to about 100.

The major interest centred on the prizes. Shrewsbury and Palmer won the batting prizes, Briggs and Bates those for bowling, but there was one other trophy, which caused a surprising, incident at the end of the match.

The last ball was bowled to William Scotton, the Nottinghamshire left-handed stone-waller who had been so miffed at the start of the first Smokers' innings, when told he would bat low in the order, that he stormed out of the ground to calm down. Scotton played the last ball of the match gently towards point and ran after it immediately to salvage it as a keepsake. Sherwin, the Non-Smokers' wicket-keeper, also a Notts player, raced him. Scotton won and picked up the ball. But, as umpire Wood had not called 'over', someone appealed. Umpire Phillips gave Scotton out, 'handled the ball'. Not that Scotton really minded. He had the match-ball as a souvenir, and if all worked out well, perhaps Briggs or Palmer would offer him a cigar from their winnings.

NON-SMOKERS

A. Shrewsbury c Duffy b Briggs	236
W. Bruce lbw b Palmer	131
W. Bates b Palmer	4
W. Gunn b Boyle	150
R.G. Barlow b Palmer	29
R. Houston c and b Briggs	57
H. Musgrove st Lewis b Briggs	62
J. Worrall b Read	78
W.H. Cooper c and b Briggs	46
M. Sherwin not out	5
W. Barnes absent	0
Extras (3 byes, 1 wide, 1 leg-bye)	5
	803

Bowling: (4-ball overs): Briggs 55.1–11–141–4, Palmer 54–10–189–3, Boyle 31–14–60–1, Lohmann 48–16–113–0, Flowers 38–12–93–0, Scotton 26–4–82–0, Duffy 15–2–52–0, Read 26–10–43–1, Walters 9–4–25–0.

Fall of wickets: 196, 204, 514, 524, 575, 656, 686, 788, 803.

SMOKERS

J.M. Read st Sherwin b Cooper	30	
G.E. Palmer c Worrall b Bruce	11	(1) c Houston b Worrall ..24
J. Briggs c Shrewsbury b Bates	86	(2) st Sherwin b Bates 54
W. Flowers run out	69	(3) b Houston 25
G. Lohmann c Sub (Briggs) b Bates	19	(5) lbw b Gunn 2
W. Scotton c Bruce b Bates	11	(4) handled ball 18
H. F. Boyle b Bruce	7	(6) not out 0
G. Browning b Bates	1	
F. Walters st Sherwin b Bates	0	
P. Lewis c Houston b Bates	2	
W. Duffy not out	0	
Extras	18	12
	356	**135–5**

Bowling: *First Innings*; Bates 49–18–73–6, Cooper 29–5–85–1, Bruce 36.3–10–92–2, Worrall 15–7–30–0, Gunn 12–4–27–0, Houston 9–2–31–0. *Second Innings*; Bates 21–8–40–1, Barnes 8–3–14–0, Bruce 14–7–15–0, Worrall 12–5–22–1, Cooper 4–0–18–0, Gunn 6–5–1–1, Houston 5–1–13–1, Shrewsbury 1–1–0–0.

GETTING
THEMSELVES OUT
NOTTINGHAM, MAY AND JUNE 1887

Nottinghamshire, the 1886 County Champions, played host to the much-improved Surrey team, which had its eye on the 1887 Championship. In fact this game went some distance towards helping Surrey win the title.

On the first day only 163 runs were scored on a slow wicket. Surrey, shaken by the unknown fast bowler Mee, slumped to 27 for six and then partially recovered to reach 115. Nottinghamshire were 48 for two at the close of play, seemingly in control.

The second day belonged to Surrey. Bowley and Lohmann bowled them to a first-innings lead of 26 runs, and Bobby Abel batted over three and a half hours in an anchor role. Surrey ended the day on 157 for three.

Wisden described the last day as 'a curious and most interesting day's cricket'. Rain delayed the start, then caused a 15-minute interruption, before Surrey settled in to bat well ... too well, because the team looked like batting through to the close and the game appeared a certain draw. A big stand by the two Reads took the score to 264 before the fourth and fifth wickets fell within two balls, Maurice Read bowled for 28, W.W. Read caught at long slip for 92. It was then that John Shuter, the Surrey captain, activated his contentious tactic.

It was not for another two years that the option of declarations was introduced, so it was up to Nottinghamshire to bowl out Surrey, until Shuter devised his alternative plan. Why couldn't Surrey get themselves out?

Shuter set a captain's example, leading from the front. After swashbuckling ten runs very quickly he deliberately swatted his own wicket as Mee sent down the ball. The crowd thought it very funny, but they didn't see the cunning behind his plan.

The other Surrey batsmen hardly concealed their intentions – hit and get out. Jones made a couple and clouted his own stumps, Wood and Beaumont strolled down the track and gave wicket-keeper Mordecai Sherwin, the Nottinghamshire captain, plenty of time to stump them, and Lohmann knocked up a friendly catch. The last seven wickets fell for 25 runs. But this meant that Surrey now had time to bowl out Nottinghamshire.

After a delay for rain, George Lohmann was among the wickets again. With 45 minutes to play, Nottinghamshire were 133 for seven but Sherwin and Gunn looked to have their batting under control. Lohmann broke through 25 minutes before the close with the valuable wicket of William Gunn, who had made 72. Sherwin and Shacklock soon followed. The game was over at 17 minutes past six. Surrey had won because of sacrificing their wickets, a tactic which created much controversy.

SURREY

Batsman	1st innings	2nd innings
Mr K.J. Key	lbw b Attewell ... 4	b Shacklock ... 42
R. Abel	c Barnes b Attewell ... 0	run out ... 44
Mr W.E. Roller	b Mee ... 4	b Flowers ... 53
Mr W.W. Read	b Mee ... 7	c Butler b Flowers ... 92
Maurice Read	c Daft b Attewell ... 48	b Mee ... 28
Mr J. Shuter	b Mee ... 0	hit wkt b Mee ... 10
Lohmann	c Sherwin b Attewell ... 1	c Attewell b Flowers ... 6
Wood	c Sherwin b Shacklock ... 36	st Sherwin b Mee ... 3
G. Jones	c Sherwin b Attewell ... 5	hit wkt b Flowers ... 2
J. Beaumont	not out ... 7	st Sherwin b Flowers ... 4
T. Bowley	c Gunn b Flowers ... 0	not out ... 0
Extras	3	5
	115	289

Bowling: *First Innings*; Attewell 37–27–36–5, Mee 51–27–52–3, Shacklock
13–8–17–1, Flowers 11.3–6–7–1. *Second Innings*; Attewell 46–29–45–0, Mee
25–9–41–3, Shacklock 50–26–51–1, Flowers 41–23–55–5, Barnes 40–15–64–0,
Gunn 4–0–8–0, Scotton 7–2–13–0, Mr H.B. Daft 11–6–7–0.

NOTTINGHAMSHIRE

W. Scotton b Lohmann	20	b Lohmann	12
A. Shrewsbury c Abel b Bowley	17	c and b Bowley	5
W. Barnes b Bowley	1	b Lohmann	15
W. Gunn c Roller b Bowley	8	lbw b Lohmann	72
W. Flowers b Bowley	6	b Lohmann	3
Mr H.B. Daft b Lohmann	6	c Abel b Jones	12
F. Butler b Lohmann	0	run out	5
W. Attewell b Lohmann	6	b Beaumont	12
Shacklock b Lohmann	8	c Sub b Roller	1
M. Sherwin run out	12	c Wood b Lohmann	13
R. Mee not out	0	not out	0
Extras	5		9
	89		159

Bowling: *First Innings*; Lohmann 47.2–27–39–5, Beaumont 12–10–4–0, Bowley
51–41–25–4, Mr Roller 6–2–14–0, Jones 10–9–2–0. *Second Innings*; Lohmann
60–31–66–5, Beaumont 22–13–28–1, Bowley 36–21–36–1, Mr Roller 3–2–1–1,
Jones 10–6–12–1, Abel 3–1–7–0.

A TEAM OF '50
OR MORE FARMERS'
YATTON, NEAR BRISTOL, OCTOBER 1887

It is a rare game that has as many as 23 ducks in one innings, but here we have an example. The game was billed as Yatton against '50 or more farmers' and there is little indication of how many farmers turned up to play the regular cricketers. The scorecard shows that 41 batted, and the Yatton bowling figures must have been impressive.

The wickets were shared between eight bowlers, Radcliffe taking 11, Chamberlayne and Gage five each, Blew and Shiner four apiece, Atherton three, Winter two and Clapp one. Five batsmen were run out, and there was an amazing dearth of catches, unless the scorecard fails to record the full details of the innings.

It is unlikely that all the 40-plus farmers fielded during the Yatton innings. That would have been some field for a radio commentator to describe. Yatton, a team including some renowned local cricketers, batted to make 75 for six (including two men retired) so we can assume the game was a draw.

The scorecard is reproduced from *Cricket* (27 October 1887), which also includes a brief background to the game: 'Mr Tankerville Chamberlayne, of Cranbury Park, Manchester, and of yachting renown, who has for many years done so much by purse and presence to uphold and support cricket, both in Hampshire and Somerset, was again to the fore on Friday October 14, at his pretty seat at Yatton, near Bristol, catering for his many guests with unbounded liberality. This was the third successive year of the festivities. The day was very cold, but this did not deter the many hundreds of both gentlemen and ladies attending and witnessing the novel sight, and partaking of the good things provided. Nearly 300 sat down to luncheon, the self-esteemed host presiding, supported by the well-known amateur cricketer, Mr O.G. Radcliffe, Rev. O. Puckridge, Frank Wills, J.H. Fowler ... About 500 partook of tea and indulged in the dancing until a late hour.'

This is just one example of a game of unbalanced teams, some of which were responsible for what now appear as astonishing bowling figures. Perhaps the most sensational was Johnny Briggs's 15 for four (match figures of 27 for 23) against 22 of the Cape Mounted Riflemen at Williams Town, South Africa, in 1888–9. As late as 1923 MCC beat 15 of Northern Orange Free State by an innings and 35 runs.

The many early matches where numbers were unbalanced include an All England XI's victory by an innings against 33 of Norfolk on Swaffham Racecourse in 1797 and Lord Winterton's XI against 37 Labourers at Shillinglee Park in 1843, the Lord's team winning by five wickets. Three years later, Lord Winterton's XI took on 56 Labourers and this game was drawn.

THE FARMERS

Marshall b Chamberlayne 20
B. Burgess run out 1
Hawkins b Radcliffe 0
J. Pavey run out 0
J. Hill b Radcliffe 0
S.B. Griffin run out 2
J. Edgell c Clapp b Radcliffe 2
A. Williams c and b Radcliffe 4
T. Price c and b Radcliffe 0
A. Osmond b Chamberlayne 0
T. Champion b Radcliffe 0
W. Cavill b Chamberlayne 0
H. Wall b Gage 0
W. Marsh b Radcliffe 0
R. Wilcox b Gage 0
M.H. Thatcher b Winter 0
W. Gill b Clapp 11
J. Wallis b Winter 0
W. Hennessy b Gage 0
R. Harding b Blew 0
F.W. Wills run out 1
C. Burgess b Clapp 0
J. Gage b Clapp 10
G. Hardwick b Blew 3
W. Luff b Blew 0
G. Badman b Blew 0
S.M. Harding run out 2
A. Batt b Radcliffe 4
T. Pearce b Shiner 12
C. Griffin b Radcliffe 0
H. Morgan b Shiner 0
T. Nicholls b Radcliffe 2
A. Hardwick b Shiner 0
A. Williams b Radcliffe 1
C. Sayer b Atherton 2
J. Bisder b Shiner 2
C. Young b Atherton 0
H. Macey b Atherton 0
W. Petheran b Gage 4
J.H. Fowler b Gage 0
S. Hurley not out 1
Extras 8
92

YATTON

C. Knowles b Luff 7
A.E. Clapp retired 20
E.W. Blew c Gill b Luff 18
H. Gage retired 23
T. Chamberlayne b Luff 0
W.A. Winter run out 3
W.H. Shiner not out 1
Extras 3
75–6

24

A.J. Atherton, C.R. Knowles, O.G. Radcliffe and B. Crossman did not bat.

THE DRESSING-ROOM FLOOD

DEWSBURY, JUNE 1899

Apart from the unusual setting (by today's expectations), there was little odd about this county championship game between Yorkshire and Derbyshire until the final day. In beautiful weather, in front of a 7,000 crowd, Yorkshire put on a fine batting display on the first day and scored 343 in four-and-a-half hours. Derbyshire's toil in the field was not helped by Young's late arrival at lunchtime. A substitute was used for the first session.

Derbyshire retained optimism for a draw at the end of the first day (36 for one) and again at lunchtime on the second day (197 for six) when Storer was 96 not out, but the last four wickets mustered a mere six runs after lunch. Derbyshire, 140 runs behind, followed on.

Derbyshire's second innings (171 all out) narrowly averted the innings defeat and ended just before the close of play on the second day. Yorkshire required only 32 for victory on the final day. If the Derbyshire team prayed for rain, that was certainly what they received, but the rain came in the worst possible place – the dressing room.

On the Friday night, after the second day's play, the water in the pavilion was turned off at the mains. Unfortunately a tap upstairs, in the catering department, was left turned on. The next morning, when the mains was switched back on at 6a.m., water began to pour through the open tap upstairs. The groundstaff, working on the ground, didn't notice.

The upper room was quickly flooded. Water seeped through the floor to the room below, which was the dressing-room for the away-team professionals. Nine Derbyshire players – the two amateurs changed separately – got the rain they prayed for, all over their cricket gear. It was like a shower-bath, covering the whole room and running down the walls, and, because the floor was a few inches below the level of the door, the water collected like that in a swimming-pool. When the Derbyshire professionals arrived for work, later that Saturday morning, they discovered saturated cricket gear unfit for human wear.

What should they do now? The Dewsbury officials were very apologetic, but Yorkshire still needed 32 to win and Derbyshire had no cricket clothes to wear. Fortunately, common sense prevailed, given the state of the game, and Derbyshire agreed to take the field wearing ordinary clothes. Had Yorkshire needed, say, 250 on the final day, it might have been an interesting debate.

'It was out of no disrespect to Yorkshire that the Derbyshire professionals turned out in their every-day clothes,' pointed out the *Dewsbury Reporter*, 'but because they themselves were the victims of an unfortunate accident which soaked their white apparel and seriously damaged not a little of their cricketing material in the way of boots, bats, etc.'

The wet clothing was hung out on every conceivable clothes-line and clothes-rack around the Dewsbury ground. Flannels and shirts fluttered in the breeze, sweaters were strewn across the pavilion rails, and boots and equipment littered the grass around. Nine professionals wearing everyday clothes, and two amateurs clad in proper gear took the field to stop Yorkshire making 32 runs in a day. The amateurs had to bowl. They were the only players with boots that could grip the surface.

The fielders rolled up their sleeves but exercised caution in case they grass-stained their trousers. Mr Higson, a reasonably regular bowler, took a wicket. Mr Wright, an irregular bowler, conceded some runs. Yorkshire won by nine wickets and the Derbyshire players hung around, waiting for clothes to dry. Harry Bagshaw's pullover shrank so much that it wouldn't have fitted a small boy.

Rumour suggests that a stranger wandered into the Dewsbury ground that Saturday morning.

'Who's playing?' he asked.

'Yorkshire and Derbyshire.'

'Which is which?'

'Yorkshire are in white.'

There has been one other occasion when a county team took to the field wearing ordinary clothes, in 1930, when Hampshire needed one to win at the start of the third day of their match against Nottinghamshire.

YORKSHIRE

Mr J.T. Brown sen, c Humphries b Hulme ... 16	b Higson 13
J. Tunnicliffe c Wright b Berwick 43	not out 19
L. Whitehead c Higson b Storer 25	not out 1
Mr F.S. Jackson c Humphries b Bestwick 82	
Mr F. Mitchell lbw b Berwick 11	
E. Wainwright b Bestwick 46	
Lord Hawke b Berwick 8	
G.H. Hirst not out 63	
S. Haigh b Berwick 2	
W. Rhodes c Humphries b Berwick 12	
D. Hunter c Humphries b Bestwick 10	
Extras 25	
343	33–1

Bowling: *First Innings*; Hulme 34–4–75–1, Bestwick 27–7–44–3, Hancock 21–4–48–0, Storer 11–1–39–1, Berwick 25–3–82–5, Higson 5–0–22–0, Young 5–2–8–0. *Second Innings*; Higson 4.3–0–10–1, Wright 4–0–23–0.

DERBYSHIRE

Mr L.G. Wright b Rhodes	4	c Hirst b Wainwright	22
H. Bagshaw c Jackson b Haigh	15	b Hirst	40
W. Storer lbw b Jackson	96	c Rhodes b Hirst	33
W. Ellis b Haigh	0	c Hawke b Hirst	11
Mr T.A. Higson c Hunter b Rhodes	31	c Rhodes b Hirst	6
J. Hancock b Whitehead b Rhodes	0	c Hunter b Rhodes	14
J. Hulme b Hirst	38	c Wainwright b Rhodes	16
Berwick not out	11	c Haigh b Hirst	1
J.H. Young c Tunnicliffe b Rhodes	0	c and b Rhodes	0
J. Humphries c Hirst b Rhodes	0	not out	12
W. Bestwick b Jackson	2	st Hunter b Rhodes	8
Extras	6		8
	203		171

Bowling: *First Innings*; Rhodes 32–12–65–5, Haigh 21–6–49–2, Jackson 17.3–6–39–2, Wainwright 8–3–18–0, Hirst 16–6–26–1. *Second Innings*; Rhodes 14.2–4–50–4, Jackson 9–4–12–0, Wainwright 15–5–29–1, Hirst 24–4–57–5, Whitehead 4–0–15–0.

THE FIRST NETTING-BOUNDARY GAME

LORD'S, MAY 1900

The game between MCC & Ground and Nottinghamshire, played at Lord's in the first week of May, 1900, was the first under the experimental netting-boundary rules and the last under the old follow-on rule (120 rather than 150 behind).

Netting, 2–3ft (61–91cm) high, was erected all the way around the Lord's boundary. If the ball reached the netting, two runs were added to all the batsmen ran. If the ball cleared the netting, only three runs were scored. The system was designed to reward gentle ground-strokes rather than slogs or powerful hits. The ageing Arthur Shrewsbury, pre-judging the idea (or perhaps realising the extra running involved?) decided not to take part in the game.

Nottinghamshire, also missing Gunn and Attewell, batted first on a dry, firm wicket. Their total of 249 was considered good for so early in the season. The fielding team admitted to being tired at the end, as there was no such thing as a lazy stroll towards the boundary to collect the ball from a spectator after a four had been scored; everything had to be chased. The fielders were thankful that there weren't any exceptionally long partnerships.

It was a perverse reward system. Dench heaved one ball into the grandstand for three, whereas, on several other occasions, an edge through the slips sent the ball rolling up to the netting for six or seven runs. By the end of the day, when MCC were 111 for nine, there weren't many takers for the netting idea. It was also a nuisance for the incoming and outgoing batsmen, who had to step over the netting to walk on to the field. 'This MCC scheme of netting the boundaries has been tried and has failed,' reported *The Times* after that first day's play.

When play resumed on the second morning, MCC needed a further 19 runs to avoid the follow-on (whereas they would have been safe under the new law). They failed by five, so batted again, avoiding an innings defeat but setting Nottinghamshire a comfortable target of 60 runs. At 6.30p.m., when 25 were still needed, it was decided to play out the game that evening.

Despite opposition from participants in this first match, the netting-boundary idea was given a fair trial before it was rejected. Later that month, Storer hit an undefeated 175 for Derbyshire against MCC & Ground, but that achievement was overshadowed by a bizarre event in the same innings. While scoring 43, Wood collected ten of his runs in one hit from a ball by Burnup. Had the system been received more favourably, the game just wouldn't have been the same again.

NOTTINGHAMSHIRE

Mr A.O. Jones c Bromley-Martin (E.) b Trott... 47	c Trott b Hearne (J.T.) 4
Mr G.J. Groves c and b Young 28	not out 36
Mr W.B. Goodacre b Young 0	c Russell b Hearne (J.T.) 4
Dench lbw b Trott 29	not out 8
Carlin c and b Relf 23	
Mason c Russell b Relf 15	
Guttridge c Somerset b Trott 0	
J. Gunn not out 53	
Iremonger b Hearne (J.T.) 31	
Mr J.C. Snaith c Carpenter b Young 21	
T. Wass b Young 0	
Extras 2	 8
249	60–2

Bowling: *First Innings*; Young 20.2–7–48–4, Trott 34–11–111–3, Hearne (J.T.) 24–7–65–1, Relf 10–5–17–2, Hearne (A) 4–3–6–0.

MCC

Mr C.W. Wright b Wass	0	c Snaith b Gun	0
Mr G. Bromley-Martin b Wass	10	b Gunn	9
A. Hearne b Gunn	2	b Wass	3
Carpenter b Gunn	6	c Carlin b Gunn	15
A.E. Trott c Carlin b Gunn	7	st Carlin b Gunn	53
Mr E. Bromley-Martin b Wass	32	c and b Gunn	7
Relf b Gunn	3	not out	48
Mr A.F. Somerset not out	29	b Wass	23
Russell c Carlin b Wass	5	b Wass	15
J.T. Hearne c Groves b Gunn	6	b Wass	0
Young c Carlin b Gunn	17	run out	1
Extras	8		9
	125		**183**

Bowling: *First Innings*; Wass 23–5–43–4, Gunn 27–6–67–6, Dench 4–0–7–0.
Second Innings; Wass 19.3–0–84–4, Gunn 26–6–67–5, Dench 7–1–23–0.

REACHING EADY HEIGHTS
HOBART, AUSTRALIA,
MARCH AND APRIL, 1902

The game between Break o' Day and Wellington, arranged to decide the Tasmanian championship, was a one-innings match which took place on four Saturdays – 8 March, 15 March, 22 March and 5 April. The committee decided that the result wouldn't be valid until each team had completed at least one innings. That led to a bizarre final Saturday, when the Wellington team (including three substitutes) turned up to allow Break o' Day to complete their innings with the result predetermined. However, that final Saturday permitted an astonishing record which still stands.

Wellington's Kenny Burn won the toss and opened his team's batting. Good wicket, good weather, and good batting from Burn, but, at the other end, wickets fell fairly regularly. By stumps on the first Saturday, Wellington were 218 for six. Burn had reached his century, while Eady, making his first impact on the game, had five wickets.

The third Saturday took the game into the realms of fantasy. Wellington had by now completed their innings, Burn performing heroically, and Break o' Day finally overhauled the Wellington total of 277 before assaulting the record books. Burn was absent with illness on this particular Saturday, so he didn't see Abbott join Eady with the score on 312 for six. Abbott was out before scoring a run, but the umpire, unable to see Abbott's stroke, gave him the benefit of the doubt. By the end of the day, Eady and

Abbott had added 340 runs, Abbott completing a century and Eady taking his score to 419, in the process beating an Australian record, Worral's 417 in a game between Carlton and University.

In the circumstances it was very sporting for Wellington to come back for a fourth day a fortnight later. Charles John Eady, a man of 6ft 3in (1.91m) and 15 stone (95.3kg), overcame the individual scores by MacLaren (424 for Lancashire) and Stoddart (485 for Hampstead), taking the record to 566, an innings which contained 13 fives, 67 fours and 33 threes. He batted eight hours and gave six chances (two very difficult) and the *Hobart Mercury* summarised his innings as follows: 'His style of batting was varied, clean, and good, while he severely punished the loose bowling, a fair quantity of which was sent down to him.' There were many who thought Eady, who had played two Test matches in England in 1896, would have been on the boat to England with the Australian touring party but for the prejudice shown against Tasmania. Presumably the Wellington players would have been happy had he been on a boat to anywhere. In helping Break o' Day win the championship Eady had compensated for losing the toss by taking seven wickets and scoring a mere 566. I doubt if anyone can name another one-innings match where the two captains scored 727 runs between them.

WELLINGTON

Burn c Gill b Eady	161
M. MacLeod b Eady	0
O. Douglas b Eady	19
N. Dodds b Eady	11
S. Ward c Butler b Maxwell	23
L. MacLeod b Eady	29
B. Burgess b Eady	7
D. McDowall c Lucas b Chancellor	6
A. Seagor b Eady	4
J. Donoghue c Byfield b Maxwell	0
A. Hayton not out	8
Extras	9
	277

Bowling: Eady 46–21–87–7, Chancellor 29–3–83–1, Maxwell 16–2–56–2, Hale 8–1–29–0, Butler 7–1–13–0.

BREAK O' DAY

C.J. Eady st Burgess b MacLeod (L.)	566
W. Gill c and b MacLeod (L.)	10
E. Lucas b Burn	38
H. Hale c Dodds b Donoghue	17
F. Pocock b Donoghue	0
Maxwell c Donoghue b MacLeod (L.)	8
Chancellor c Burgess b Dodds	0
W. Abbott c MacLeod (L.) b Hayton	143
N. Douglas c Douglas (O.) b MacLeod (L.)	49
J. Bayfield not out	4
C.W. Butler b Hayton	1
Extras	75
	911

Bowling: Dodds 39–7–144–1, Donoghue 16–4–86–2, MacLeod (L.) 27–1–218–4, Hayton 40–3–136–2, McDowall 4–0–38–0, Ward 9–0–50–0, Douglas (O.) 17–1–101–0. MacLeod (M.) 5–0–39–0, Burn 8–2–25–1.

CRICKET ON DECK
THE MEDITERRANEAN SEA, JUNE 1904

There is a story about a seasick ship's passenger who endures a stormy crossing and is received at the other end by someone who asks a stupid question: 'Did you find plenty to do on the voyage?'

'Yes,' he replies, testing the intelligence of the questioner. 'In the evenings we played snooker below deck, and during the daytime we played baseball and cricket on the deck.'

The point of this story is that the idea of playing these sports on a rocking and rolling ship is beyond comprehension for the connoisseurs, but, with cricket, where there is a will there has to be a way ... and usually a strange game is the result.

Take the crew of the HMS *Irresistible*. They invented an evening game to play at sea or in harbour. The first problem, of course, is the possibility of the ball going overboard. This was solved by hanging the seine net around the deck, suspended from the wire running along the edge of the awning. Portable wickets were then pitched on deck and creases marked with chalk. So as not to encourage big hitting with the risk of the ball clearing the top of the net, the game took on a 'tip and run' identity. Should someone put the ball in the sea, the rule was that the whole team would be given out. Not a case of six and out but nought and all out.

Playing with home-made bats and balls, or, rather, made-at-sea bats and balls, the teams were usually seven or eight a side. The fielding team were allowed to bowl from the most convenient end, which put pressure on the batsmen to complete their run before the next ball. They had to run at least one for each ball. If either batsman was run-out on the first run, then the striker was always the batsman out. He was held responsible for guaranteeing a run off each ball. Run-outs on subsequent runs would follow normal practice. The best shot, risky but rewarding, was to chip the ball down a hatchway as it wasn't easy to find and runs were there for the taking. Predictably, it was a tiring game. Teams would knock up perhaps 50 runs in only 15 minutes' batting. It was good exercise.

A RECORD LOW
GLOUCESTER, JUNE 1907

If Northamptonshire were still novices to the County
Championship, which they joined in 1905, it showed in this
game against Gloucestershire when they were bowled out
for a baseball score by the home county. It happened on an
astonishing second day's cricket which retains its place in
the record books today.

This was the first meeting between Gloucestershire
and Northants, set up by a falling-out of Gloucestershire
and Lancashire. Northants were missing Vials, but
Gloucestershire had two new men in Parker and Mackenzie.

Gilbert Jessop won the toss, Gloucestershire batted, and
both teams sent for weather forecasts. The second break
for rain, when Gloucestershire were 20 for four, ended play
for the day. Northants had started well, although Jessop was
the not-out batsman.

The second day was one of the most sensational ever – 33
wickets for 180 runs in 260 minutes. It was a particularly
unforgettable day for Gloucestershire's slow left-arm bowler
George Dennett, who was unplayable. In the course of that
day Dennett took 15 wickets (out of 17) for 21 runs and scored
a pair. Oddly enough, considering the Northamptonshire
totals, Dennett's was the only pair of the game.

Gloucestershire took their overnight score to 60 before
the innings finished after only 95 minutes' batting, Jessop
contributing 22 of the runs. Northamptonshire soon

reached a respectable total of ten for one. Crosse, the captain, was caught at the wicket when the total was six, but Pool took a single and then steered Jessop to leg for three. What happened next was unbelievable. Never has first-class cricket had such a dramatic collapse.

Pool was out (ten for two), Buswell scored a run and Cox was out (11 for three). Driffield was bowled first ball (11 for four) but Thompson prevented the hat-trick. Even so, Dennett picked up his third wicket in four balls when Thompson was bowled (11 for five). In his next over Dennett was on another hat-trick, having trapped both Hawtin and East (11 for seven). Beasley turned him for a single, but Buswell fell next ball to give Dennett three in four for the second time in the innings (12 for eight).

Dennett had thus taken the first eight wickets. This wasn't entirely unusual – he had taken ten for 40 against Essex the previous season – and on a drying wicket the spinner showed why he was the main left-arm rival of Kent's Colin Blythe. In fact it is astonishing that he never played for England. On this occasion his chance of ten wickets was spoiled by Jessop, who bowled Beasley and had Wells caught at extra-cover in the same over. Northamptonshire were all out for no more than a dozen runs, emulating the 'achievement' of Oxford University in 1877. Unlike Oxford, Northants had had 11 batsmen rather than only ten. Morally, this was a new record low.

Dennett and Jessop had bowled 57 balls in 40 minutes. Jessop must have achieved some sort of record by bowling through an innings and conceding only three runs, and Dennett took his eight wickets for three runs in his last 25 balls. The following is the best estimate of the two bowlers' performances, adapted slightly from that produced in the *Northamptonshire Chronicle* to take account of the clear evidence that Dennett twice took three wickets in four balls:

Dennett: . 2 1 . 1 . / . 1 . . 1 W / . . . . 1 . / W 1 . . . . / W W . W . . / . . W W 1 W /
Jessop: . . . . . . / . . . . . . / . . . . 3 / . . . . . . / . . . . . . / W . W

When Gloucestershire batted again, they had plenty of trouble with the pitch too. Mackenzie and Jessop formed the backbone of the score of 88, and Northants were set 137 to win, a daunting prospect for a team scoring 12 in its first innings, rendered more so when they made a worse start, Crosse going without scoring.

Hawtin, a notorious stone-waller, was sent in early in a bid to avert the danger. He lasted an hour, and provided Dennett with the first victim of a deserved hat-trick, Beasley and Buswell being the others. Beasley's was the ninth Northants duck of the game, yet, amazingly, none of them put together a pair of ducks, although Driffield and Buswell were still in with a chance and East was dropped off the first ball he received, which would have meant four in four for Dennett. At 6 o'clock, when play ended for the day at Gloucester, Northants were 40 for seven, needing another 97 to win. George Thompson, the one batsman who could turn a game, was still there after taking 30 minutes to score his first run.

At close of play, Jessop offered Crosse the chance to continue. Crosse declined politely. You never know in Britain, it could rain all the next day. Indeed it did. At 4.30p.m. on the third day, the game was given up as a draw.

39

GLOUCESTERSHIRE

H. Wrathall b Thompson	4	b Thompson	7
Mr E. Barnett lbw b Thompson	3	b East	0
J.H. Board b Thompson	3	lbw b Thompson	5
Mr M.G. Salter c Buswell b East	3	c and b East	3
Mr G.L. Jessop b East	22	c Hawtin b East	24
Mr R.T.H. Mackenzie b East	0	c King b East	21
T. Langdon b East	4	lbw b Thompson	4
J.H. Huggins c Crosse b East	8	c Buswell b East	3
E. Spry lbw b Thompson	6	b East	4
Parker not out	2	not out	8
G. Dennett c Pool b Thompson	0	b East	0
Extras	5		9
	60		88

Bowling: *First Innings*; Thompson 16.5–7–29–5, East 16–5–26–5. *Second Innings*; Thompson 15–2–43–3, East 14.2–4–36–7.

NORTHAMPTONSHIRE

Mr E.M. Crosse c Board b Dennett	4	c and b Dennett	0
M. Cox lbw b Dennett	2	c Barnett b Dennett	12
Mr C.J.T. Pool c Spry b Dennett	4	st Board b Dennett	9
W.A. Buswell st Board b Dennett	1	c Langdon b Dennett	0
Mr L.T. Driffield b Dennett	0		
G.J. Thompson b Dennett	0	not out	5
Mr R.W.R. Hawtin lbw b Dennett	0	lbw b Dennett	8
W. East st Board b Dennett	0	lbw b Dennett	2
Mr R.N. Beasley b Jessop	1	b Dennett	0
Mr S. King not out	0	not out	1
W. Wells c Parker b Jessop	0		
Extras	0		3
	12		40–7

Bowling: *First Innings*; Dennett 6–1–9–8, Jessop 5.3–4–3–2. *Second Innings*; Dennett 15–8–12–7, Jessop 10–3–20–0, Parker 5–2–5–0.

AUTHORS AGAINST
ACTORS
LORD'S, AUGUST 1907

The annual fixture between a team of Authors and a team of Actors owed much to the enthusiasm of the two captains, Major Philip Trevor, the cricket correspondent of *The Daily Telegraph*, and C. Aubrey Smith, a cricket-fanatic actor who had played first-class cricket for Sussex and led the first touring team to South Africa. Aubrey Smith, who earned the sobriquet 'Round the Corner' Smith from his meandering run-up to the wicket while bowling, later initiated Hollywood CC, but was just one of many actors who grew up on the game and did their best to play. It is rumoured that one theatre company, when advertising for a Shakespearean actor, indicated they would give preference to a slow left-arm bowler. On another occasion, a team of 11 Hamlets challenged a team of 11 Macbeths at Manchester.

For three successive years in the late 1900s, rain affected play in the Authors–Actors game. In 1908, rain permitted only an hour's play, and the Actors, for once, were in trouble, at 25 for three. The previous year's game, our concern here, was played to a finish even though it rained for two hours. In fact the loss of time provoked some sensational batting.

The Authors batted first, but half of the experienced opening pair failed. Sir Arthur Conan Doyle, who had played a few games for the MCC but was better known for his Sherlock Holmes stories, was out for four. Major Guggisberg, whose books on the military included *Modern Warfare* under the pseudonym of 'Ubique', made a good 50, but the innings collapsed to the bowling of Aubrey Smith. The young men in their twenties, like A.A. Milne, then assistant editor of *Punch*, and P.G. Wodehouse, who already had books to his credit, failed to stem the tide. It was left to Major Trevor, then in his mid-forties, to bolster the bottom order and bring round the score from 150 for eight, helped by last-man E.W. Hornung, a cousin of Conan Doyle and the creator of Raffles, a fictional cricketer.

The Actors, set 194 to win, did not start their innings until 4.40p.m. when Doyle and Guggisberg opened the bowling. Apart from a dropped catch off Doyle, when O'Connor was 30, the two opening batsmen looked in no trouble, especially Basil Foster, one of the famous cricketing Worcestershire Foster brothers. When Wood came on to bowl, he was hit for 36 from his two overs. He gave way to Wodehouse, who broke the partnership by bowling O'Connor.

The Actors reached 150 in less than an hour. After Foster had completed his century, he was caught off a skier, well taken by A.A. Milne, who was undoubtedly the best fielder on the Authors' team. After passing the Authors' total with three wickets down, the Actors batted on, eventually making 253 for four in 95 minutes off only 26 overs. The game had to finish reasonably early as most of the Actors had to be on stage that evening.

AUTHORS

Sir A. Conan Doyle c and b Egerton	4
Major F.G. Guggisberg lbw b Smith	56
Mr Arthur Anderson b Foster	22
Mr C.C. Headlam b Smith	29
Mr A.H. Wood b Smith	0
Mr E.B. Noel c Pearce b Smith	17
Mr A.A. Milne st Knox b Smith	5
Major Philip Trevor b Smith	25
Mr P.G. Wodehouse b Wilde	1
Mr P. Graves c and b Smith	19
Mr E.W. Hornung not out	7
Extras	8
	193

Fall of wickets: 4, 41, 105, 105, 122, 130, 139, 144, 172, 193.

ACTORS

Mr V. O'Connor b Wodehouse	51
Mr B.S. Foster c Milne b Wodehouse	100
Mr H.E. Pearse c Anderson b Doyle	39
Mr Oscar Asche run out	0
Mr H. Wilde not out	48
Mr C. Aubrey Smith not out	15
Mr D. Ferguson	
Mr P.F. Knox	
Mr Henry Ainley	
	253–4

Fall of wickets: 129, 164, 168, 204.

WHEN WOMEN MET MEN AT TRENT BRIDGE

NOTTINGHAM, SEPTEMBER 1907

At the end of a season which saw Nottinghamshire crowned as County Champions, it is intriguing to note that the game described by the *Nottingham Evening Post* as 'one of the most interesting cricket matches witnessed on the Trent Bridge Ground this season' did not involve the county team. It was a charity game between Notts Crimea & Indian Mutiny Veterans and Nottinghamshire Ladies. There were about 1,500 witnesses.

The umpires were the Sheriff of Nottingham, Councillor Ball, and Mr A.O. Jones, captain of the Nottinghamshire champions. The Veterans won the toss and invited the ladies to bat. The ladies, incidentally, included one man, Councillor Swain, an organiser of the game, which was played for the benefit of poor children in the city. The proceeds of the match went towards a holiday home at Skegness.

Bearing in mind the dates of the Crimean War, which began in 1853, and the Indian Mutiny, which started four years later, it is understandable that the Veterans of these actions did not show too much élan in the field in 1907. Corner and Cox bowled underarm, and Alice Watts and Miss Pawlett made runs easily, in a manner which was technically correct. Miss Hickling and Councillor Swain put together a good partnership, but when both woman and man had reached their twenties they were out, Miss Hickling caught at mid-on, Councillor Swain deliberately hitting all round a ball from Cox. The consensus was that the Ladies' 106, made in an hour and a half, would take some matching.

The Ladies' team, with the exception of Councillor Swain, took to the field wearing long white skirts, white shirts and green ties. The Veterans batted more slowly than the Ladies, wary of taking a single unless there was an easy two or three. Trooper Holland, a survivor of the Charge of the Light Brigade, sent in to seal up one end, used his own bat, which was as wide as the wicket. A wicked spinning ball from Miss Hickling still did for him, and the Ladies took a commanding position, except for the resistance of the Veterans' one 'ringer', Mr Whitby, who, earlier in the day, had caught out his wife (in the context of a cricket match, that is).

Games between men and women are abundant throughout cricket history, and various rule-changes have been incorporated for such occasions. Men have batted and bowled with their unorthodox hand, or bowled underarm. Women have been allowed to catch the ball in their skirts, men have been penalised three runs for fielding the ball with their stronger hand. Men have batted with broomsticks, women have broomsticked with bats. Men have dressed in women's clothing and vice versa. But, in recent years, international women cricketers have shown themselves capable of taking on good club cricketers on equal terms.

NOTTINGHAMSHIRE LADIES

Miss A.M. Watts b Corner	9
Miss L. Pawlett b Cox	8
Miss Hickling c Whitby b Corner	24
Miss Mutch b Corner	1
Miss Taylor b Corner	4
Councillor R.H. Swain b Cox	23
Miss E.M. Vaulkhard c Whitby b Taylor	6
Mrs H.S. Whitby c Whitby b Corner	5
Mrs J. Gaskin b Taylor	17
Miss D. Hutton c Tomlinson b Taylor	2
Miss L. Simpkin not out	0
Extras	7
	106

NOTTS CRIMEA & INDIAN MUTINY VETERANS

Sgt-Major G. Watson (11th Hussars) c and b Hickling 1
Private G. Corner (84th Foot) run out 18
Private T. Cox (34th Foot) b Pawlett 0
Trooper M. Holland (11th Hussars) b Hicklin 0
Sgt G. Willbond (K.R. Rifles) b Pawlett 1
Mr H.S. Whitby b Watts 52
Private W. Tomlinson (Land Transport Corps) b Pawlett 0
Private W. Taylor (95th Foot) not out 6
Private S. Baxter (81st Foot) not out 0
Extras 4

<u>82–8</u>

A FIRST FIXTURE WITH YORKSHIRE

NORTHAMPTON, MAY 1908

'Northamptonshire, it is safe to declare, will long remember the first visit they received from Yorkshire,' wrote the *Athletic News*, but in case they have forgotten, here is a reminder.

After the glee at obtaining the fixture, and the optimism before the contest, there was let-down for the Midlands county, who were without three key players, Pool, Driffield and East. In addition, it turned out that George Thompson and Vials were both below fitness, although Vials could later claim the dubious honour of scoring Northamptonshire's only boundary in two completed innings.

Yorkshire batted first on a wicket that wasn't wonderful. Batting became easier during a day beautified by a faultless innings from Denton. In hitting the season's first century, Denton scored nine fours and batted a little more than three hours. In one over by George Thompson, who was already handicapped by lumbago, Denton hit three fours and two twos from successive deliveries. By the end of the day, Yorkshire were 333 for eight.

The next day it rained. Play resumed at 2.30p.m. and the game was finished by 5.50. After Yorkshire had batted on, adding 23 runs before Kaye's declaration, Northamptonshire were dismissed twice within 135 minutes. Thompson was unable to bat in either innings, his colleagues not giving him much time to recover from his back problem.

There were some astonishing statistics from the two

innings. George Hirst took 12 for 19 and Schofield Haigh six for 19 as Northamptonshire scored 42 for the loss of 18 wickets. It was a powerful display of left- and right-arm bowling. Only one dismissal required the help of other players, Vials being caught by Myers in the second innings. Even more astounding was the fact that seven Northants batsmen were out in exactly the same manner in both innings. In the second innings every batsman came within five of his first-innings score. It was consistency at its worst.

That second Northants innings started cautiously. Kingston and Cox scored three in the first 25 minutes before Kingston was out. Cox stayed a further 20 minutes for his two runs. It turned out to be the third highest score as Northants went down by an innings and 312 runs. One reporter, delving into the record books, came up with two interesting precedents from the Nottinghamshire season of 1800 – the totals of Leicester (15 and 8) and Sheffield (24 and 22) in games played at Leicester and Mansfield respectively. In first-class cricket, however, Northamptonshire created a new record, not surpassed (if that is the correct word) until Border's performance in South Africa in 1959.

About three weeks after the emphatic defeat by Yorkshire, Northamptonshire took on Lancashire and won a thrilling encounter by one wicket, the last pair, Wells and Hardy, forming an unbeaten stand of 23 to win the game.

YORKSHIRE

W. Rhodes b Hawtin (R.)	40
J.W. Rothey by Hawtin (R.)	27
D. Denton b Wells (R.)	110
W.H. Wilkinson c Thompson (A.R.) b Hawtin (R.)	36
G.H. Hirst c Thompson (A.R.) b Hawtin (R.)	44
W.E. Bates b Cox	12
Mr H.S. Kaye c Hawtin (A.) b Hawtin (R.)	15
S. Haigh b Falconer	13
H. Myers not out	14
J.T. Newstead not out	19
Extras	26

(declared) 356–8

Bowling: Thompson (G.J.) 26–6–77–0, Wells 31–10–86–1, Hawtin (R.) 25–3–78–5, Falconer 21–4–62–1, Cox 18–5–27–1.

NORTHAMPTONSHIRE

Mr W.H. Kingston b Hirst	8	b Hirst	3
M. Cox b Hirst	0	b Hirst	2
Mr A.P.R. Hawtin lbw b Hirst	2	lbw b Hirst	0
Mr G.A.T. Vials b Haigh	0	c Myers b Hirst	5
Mr R.W.R. Hawtin b Hirst	1	lbw b Hirst	2
Mr A.R. Thompson b Haigh	1	b Haigh	1
Mr T.E. Manning b Hirst	0	lbw b Haigh	2
W.A. Buswell b Haigh	4	b Haigh	0
W. Wells not out	5	not out	0
R. Falconer b Hirst	2	b Hirst	0
G.J. Thompson absent	0	absent	0
Extras	4		0
	27		15

Bowling: *First Innings*; Hirst 8.5–4–12–6, Haigh 8–1–11–3. *Second Innings*; Hirst 11.2–8–7–6, Haigh 11–6–8–3.

ALLETSON'S INNINGS

HOVE, MAY 1911

One might expect the possibility of a hard-hitting sensation from an Ian Botham or a Kapil Dev, but not a Nottinghamshire nonentity at number nine. What made Ted Alletson's innings so phenomenally strange was that he had been in and out – more often out – of the Nottinghamshire team during his five years as a professional.

When Alletson went out to bat, in Nottinghamshire's second innings at Hove, his team were nine runs ahead with only three wickets left. There were 50 minutes before lunch on the third day. Sussex could reasonably expect that the game would soon be over. In the first innings the last three Notts batsmen had contributed 13 runs, and Alletson's share had been seven.

The son of a wheelwright on the Duke of Portland's estate in the Nottinghamshire Dukeries, Ted Alletson was a strapping 27-year-old. He had played local cricket for Welbeck and then had one season as a professional in the Huddersfield Alliance before joining Nottinghamshire in 1906. He was more a bowler than a batsman, and his opportunity in the game at Sussex came mainly because Wass, the front-line Notts bowler, was injured. Alletson himself was nursing a sprained wrist and was barely passed fit.

At 185 for seven, therefore, on a grey Hove day, Alletson went out to join Lee. Alletson kept the Notts innings going until lunch, when the score was 260 for nine. He had made 47 in 50 minutes, hitting five fours, two threes, four twos and 13 singles. It was nothing out of the ordinary, but a useful innings for his team. There were a couple of strokes of good fortune – a skier not going to hand at 25, and a difficult slip catch being put down at 42 – and Alletson was free to come out after lunch and deliver the most extraordinary display of sustained hitting ever seen in cricket. He was not a technically good batsman, but he could drive harder than anyone, using his powerful physique and the leverage of his 6ft 6in (1.98m) arm span.

John Arlott, in his delightful monograph *Alletson's Innings*, reconstructs (with the help of Roy Webber) the best estimates of what happened in the 40-minute period after lunch. Leach had four balls left of his interrupted wicket-taking over. Riley, the number 11 bat, survived them without scoring.

The next 65 balls brought 152 runs. Then a wicket fell, and Nottinghamshire were all out.

Edwin Boaler Alletson faced 51 balls after lunch, according to the Arlott-Webber interpretations of patchwork evidence remaining from the scorebooks. He scored 142 runs and was caught on the boundary by Smith, who was allegedly over the boundary ropes. By then Alletson was almost glad to be out, perhaps sensing that Nottinghamshire, 236 ahead, had a chance of victory.

The 51 balls brought Alletson eight sixes, 18 fours, two threes, six twos and four singles. He failed to score off 12 balls and was caught from the fifty-first with his score on 189. The full details of those post-lunch balls are as follows: 0 4 4 1 2 4 2 0 1 6 0 4 2 4 6 4 0 6 3 4 4 0 2 1 4 6 0 4 3 4 6 6 0 4 4 4 6 0 0 0 0 4 4 2 2 6 1 4 4 0 W.

Perhaps the most incredible spell came in the middle of the 40-minute period after lunch. In the course of five overs, three by Killick and two by Leach, Nottinghamshire picked up 100 runs, 97 to Alletson and three to Riley. One over from Killick, which included two no-balls, went for 34 runs – 4, 6, 6, 0, 4, 4, 4, 6 – a record for an over until Gary Sobers went to work on Malcolm Nash.

Sussex were left to make 237 in three and a quarter hours. They finished 24 short with two wickets to fall.

Ted Alletson stayed with Nottinghamshire for just three more years. When his career ended he had made 3,217 runs at an average of 18.59. His 189 at Hove was his only century, although he hit Wilfred Rhodes for three consecutive sixes at Dewsbury in 1913 and there were other occasions when his powerful driving had fielders cowering for cover. During the First World War he served in the Royal Garrison Artillery and later he worked at Manton Colliery.

NOTTINGHAMSHIRE

Mr A.O. Jones b Cox	57	b Leach	0
J. Iremonger c and b Relf (A.E.)	0	c Tudor b Killick	83
G. Gunn st Butt b Cox	90	st Butt b Relf (R.)	66
J. Hardstaff b Cox	8	c Butt b Relf (A.E.)	7
J. Gunn c Relf (R.) b Killick	33	b Relf (R.)	19
W. Payton c Heygate b Killick	20	lbw Relf (A.E.)	0
W. Whysall b Killick	1	c Butt b Relf (A.E.)	3
G.M. Lee c and b Killick	10	c Cox b Leach	26
E. Alletson c Killick b Relf (A.E.)	7	c Smith b Cox	189
T. Oates not out	3	b Leach	1
W. Riley c Smith b Killick	3	not out	10
Extras	6		8
	238		**412**

Bowling: *First Innings*; Relf (A.E.) 19–5–40–2, Leach 11–2–53–0, Vincett 4–0–31–0, Relf (R.) 11–0–36–0, Cox 25–4–58–3, Killick 10.2–4–14–5. *Second Innings*; Relf (A.E.) 33–13–92–3, Leach 19–2–91–3, Vincett 3–1–25–0, Relf (R.) 19–6–39–2, Cox 9.4–2–27–1, Killick 20–2–130–1.

SUSSEX

R. Relf b Jones	42	c Oates b Jones	71
J. Vine b Jones	77	c Payton b Riley	54
Mr R.B. Heygate c Lee b Iremonger	32	b Gunn (J.)	13
G. Cox b Riley	37	st Oates b Riley	5
A.E. Relf c and b Jones	4	c Oates b Riley	0
Mr C.L. Tudor c Oates b Riley	23	b Gunn (J.)	4
E.H. Killick c Hardstaff b Lee	81	c Lee b Riley	21
G. Leach b Lee	52	b Gunn (J.)	31
Mr C.L.A. Smith not out	33	not out	12
J.H. Vincett c Iremonger b Lee	9	not out	1
H.R. Butt b Riley	13		
Extras	11		1
	414		**213–8**

Bowling: *First Innings*; Iremonger 34–7–97–1, Riley 29.4–5–102–3, Gunn (J.) 29–2–87–0, Jones 22–2–69–3, Alletson 1–0–3–0, Lee 14–1–45–3. *Second Innings*; Iremonger 14–2–34–0, Riley 33–9–82–4, Gunn (J.) 25–9–41–3, Jones 5–1–24–1, Lee 4–0–31–0.

DRAKE'S FINE BOWLING
WESTON-SUPER-MARE, AUGUST 1914

War had broken out. Cricket was already affected, and County Championship games were under threat of abandonment and postponement. The impact of war on the Somerset–Yorkshire game at the start of the first Weston-super-Mare festival was relatively slight but interesting. Yorkshire, without regular captain A.W. White, who was on military service, fielded a team of 11 professionals. George Hirst took over as captain.

Yorkshire spent an amazing week in the West Country. The first game, against Gloucestershire, was won by an innings and 227 runs. The opening bowlers, Major Booth (Major was his Christian name) and Alonzo Drake, bowled unchanged through both Gloucestershire innings, the first time this had happened in a Yorkshire match for four years. Booth had match figures of 12 for 89, Drake eight for 81. More was to follow.

Somerset were likely whipping-boys too. The previous season Yorkshire had beaten Somerset by an innings and 132 runs, and Drake had finished with sensational match figures of 10.4–5–7–7, taking four for four in the first innings and three for three in the second. He must have been relishing the contest at the Weston-super-Mare festival.

The newly laid pitch had suffered from the rain, encouraging the bowlers to harbour optimistic smirks. Yorkshire batted first and were thankful to reach 162, depending largely on fifties from Denton and Drake, Yorkshire's opening bowler having a good chance to see what the wicket could do.

Booth and Drake skittled Somerset in about an hour, sharing the wickets equally. For the third time in the week they bowled unchanged through an innings, Booth fast and right-handed, Drake slower and left-handed.

When Yorkshire batted again, Wilfred Rhodes fought his way to top score of 25, Drake managed another 12, and a three-figure total looked to be worth the equivalent of 300 on a normal wicket. Somerset were set 231 to win. Not much chance.

That they reached 90 was down to a ninth-wicket stand between Hope and Harcombe, who added 37. Harcombe was particularly severe on Drake, taking 11 from one over, but Drake had his reward. Not only did he bowl through an innings unchanged with Booth for the fourth successive time, but he took all ten wickets while Booth took none for 50. It was the first time a Yorkshire bowler had taken ten in an innings, although it could hardly compare with an achievement the previous season in Australia when Davidson had taken ten for nought for Williamstown against Fitzroy in the Victoria Scottish Cricket Competition.

Yorkshire's week in the West Country in 1914 saw them use only two bowlers while they were dismissing Gloucestershire for 94 and 84, and Somerset for 44 and 90. Booth's statistics for the week were 57–8–166–17 and Drake's were 55.2–12–132–23. This was the pinnacle of their careers. Drake suffered from ill health, and Booth was killed in action in France in July 1916.

YORKSHIRE

M.W. Booth c Poyntz b Bridges	1	b Bridges	9
B.B. Wilson c Saunders b Bridges	20	b Bridges	9
Denton c Chidgey b Hylton-Stewart	52	c Saunders b Bridges	0
R. Kilner b Hylton-Stewart b Bridges	2	c Braund b Bridges	4
W. Rhodes c and b Hylton-Stewart	1	lbw b Robson	25
T.J. Birtles lbw b Braund	16	b Robson	10
A. Drake c Harcombe b Braund	51	c Hope b Robson	12
P. Holmes b Bridges	7	not out	3
G.H. Hirst c Bisgood b Bridges	5	c Saunders b Robson	10
E. Oldroyd not out	0	b Hylton-Stewart	23
A. Dolphin b Braund	0	b Robson	0
Extras	7		7
	162		**112**

Bowling *First Innings*; Robson 14–5–45–0, Bridges 17–1–59–5, Hylton-Stewart 9–0–38–2, Braund 8.4–2–13–3. *Second Innings*; Robson 14–2–38–5, Bridges 14–1–54–4, Hylton-Stewart 2–0–6–1, Braund 4–2–7–0.

SOMERSET

Mr B.L. Bisgood c and b Booth	6	c Dolphin b Drake	11
L.C. Braund b Drake	1	b Drake	9
E. Robson c Rhodes b Booth	19	c Birtles b Drake	3
Mr B.D. Hylton-Stewart b Drake	1	st Dolphin b Drake	3
W. Hyman b Drake	1	st Dolphin b Drake	4
Mr E.S.M. Poyntz b Drake	0	c Oldroyd b Drake	5
Mr P.P. Hope b Booth	3	c and b Drake	19
Mr H.W. Saunders b Drake	0	b Drake	0
Mr H.D. Harcombe not out	5	b Drake	26
J.F. Bridges c Drake b Booth	7	not out	1
H. Chidgey c Holmes b Booth	0	b Drake	4
Extras	1		5
	44		**90**

Bowling: *First Innings*; Booth 8–0–27–5, Drake 7–1–16–5. *Second Innings*; Booth 9–0–50–0, Drake 8.5–0–35–10.

HEYGATE'S LAST STAND
TAUNTON, MAY 1919

The 1919 Somerset–Sussex match was as equal as a game could be. Somerset batted first, in front of their own crowd, and reached 243 with the help of a good innings by Dudley Rippon, one of the Rippon twins, some hard hitting by Hope, the Bath rugby captain, and a few hefty lunges by Bridges, including one that put a ball into the river. Somerset were hindered by George Cox's left-arm slow bowling and three good catches by Miller, the new Sussex wicket-keeper.

Cox also performed well in the Sussex batting. His unbeaten 24 helped Maurice Tate (69) bring the total to within one of Somerset's. But the most significant contribution, or lack of contribution, came from Mr H.J. Heygate, who batted at 11 for Sussex and was bowled by White without scoring. Mr Heygate, crippled by rheumatism, was unable to field during the Somerset second innings. The significance of this came later.

Somerset batted with more difficulty the second time around. Cox, turning the ball sharply, was again among the wickets – he finished with match figures of nine for 77 – and Somerset managed only 103, Bridges top-scoring with 14.

Sussex were favourites when they went in chasing 105 to win, and opening bat Herbert Wilson stayed as solid as a rock. At the other end, wickets tumbled to miraculous fielding. Braund made two excellent slip catches, and Bridges dismissed Bourdillon with an incredible low catch.

In no time Sussex were 48 for six, wanting another 57 to win.

Roberts (28) stayed with Wilson long enough to swing the game Sussex's way. The score crept to 102, within three of victory. Somerset looked defeated when Dudley Rippon came on to bowl, but, after conceding a single, he bowled Roberts and picked up Stannard's wicket immediately: 103 for eight. Another single from Wilson, now 42 not out, brought the scores level. Then Miller, batting lower down the order, was caught one-handed by Bridges. One wicket to fall, and still one to win.

Inside the pavilion, the 34-year-old Mr Heygate was still suffering from rheumatism. He was asked if he would like to bat. Heygate, dressed in his everyday clothes, agreed, even if he had to crawl to the wicket. It was a rush to get him ready.

Out on the pitch, the Sussex fielders, recognising that Heygate had not fielded, presumed he would not be batting. Four minutes went by, then a Sussex player appealed under Law 45, which allowed batsmen only two minutes to reach the wicket.

Heygate came out of the pavilion, still wearing ordinary clothes, to discover that he was already out. The umpires had delighted the home crowd by pulling up the stumps. Some people were uncertain about the result – a rigid interpretation of Law 45 implied that Sussex could lose the match – but the game was declared a tie, the first since Surrey and Kent in 1905. Heygate's dismissal was an ignominious end to his first-class career, this being the last of six matches he played for Sussex. It provoked much discussion. 'An extraordinary and in some respects very regrettable incident,' said *Wisden*, but the MCC committee upheld the umpire's decision.

Some weeks later the same umpire stood in another Somerset game, so several players padded up and ran out to meet a dismissed batsman 20 yards (18.3m) from the pavilion gate.

SOMERSET

Mr A.E.S. Rippon c Miller b Stannard	26	b Cox	8
Mr A.D.E. Rippon c Miller b Vincett	60	b Cox	8
Mr J.C.W. McBryan lbw b Cox	18	b Cox	0
E. Robson b Cox	14	b Roberts	11
L. Braund b Roberts	3	b Roberts	11
Mr J.D. Harcombe c H. Wilson b Cox	0	run out	5
Mr P.P. Hope c Tate b Vincett	48	c Stannard b Vincett	6
J.F. Bridges c Miller b Vincett	34	st Miller b Vincett	14
Capt. Amer b Cox	14	c Cox b Tate	13
Mr J.C. White b Cox	12	not out	11
H. Chidgey not out	1	c Vincett b Cox	10
Extras	13		6
	243		**103**

Bowling: *First Innings*; Roberts 17–4–51–1, Vincett 31–4–69–3, Stannard 8–0–27–1, Tate 12–3–32–0, Cox 15.4–4–51–5. *Second Innings*; Roberts 16–1–40–2, Vincett 9–0–20–2, Tate 6–1–11–1, Cox 18.4–6–26–4.

SUSSEX

Mr H.L. Wilson b Bridges	56	not out	42
Mr A.K. Wilson c Braund b Bridges	4	c Braund b Robson	4
Mr T.E. Bourdillon b Bridges	21	c Bridges b Robson	7
Mr A.C. Somerset b Robson	33	c Braund b Robson	0
Mr R.A.T. Miller b Bridges	2	c Bridges b White	0
Mr J.H. Vincett b Bridges	14	b Bridges	6
H.E. Roberts b Robson	5	b D. Rippon	28
M.W. Tate c Braund b Robson	69	c Chidgey b Bridges	11
G. Stannard b D. Rippon	3	c McBryan b D. Rippon	0
G. Cox not out	24	b Bridges	0
Mr H.J. Heygate b White	0	not allowed to bat	0
Extras	11		6
	242		**104**

Bowling: *First Innings*; White 18.4–1–76–1, Robson 15–3–49–3, Bridges 22–4–84–5, D. Rippon 9–2–22–1. *Second Innings*; White 33–0–14–1, Robson 14–2–51–3, Bridges 12–2–32–3, D. Rippon 2–1–1–2.

FIFTEEN
ALL OUT AND THEN ...
BIRMINGHAM, JUNE 1922

Hampshire won the toss and put Warwickshire in. Thanks to a steady innings from Santall (84), who broke a tile on the pavilion roof with a six, and some lusty blows from Calthorpe (70), whose three sixes included one over the pavilion into a field, the home county reached 223 all out. Hampshire's opening bowlers, Jack Newman and Alec Kennedy, were typically united, the former penetrative and slightly erratic, the latter persistently accurate. Warwickshire's disappointments came in the middle of their batting. Reverend E.F. Waddy was out without scoring, and the younger Quaife also went for a duck. As it happened they were good role models for the Hampshire innings later that same day.

Hampshire lasted 53 balls and 40 minutes. The slow over rate was no fault of Warwickshire's Howell and Calthorpe. There was a lot of walking about – on and off the field. Kennedy went to the third ball of Calthorpe's first over and Hampshire were soon nought for three. Mead managed a single, and Lionel Tennyson, the Hampshire captain, streaked a four through the slips before being caught. Brown was immediately bowled, and Hampshire were five for five. Mead batted steadily and took his own score to five. With the total on nine, Newman was caught in the slips, a run later Shirley went the same way and McIntyre was leg before wicket. Ten for eight. Hampshire were in grave danger of recording the lowest score of all first-class cricket which was – and still is – 12.

They were saved by four byes which, after Mead had notched another single, took the score to 15. The last two wickets then fell, leaving Mead unbeaten on six – quite an astonishing achievement considering he had lost eight partners. Eight of the team were out without scoring. Had it not been for four byes and a lucky four through the slips, Hampshire would have made only seven.

There was nothing sensational about the wicket. It was purely an accident of cricket. Hampshire batted badly, and the innings accumulated failure. They followed on, and at the close of play on the first day were 98 for three, which showed that runs could be made, although not enough.

When Mead was out early the next day (127 for four) Hampshire needed another 81 to avoid an innings defeat. Just before lunch they were 177 for six, still 31 behind. The five remaining batsmen had scored one run between them in the first innings. They evoked memories of Tennyson's comments about the late-order batting early in the season.

Observers early that Thursday afternoon, recognising that less than half the allotted time had been used, were quite pleased when Hampshire started to make a bit of a fight. Brown and Shirley put on 85 for the seventh wicket, and Brown and McIntyre cobbled together a further 13 for the eighth. At 274 for eight, however, 66 ahead, Hampshire seemed to be showing token resistance.

The ninth-wicket stand brought together George Brown, a notable left-handed battling batsman, and wicket-keeper Walter Livsey, Tennyson's valet, who had chalked up a pair against Sussex in the first match of the season. The stand was worth 177 runs. Brown hit 18 fours in his 172, and at the end of the day Hampshire were 475 for nine, 267 ahead. Brown's century was reminiscent of his fighting effort against Essex in 1913, when his unbeaten 140 saved Hampshire from the unenviable position of 119 behind with four second-innings wickets left. In his career, Brown was to score over 25,000 runs. Livsey, however, was moving towards unknown territory, although he had shared a last-wicket stand of 192 with Bowell the previous season.

Hampshire batted for a further 40 minutes in the morning, and Livsey was able to complete his century. Boyes (29) helped him add 70 for the last wicket.

When Warwickshire batted again they needed 314 runs to win, and there was ample time to make the runs. Bates went quickly, and in came Santall, top score in the first innings. He was bowled for nought. Suddenly the game was alive, and Hampshire had control.

Wickets continued to fall – Reverend Waddy completed his 'pair' – but Quaife, senior, kept one end intact. When last-man Howell came to the wicket, Warwickshire still needed more than 150 to win. Quaife looked solid at one end, Howell picked up a few runs and was then dropped by wicket-keeper Livsey. A few more runs, and Howell was dropped at slip. Surely the course of the game could not change again? No, Newman picked up Howell's wicket, and Quaife was left unbeaten after resisting for 100 minutes.

Hampshire, 15 all out in their first innings, had not only made a fight of the match, they had won convincingly by 155 runs. 'The victory taken as a whole,' said *Wisden*, 'must surely be without precedent in first-class cricket.'

It wasn't even the end of Hampshire's strange matches that season. Jack Newman made the news in August when he lost his temper over an umpiring decision and kicked down the stumps. Lord Tennyson ordered him off the field and, at the end of the day, sat down to help Newman compile a letter to the Nottinghamshire captain and president: 'I humbly apologise for my action on the field of play at Trent Bridge and herewith I tender my deep regret,' wrote Newman.

WARWICKSHIRE

L.A. Bates c Shirley b Newman	3	c Mead b Kennedy	1
E.J. Smith c Mead b Newman	24	c Shirley b Kennedy	41
Mr F.R. Santall c McIntyre b Boyes	84	b Newman	0
W.G. Quaife b Newman	1	not out	40
Hon. F.S.G. Calthorpe c Boyes b Kennedy	70	b Newman	30
Rev. E.F. Waddy c Mead b Boyes	0	b Newman	0
Mr B.W. Quaife b Boyes	0	c and b Kennedy	7
J. Fox b Kennedy	4	b Kennedy	0
J. Smart b Newman	20	b Newman	3
C. Smart c Mead b Boyes	14	c and b Boyes	15
H. Howell not out	1	c Kennedy b Newman	11
Extras	2		10
	223		**158**

Bowling: *First Innings*; Kennedy 24–7–74–2, Newman 12.3–0–70–4, Boyes 16–5–56–4, Shirley 3–0–21–0. *Second Innings*; Kennedy 26–12–47–4, Newman 26.3–12–53–5, Boyes 11–4–34–1, Brown 5–0–14–0.

HAMPSHIRE

A. Bowell b Howell	0	c Howell b W.G. Quaife	45
A. Kennedy c Smith b Calthorpe	0	b Calthorpe	7
Mr H.L.V. Day b Calthorpe	0	c Bates b W.G. Quaife	15
C.P. Mead not out	6	b Howell	24
Hon. L.N. Tennyson c Calthorpe b Howell	4	c C. Smart b Calthorpe	45
G. Brown b Howell	0	b C. Smart	172
J. Newman c C. Smart b Howell	0	c and b W.G. Quaife	12
Mr W.R. Shirley c J. Smart b Calthorpe	1	lbw b Fox	30
Mr A.S. McIntyre lbw b Calthorpe	0	lbw b Howell	5
W.H. Livsey b Howell	0	not out	110
G.S. Boyes lbw b Howell	0	b Howell	29
Extras	4		27
	15		**521**

Bowling: *First Innings*; Howell 4.5–2–7–6, Calthorpe 4–3–4–4. *Second Innings*; Howell 63–10–156–3, Calthorpe 33–7–97–2, W.G. Quaife 49–8–154–3, Fox 7–0–30–1, J. Smart 13–2–37–0, Santall 5–0–15–0, C. Smart 1–0–5–1.

CHAPMAN'S CAPTAIN'S INNINGS

HYTHE, KENT, SEPTEMBER 1925

Shortly after his twenty-fifth birthday, Percy Chapman, a Cambridge blue who was in his second season with Kent, recruited a team of workmen from the Hythe Brewery and captained them in a 12-a-side game against the Elham Division of the Kent County Police.

The Police batted first and scored steadily until Chapman, not known for his bowling, came on and demonstrated what a local reporter referred to as 'weird slows'. The Police were eventually all out for 151, the 11 wickets being shared between Moore (five), Chapman (four), Gubbins (one) and one run out.

It was agreed that Mr Chapman's team, the Hythe Brewery XI, would bat through until they were all out. What an amazing innings it was. Chapman, going in at number four, scored 183. The other 11 players mustered only seven between them; of these, six came from the last two.

Chapman, a tall, powerful, left-handed bat, hit seven sixes, one five and 23 fours in his 183. Last out, he was met by his team-mates and carried shoulder-high to the pavilion. The game then turned into a social occasion. Wives and families turned up, and the Police and brewery workmen began to enjoy themselves even more.

Percy Chapman, who had scored 79 and 54 for Hythe the previous week, would make his mark even more the following season, when he became an exceptionally young captain of the England team which regained the Ashes. He captained England 17 times, and altogether played in 26 Test matches, making one hundred and five fifties. Never again, though, would he dominate a game in the way he did against the Elham Division Police, and only occasionally were his 'weird slows' seen in action.

ELHAM DIVISION, KENT COUNTY POLICE

P.C. Rowe c Dray b Moore	27
P.C. Stokes run out	2
P.C. Goodall b Gubbins	28
P.C. Green b Moore	24
Sgt Burren c Dale b Moore	22
P.C. Holman c and b Chapman	4
Sgt Waters st Middleton b Chapman	0
P.C. Sheepwash b Moore	10
Sgt Marsh not out	9
P.C. Green b Moore	6
P.C. Avery b Chapman	11
P.C. Pay c and b Chapman	4
Extras	4
	151

MR CHAPMAN'S TEAM (HYTHE BREWERY)

R. Down lbw b Holman	0
C. Tugwell b Holman	0
B. Middleton b Holman	0
A.P.F. Chapman c Green b Burren	183
J. Davidson c March b Holman	0
W. Gubbins b Holman	0
C. Dray b Holman	0
A. Moore run out	0
S. Dale run out	1
F. Wright run out	0
H. Wood c and b Green	2
H. Rose not out	4
Extras	11
	201

WORLD RECORD SCORE
MELBOURNE, AUSTRALIA, DECEMBER 1926

King stepped out to Arthur Mailey and was beaten in the flight. Wicket-keeper Ratcliffe took the ball, gloved the stumps, scattered the bails untidily and appealed. The umpire's finger was triggered. Victoria had slumped from 594 for one to 657 for five.

'The rot's set in,' a local joker said to his mate.

In fact almost 500 runs were still to come, and Mailey's useful figures of three for 40 in that morning session, on the second day of the Victoria innings against New South Wales, were to become dominated by what went on elsewhere in the innings. Mailey recorded the most expensive figures of all time (four for 362).

The big score was dominated by Bill Ponsford, the 26-year-old from North Carlton who was having a prolific season (551 runs in four innings before that game). Going in first with Bill Woodfull, facing a New South Wales total of 221, Ponsford outscored his partner before lunch (Ponsford 75, Woodfull 50) and then scored at double Woodfull's pace after the interval. Woodfull was happy to give Ponsford all the strike he wanted. At that time Ponsford already held the world record individual score in first-class cricket (429 against Tasmania) and by the end of his first day's batting, when he was 334 not out, he had his sights on Clem Hill's Sheffield Shield record of 365 not out for South Australia. 'We'll meet again in the morning,' he is alleged to have told the fielders.

On the second morning Ponsford batted less assuredly. He lost his partner, 'Stork' Hendry, another centurion, after a Victorian record second-wicket stand of 219, then played a ball from Morgan on to his toe, from where it bounced into the stumps. Ponsford was out for 352, made in 363 minutes with 36 boundaries, an innings almost without blemish although he was caught off a no-ball early on and there was a possible stumping chance at 265. Love and King quickly fell to the Ratcliffe-Mailey partnership to complete 'the rot'.

Jack Ryder and Albert Hartkopf pulled Victoria through with a stand of 177 for the sixth wicket, another Victoria record. Ryder stayed to register the third Victoria record stand of the innings – 128 with Ellis for the eighth wicket – and when he was out for 295, made in only 243 minutes with six sixes and 33 fours, he had made his runs out of 449 and Victoria were 1,043 for eight. Ryder had also seen Victoria through the nervous 990s and into four figures. In the last over he faced, Ryder hit Andrews for four, six, four and six, but was caught at mid-on off the fifth ball. Morton was run out three runs later.

The next record in sight was Victoria's own – 1,059 in an innings against Tasmania in Melbourne in 1923. With Blackie content to stay there, Ellis went for the runs. A three by Ellis brought the new record, and the last-wicket pair went on to add 61 in a partnership that could best be understated as 'a nuisance' to the tired New South Wales bowlers. Hogg's fielding kept the score down to 1,107, made in ten and a half hours. New South Wales needed 886 runs to avoid an innings defeat. They held out until just after four o'clock on the fourth day. The 18-year-old Jackson made the top New South Wales score in the match – a mere 59 not out. New South Wales lost by an innings and 656 runs.

In his autobiography *Ten for 66 and All That*, Arthur Mailey tells of how he and his New South Wales colleagues vowed to measure Bill Ponsford's bat after the game because it had seemed so wide to the bowlers. 'You've been looking at it for a couple of days,' Ponsford replied with a smirk. 'You should know its width.'

In England the whinging Poms recognised the new record and immediately reckoned that the bowling must have been abysmal, although Mailey had been good enough to take six for 138 against England at The Oval the previous summer and, in 1921 against Gloucestershire, had taken his legendary ten for 66 in an innings. The other English criticism was that it must have been pretty tiresome for the crowd, seeing nothing but runs and more runs.

The 1,107 total still stands as a record for first-class cricket. The odd thing is that New South Wales reaped their revenge a month later, beating Victoria by an innings.

NEW SOUTH WALES

Phillips c Blackie b Liddicutt	52	lbw b Hartkopf	36
Morgan c Love b Liddicutt	13	c King b Liddicutt	26
Andrews st Ellis b Hartkopf	42	b Liddicutt	0
Kippax b Liddicutt	36	b Hartkopf	26
Radcliffe c Ryder b Liddicutt	2	c Morton b Hartkopf	44
Jackson c Ellis b Blackie	4	not out	59
Hogg not out	40	c Hendry b Liddicutt	13
Mailey b Ryder	20	c Morton b Hartkopf	3
Campbell lbw b Blackie	0	c Ryder b Hartkopf	8
McNamee b Ryder	8	b Liddicutt	7
McGuirk b Ryder	0	b Hartkopf	0
Extras	4		8
	221		**230**

Bowling: *First Innings*; Morton 15–4–43–0, Liddicutt 21–7–50–4, Ryder 9–1–32–3, Blackie 16–3–34–2, Hendry 2–2–1–0, Hartkopf 17–1–57–1. *Second Innings*; Morton 11–0–42–0, Liddicutt 19–2–66–4, Blackie 5–1–16–0, Hartkopf 16.3–0–98–6.

VICTORIA

Woodfull c Ratcliffe b Andrews	133
Ponsford b Morgan	352
Hendry c Morgan b Mailey	100
Ryder c Kippax b Andrews	295
Love st Ratcliffe b Mailey	6
King st Ratcliffe b Mailey	7
Hartkopf c McGuirk b Mailey	61
Liddicutt b McGuirk	36
Ellis run out	63
Morton run out	0
Blackie not out	27
Extras	27
	__1,107__

Bowling: McNamee 24–2–124–0, McGuirk 26–1–130–1, Mailey 64–0–362–4, Campbell 11–0–89–0, Phillips 11.7–0–64–0, Morgan 26–0–137–1, Andrews 21–2–148–2, Kippax 7–0–26–0.

THE DEFIANT GAME
SOUTHWICK, SUSSEX, APRIL 1932

For 200 years they had been playing cricket on Southwick Village Green, which had been bought for £25 by the local council in 1902. The Green had even produced a county cricketer, Cleverly of Sussex, who had started his career with Southwick.

In 1932 the council banned adult cricket from the Green, believing the game to be a danger to people and property. There was uproar in the village. Rarely have local politics been so closely monitored by villagers.

The council sanctioned only one game for the 1932 season – for children under 14 – but in the middle of April the village cricket team organised its first protest game, which was conveniently ignored by the council. A bigger event was planned for 30 April, one that the local council could not ignore. It was a 12-a-side game – between adults.

The cricket club and Ratepayers' Association conducted their own referendum and obtained 900 signatures – 750 in favour of the adult cricket and 150 against. The council chose not to reverse its original decision. The protesters were outraged, claiming that while there was an element of danger in cricket it had been exaggerated.

'We are defying the council because the council defy you,' said Mr W.H. Griffin, when he spoke to the crowd before the game on 30 April. The two teams took to the Green, one led by Bert Gillam, the other by W.G. Denyer.

The greenkeeper produced the official prohibition notice and took the names of all the players: 'Bowler's name, please. Fielders' names, please.' It was agreed that the addresses would also be supplied. The game was played.

In the first week of June the council decided to prosecute a select few of the defiant cricketers. They singled out five players – Gillam, Denyer, Rountree, Knowles and Mais, the last a local novelist who had been active in writing protest letters. They faced a possible penalty of a £5 fine.

The debate raged on, although one game that sneaked through, late in June, was a comic costume game staged for charity. 'All Indeer' played the Ladies, and the participants dressed appropriately. The winner of the fancy-dress competition was the spit image of Gandhi, while 'W.G. Grace', perambulating the boundary, was probably the best fancy-dressed spectator. The game was played with a tennis ball, in accordance with the council's demands.

The next year the cricketers were back in harness, and village cricket was once more seen on the Village Green.

'SMASHING CRICKET AT CARDIFF ARMS PARK'

CARDIFF, JUNE 1935

One hundred and fourteen for nine in their second innings, needing another 145 to save the innings defeat. Not good for Glamorgan. But help was on the way, described by the *South Wales Echo and Evening Express* as 'like a story from a boy's three-penny thriller'.

From the time that Wade and Rowan embarked on their huge stand of 256 on the first day of their touring match at Cardiff, the South Africans appeared totally in control of the Glamorgan team. Despite Emrys Davies carrying his bat through the first Glamorgan innings, South Africa, with a first-innings lead of 259, were able to enforce the follow-on. At ten for four in their second innings, at the end of the second day, Glamorgan were in a position of no hope. Their situation grew worse on the final morning – ten for five, 26 for six and 46 for seven. It was then that Cyril Smart started to attack the bowling. Nothing to lose, everything to gain.

With Mercer, Smart put on 68 runs in 35 minutes, reaching his 50 with a sweep to the pavilion rails that brought the first cheers of the morning. But Mercer was out, and Glover went first ball. Langton was on a hat-trick, and the only man left was a 26-year-old amateur playing his first match. Donald Wynn Hughes had failed with the bat in the first innings, and had had little success with his right-arm fast-medium bowling. The only interest centred on whether he could prevent Langton's hat-trick before the end came.

In fact Hughes hit Langton for four, then six. He smashed Tomlinson for 11 in one over, and, in no time at all, was 24 not out. When Vincent replaced Tomlinson, Hughes hit him for six too.

Tomlinson returned at the other end, but Smart cover-drove him for four, on-drove him for six, square-cut him for four and late-cut him for three. Smart, soon in the nervous nineties, hit Vincent for a six and then confidently took a single to leave Hughes to face the bowling. The debutant, a local school-teacher, survived the over, allowing Smart to reach his 100 with a cut for four from Tomlinson in the next over.

'It was wonderful cricket,' wrote the *South Wales Echo and Evening Express*, 'and men and boys stood on their seats waving their hats and shouting frantically.' Smart's next big hit sent the ball over the tennis courts and through a window of the Grand Hotel in Westgate Street. Hughes reached his 50 with two more sixes off Vincent and the century partnership came up in only 45 minutes.

The South Africans took the new ball with no real effect. By lunch the stand was worth 131 runs in an hour, and Glamorgan were only 14 behind. During the lunch interval, a collection for Smart's 100 raised slightly more than £9.

Shortly after lunch, it rained, and the game was abandoned as a draw. The astonishing last-wicket stand by Smart and Hughes had saved the game but there was no telling where it might have ended, even though Hughes's later batting form – 202 runs in 24 completed innings – was unimpressive.

SOUTH AFRICA

H.F. Wade c and b Davies (D.)	139
Mitchell c Dyson b Davies (E.)	16
E.A. Rowan c Brierley b Mercer	153
A.D. Nourse c Dyson b Lavis	12
H.B. Cameron run out	11
E.L. Dalton b Mercer	5
K.G. Viljoen b Davies (E.)	17
C.L. Vincent b Mercer	0
A.B. Langton c Mercer b Hughes	23
D. Tomlinson c Brierley b Glover	8
A.J. Bell not out	5
Extras	12
	__401__

Bowling: Mercer 27–5–82–3, Hughes 26–5–73–1, Davies (E.) 48–7–90–1, Glover 26.5–3–79–1, Lavis 10–2–23–1, Smart 5–0–31–0, Davies (D.) 6–1–11–1.

GLAMORGAN

A.H. Dyson c Mitchell b Langton	18	b Langton	1
E. Davies not out	75	b Langton	0
D. Davies b Tomlinson	5	run out	3
Mr M.J. Turnbull lbw b Langton	1	b Bell	0
R. Duckfield lbw (N.) b Tomlinson	4	b Bell	0
C. Smart c and b Tomlinson	2	not out	114
G. Lavis c Nourse b Tomlinson	8	b Langton	6
T.L. Brierley c Wade b Tomlinson	9	c Rowan b Langton	3
J. Mercer c Viljoen b Vincent	12	c Nourse b Langton	34
Mr E.R.K. Glover b Vincent	2	b Langton	0
Mr W. Hughes c Bell b Vincent	2	not out	70
Extras	4		14
	__142__		__245–9__

Bowling: *First Innings*; Bell 5–0–15–0, Langton 18–8–26–2, Tomlinson 24–4–72–5, Vincent 13.2–3–25–3. *Second Innings*; Bell 11–21–41–2, Langton 22–5–66–6, Tomlinson 9–0–69–0, Vincent 7–1–36–0, Mitchell 4–0–19–0.

TWO AGAINST 11
WITTERSHAM, ISLE OF OXNEY, SEPTEMBER 1936

This strange game, two men against an 11 from the Isle of Oxney on the Kent-Sussex border, had its origins in a bet made in the early 1830s, more than 100 years earlier. The landlord of Wittersham's Norton's Inn had been so disgusted with the boastings of the local village side that he wagered he could find two cricketers to beat the lot of them. The crafty publican turned up with two Kent professionals, Edward Wenman and Richard Mills, who beat the 11 from the Isle of Oxney by 66 runs in a two-innings match.

In 1936 someone had the idea of repeating the game. Different players, of course, but two professionals against a team of local lads. A two-innings game was planned, whereby the professionals would be 'all out' as soon as they lost a wicket, but they were given the concession of being able to change their bowling at will.

The two-man professional team consisted of Bert Wensley of Sussex and Bill Ashdown of Kent. The Isle of Oxney team, captained by coal-merchant S.J. Pridham, were mainly local workmen – three gardeners, two carpenters, one hop-dryer, two farmers, a bricklayer and a motor mechanic.

The publicity for the game was excellent and the idea caught the imagination of people in the region. The BBC decided to broadcast a radio commentary of the game. A big crowd turned out on the day – one source says 2,000 plus, another gives it at 4,000 – and the proceeds went to charity.

The game started at 11.30a.m. and the Isle of Oxney batted first. The two-man team of Wensley and Ashdown rotated between wicket-keeping and bowling. There were no other fielders, which meant there were only two gaps in the field – all the on side, and all the off. Not surprisingly, neither Ashdown nor Wensley managed to bowl a maiden over in the whole innings, which lasted 24.4 overs. When Bill Catt, the bricklayer, and one of the Bromham brothers took the Isle of Oxney score from 39 for one to 102, things looked really bleak for the professionals (and the onlookers who had betted on them), but the two men stuck at their task. Isle of Oxney were dismissed for 153.

Ashdown and Wensley went in knowing that one mistake would end the whole innings. In 36.4 overs they took the total to 186, an excellent first- and last-wicket stand. Wensley was the man out after hitting three sixes and 13 fours in his 96. Ashdown, unbeaten on 83, had hit 14 fours.

Unfortunately the rain came down, and the last two innings were never started. The professionals won on first innings, and had emulated the performance of their counterparts in the early 1830s.

ISLE OF OXNEY		THE PROFESSIONALS	
F.G.H. Pridham st Wensley		Ashdown not out	83
b Ashdown	11	Wensley c Cook b Bush (A.)	96
W. Catt b Ashdown	68		
A. Bromham run out	20		
G. Cook b Wensley	0		
C. Gorman b Ashdown	0		
C. Bush c Ashdown b Wensley	2		
A. Bush b Wensley	14		
P. Shanbrooke lbw b Ashdown	28		
F. Jenner b Wensley	0		
F. Burt b Wensley	0		
Bromham not out	5		
Extras	5	Extras	7
	153		186

Bowling: Wensley 12.4–0–66–5, Ashdown 12–0–82–4.

THE LONGEST TEST
DURBAN, SOUTH AFRICA, MARCH 1939

The final Test of the series between South Africa and England was to be played to a finish as England were one up and the rubber was still at stake. It was destined to be an unusual match from the moment England captain Wally Hammond lost the toss. That in itself was strange. Hammond, after switching from a professional to an amateur, had captained England on eight previous occasions, four against Australia, four against South Africa, and this was the first time he had lost the toss. South African captain Alan Melville surprised him by using a threepenny bit that one of the players, Norman Gordon, had won the previous evening at snooker from Len Hutton. England started the timeless Test in the field on a Friday.

On the first day, van der Byl occupied the crease all day for his century, spending one 45-minute period without scoring, and South Africa moved slowly to 229 for two on a perfect wicket.

On the second day, after only 17 had been added in the first hour and van der Byl's 435-minute marathon ended, Dalton and Nourse quickened the pace, and South Africa ended on 423 for six. The wicket was still perfect.

The next day, a Sunday, was a rest day. It rained anyway.

On the third day of the match, South Africa were all out for 530 and England finished on 35 for one when rain stopped play.

On the fourth day, a dull day, South Africa bowled themselves into a winning position. Paynter and Ames offered the main resistance, but England ended at 268 for seven.

On the fifth day, the England innings ended on 316, over 200 behind. As the Test was timeless, South Africa decided not to enforce the follow-on but make England bat last ... if they could still stand on their feet. The wicket was good enough for another week, as proved by the South African opening stand of 191 between van der Byl and Mitchell. But three wickets fell suddenly just before the close, when South Africa were 193 for three.

On the sixth day, South Africa took their score to 481 with an excellent century from Melville, the first of his four successive centuries against England, the others coming over eight years later. After lunch, Reg Perks made a pretence of crawling back to the field on his hands and knees. After tea, Paul Gibb kept wicket to give Les Ames a break. After one ball of the England innings, Hutton and Gibb successfully appealed against the light. At none for none, England needed 696 to win. On the seventh day, bespectacled Yorkshireman Paul Gibb batted through for 78 runs. He was the anchor for Hutton (55) and Bill Edrich (107 not out), and England reached 253 for one. Edrich was the big surprise. His previous highest score for England was 29 and he had been dogged by a run of failures. Now Hammond sent him in early and he came off in fine form.

On the eighth day, a Saturday, it rained. There were now signs that the England party could be pressed for time. They were booked on a return boat passage from Cape Town and would need to leave Durban on Tuesday evening to catch the boat. Three MCC touring players, not selected for the Durban Test, had already left for Cape Town.

The next day, a Sunday, was the second rest day of the Test. On the ninth day of the match, Gibb and Edrich took their stand to 280 before Gibb was out. His innings, which started on Thursday evening and ended on Monday afternoon, lasted nine hours and contained only two fours and a five (four overthrows) in boundaries. Edrich's 219 set up England for a possible winning position. At the close they were 496 for three, needing another 200 to win. The next day, the tenth, would have to be the last, so the party could ensure their passage on the *Athlone Castle*. There was no other boat for a fortnight if they missed it.

Hammond, 58 not out overnight, played a superb innings in the morning. Paynter stayed until the score was 611, and, when a very tired Newson took the new ball, the twelfth of the match, England were 619 for four. After being over 400 behind on the fifth day, with ten South African wickets still to fall, they were now within range. Then a couple of short stoppages for rain interrupted the concentration of Hammond, who went for 140. At tea, when England needed another 42 with five wickets remaining, it rained. This time it didn't stop.

The South African Board of Control met with the two captains and at 5.45p.m. issued a statement: 'The South African Cricket Association Control Board, in consultation with the captains, agreed that the match should be abandoned, the Board recognising that the MCC would otherwise not have the requisite number of hours in Cape Town before sailing home.' After ten days, and over 43 hours of play, the final Test of the series was a draw, which is probably not easy for an American to understand.

The last timeless Test has left its legacy in the record books. The major records include the highest aggregate number of runs (1,981) for a first-class match (since exceeded, though not in a Test match), Edrich and Gibb's record stand for any wicket against South Africa (still a record for the second wicket), the highest fourth-innings total in a Test, the longest first-class match (beating the nine-day epic in the West Indies in 1930) and Paul Gibb's slowest-ever century (since 'beaten' by Jackie McGlew of

South Africa). The total of 16 fifties was a record for Tests, as was Verity's achievement of bowling as many as 766 balls.

SOUTH AFRICA

P.G. van der Byl b Perks	125	c Paynter b Wright	97
A. Melville hit wkt b Wright	78	(6) b Farnes	103
E.A. Rowan lbw b Perks	33	(3) c Edrich b Verity	0
B. Mitchell b Wright	11	(2) hit wkt b Verity	89
A.D. Nourse b Perks	103	(4) c Hutton b Farnes	25
K. Viljoen c Ames b Perks	0	(5) b Perks	74
E.L. Dalton c Ames b Farnes	57	c and b Wright	21
R.E. Grieveson b Perks	75	b Farnes	39
A.B.C. Langton c Paynter b Verity	27	c Hammond b Farnes	6
E.S. Newson c and b Verity	1	b Wright	3
N. Gordon not out	0	not out	7
Extras	20		17
	530		**481**

Bowling: (8-ball overs): *First Innings*; Farnes 46–9–108–1, Perks 41–5–100–5, Wright 37–6–142–2, Verity 55.6–14–97–2, Hammond 14–4–34–0, Edrich 9–2–29–0. *Second Innings*; Farnes 22.1–2–74–4, Perks 32–6–99–1, Wright 32–7–146–3, Verity 40–9–87–2, Hammond 9–1–30–0, Edrich 6–1–18–0, Hutton 1–0–10–0.

80

ENGLAND

Hutton run out	38	b Mitchell	55
P.A. Gibb c Grieveson b Newson	4	b Dalton	120
Paynter lbw b Langton	62	(5) c Grieveson b Gordon	75
W.R. Hammond st Grieveson b Dalton	24	(4) st Grieveson b Dalton	140
Ames c Dalton b Langton	84	(6) not out	17
Edrich c Rowan b Langton	1	(3) c Gordon b Langton	219
B.H. Valentine st Grieveson b Dalton	26	not out	4
Verity b Dalton	3		
Wright c Langton b Dalton	26		
K. Farnes b Newson	20		
Perks not out	2		
Extras	26		24
	316		**654–5**

Bowling: (8-ball overs): *First Innings*; Newson 25.6–5–58–2, Langton 35–12–71–3, Gordon 37–7–82–0, Mitchell 7–0–20–0, Dalton 13–1–59–4. *Second Innings*; Newson 43–4–91–0, Langton 56–12–132–1, Gordon 55.2–1–174–1, Mitchell 37–4–133–1, Dalton 27–3–100–2.

A WIN AT LAST

NORTHAMPTON, MAY 1939

More than 2,000 spectators streamed on to the pitch, boys and old men together, the best runners grabbing stumps as souvenirs, the rest bolting for the pavilion to cheer their team's success.

'Speech, speech,' cried the crowd.

'Three cheers for the team,' someone shouted, and thousands of simultaneous cheers erupted.

Robert Nelson, the Northamptonshire captain, stood at the top of the pavilion steps and thanked the crowd for their loyal support. Their achievement had finally come. It would be the first of many, he assured them, and that night even the non-drinkers in the team got drunk.

It could have been the scene at the end of the final of a major limited-overs competition, but it wasn't. It was simply a victory for Northamptonshire in the County Championship, the county's first for four years, their first win in Northamptonshire since midway through the 1934 season and their first win at the County ground headquarters for six years. Since their last win, Northamptonshire had played 101 games. No wonder the crowd felt like celebrating.

From the start, the game against Leicestershire on the Whitsuntide week-end was a strange match, and not only because it took place during the one-year experiment of eight-ball overs. Within 35 minutes, Leicestershire were reduced to eight for five without help from fielders, and

Northamptonshire's unenviable record – the lowest first-class total of 12 – was under threat. Partridge took wickets with the fourth ball of his first over (Watson) and the fourth ball of his second (Armstrong). Buswell took wickets with the first ball of his third over (Berry) and the first of his fourth (Dempster). By lunch, though, Leicestershire had recovered to reach 97 for seven.

The rest of the day belonged to Northamptonshire. Bowling out Leicestershire – almost literally, as eight were bowled – for 134, they reached 280 for two by the close.

The next day, a Bank Holiday Monday, there were 6,352 paying spectators at the County ground. Northants extended their innings to just over six hours for 510 runs, Nelson declaring at 3.20p.m. Dennis Brookes scored 24 fours in his 187, helping his county to their highest score for six years.

Leicestershire worked their way to 53 without loss by tea-time, but the final session of the second day was sensational. Merritt spun through the rest of the team, and, after 20 minutes of the extra half-hour, Northamptonshire had an emphatic victory, worth waiting four years for. The inclusion of the game in this book is a testimony to those people who have answered my queries about strange games with the familiar retort: 'It would be a strange game if our lot won.'

Nelson's optimism in his closing speech was justified, for Northants now had a regular captain and some useful young players, like the underrated Brookes. The late 1930s had been an erratic period of captaincy, and the team had suffered from a tragic 1936 motor accident which had killed Northway and seriously injured Fred Bakewell, preventing the county's star batsman from playing again. The situation had been aggravated by the county's financial concerns, but with the win came hope. Unfortunately, the war soon came and, in October 1940, Robert Nelson, still only 28, was killed on service with the Royal Marines. Northamptonshire's next win in the County Championship was not until 16 July 1946.

LEICESTERSHIRE

L.G. Berry b Buswell	3	b Buswell	31
Watson b Partridge	1	st James b Merritt	36
N.F. Armstrong b Partridge	1	lbw b Buswell	20
F. Prentice lbw b Partridge	1	lbw b Buswell	1
Mr C.S. Dempster b Buswell	0	b Partridge	10
M. Tompkin run out	32	st James b Merritt	13
G. Dawkes b Timms	16	c James b Merritt	1
G. Lester not out	44	c Greenwood b Merritt	29
Mr J.E. Walsh b Buswell	14	c. Partridge b Merritt	4
H.A. Smith b Nelson	13	st James b Merritt	8
W. Flamson b Nelson	0	not out	10
Extras	9		20
	134		**183**

Bowling: *First Innings*; Buswell 14–2–43–3, Partridge 13–2–38–3, Merritt 6–0–21–0, Timms 5–0–22–1, Nelson 1.6–0–1–2. *Second Innings*; Buswell 12–2–47–3, Partridge 12–3–45–1, Merritt 10.7–0–56–6, Timms 6–2–15–0, Nelson 1–1–0–0.

NORTHAMPTONSHIRE

H.W. Greenwood c Smith b Flamson	8
P. Davis st Dempster b Walsh	84
D. Brookes c Armstrong b Lester	187
J.E. Timms c Tompkin b Flamson	55
Mr R.P. Nelson run out	44
L.P. O'Brien b Walsh	10
K.C. James not out	42
M. Dunkley c Smith b Flamson	12
W.E. Merritt lbw b Flamson	7
R.J. Partridge not out	20
Extras	41
(declared)	**510–8**

Bowling: Flamson 27–2–125–4, Smith 31–1–99–0, Walsh 33–1–157–2, Lester 13–0–60–1, Armstrong 3–0–7–0, Prentice 4–0–21–0.

'IS HUNT'S FEAT
A WORLD RECORD?'
LINLITHGOW, SCOTLAND, JULY 1939

'Is Hunt's feat a world record?' asked the reporter from Aberdeen's *Evening Express* after Alma Hunt's astonishing one-man effort in the one-innings game between West Lothian and Aberdeenshire.

Hunt, a Bermudan, bowled throughout the West Lothian innings and finished with the excellent figures of 12.7–6– 11–7, this being the year of the experiment with eight-ball overs. These statistics demonstrate both parsimony (only 11 runs off 103 balls) and penetration (only one of the seven wickets was caught). He took his last three wickets in four balls.

Alma Hunt's bowling performance would have been enough to satisfy most mortals, but Hunt's batting was even more amazing. He knocked off the 49 runs needed for victory literally on his own.

It is worth looking at the details of this amazing innings. Dumbreck opened the bowling for West Lothian, and Hunt faced the first five balls without scoring. A four and a single meant that Findlay faced only the last ball of that first over. However, a single by Hunt from the first ball of Benham's opening over gave Findlay seven balls to face. He failed to score. Aberdeenshire were six for none at the end of two eight-ball overs.

Hunt did not score from the next six balls, bowled by Ford, but a single left Findlay the last ball to play. At this stage, therefore, there was nothing particularly odd about the score – seven for none from three overs (Hunt seven, Findlay nought). In the next over, bowled by Benham, Hunt let rip, pulling and driving powerfully. The over brought 0, 4, 6, 4, 4, 0, 0 and 1, and the Aberdeenshire score moved to 26 (Hunt 26 not out). Any collusion can be discounted by the details of the next over, bowled by Ford. Hunt hit the third ball for four, then took a single from the fourth. This left Findlay on strike, and, though he was trying to get off the mark, the opening bat failed to score from the last four balls of the over. This left Aberdeenshire 31 for none (Hunt 31 not out).

Dumbreck came back into the attack, and Hunt finished the match in six balls, hitting 6, 0, 0, 4, 4, and 4. Aberdeenshire had reached the winning target of 49 without loss. Hunt was 49 not out. He had faced 33 balls compared with Findlay's 13. The innings was over in 25 minutes.

Is Hunt's feat a world record?

WEST LOTHIAN
F.C. Benham lbw b Hunt 8
R.R. Philip c Mellis b Donaldson 4
J. Dumbreck c Rice b Donaldson 1
Benham c Robertson b Hunt 5
A.C. Ford b Hunt 10
J.H. Matheson c Findlay b Catto 8
W. Summerville b Hunt 1
W. MacKay not out 2
J. Clarke b Hunt 5
A.J. Benham b Hunt 0
J. Smart b Hunt 0
Extras 4
                                                      48

ABERDEENSHIRE
A. Hunt not out 49
T.A. Findlay not out 0
Extras 0
                                                    49–0

FOUR A SIDE
AT FENNER'S

CAMBRIDGE, JUNE 1940

Mr Baylis's team went in first, batting one at a time, doing their best to remember the innovative rules of this four-a-side contest. Each team had 50 minutes to bat and no boundaries were allowed.

Mr Thompson's four-man team spread themselves around Fenner's. One man bowled, one kept wicket, two men fielded. There were plenty of gaps in the field. Runs piled up.

The Baylis team notched 106 in 40 minutes, which, not surprisingly, was a fairly good scoring rate. Unusually, there was no not-out batsman. All four wickets fell. That was an agreed rule. The innings lasted almost to the end of the eighth eight-ball over.

When Mr Thompson's team batted, the opening bat, Crawford, obviously pondering his tactics while running around in the field, opted for a new strategy – pushing ones and twos, keeping both the fielders busy. His departure, for 50, precipitated a collapse. When the last man, Bower, came to the wicket, at 82, his team expected defeat. Twenty-five were needed to win, and Bower wasn't known for his batting. He wasn't known for his bowling either. He was the team's wicket-keeper.

Bower slowly picked his way towards the target. When the last over was called, his team needed five to win off the eight balls. The field placing was interesting – two on the off and none on the leg side. It was canny enough to make it difficult for Bower, who swung unsuccessfully at the first six balls, one of which offered a difficult stumping chance.

Two balls to go. Five runs still needed. Somehow Bower contrived to heave the seventh ball round to square leg and it disappeared towards the trees. The bowler took the responsibility for the long chase. Bower ran four.

One needed from the last ball, bowled by a very tired Bridger. Bower hit it to mid-on. It was worth four more. Bower's last-wicket stand of 28 had won the strange game.

G.P. BAYLIS'S IV
J.R. Bridger st Bower b Thompson 75
G.P. Baylis lbw b Webster 12
C.E. Coote b Thompson 5
M.R.G. Earle Davis b Thompson 3
Extras 11
                                                                      106

Bowling: Webster 4–0–43–1, Thompson 3.7–0–52–3.

J.R. THOMPSON'S IV
M.G. Crawford c Bridger b Earle Davis 50
J.R. Thompson lbw b Bridger 0
J. Webster c Bridger b Earle Davis 19
A.J. Bower not out 28
Extras 13
                                                                   110–3

Bowling: Earle Davis 5–0–27–2, Bridger 5–0–70–1.

LORD'S UNDER FIRE
LORD'S, LONDON, JULY 1944

The game between the Army and the RAF, at Lord's in 1944, is memorable for a couple of key *incidents* and may not be considered, strictly speaking, a strange *game*. However, it does give a flavour of the background to wartime cricket.

The key incidents occurred early in the game, which started at 2p.m. The Army, having won the toss, had progressed to 57 for one when an all-too-familiar noise was heard in the sky. Hidden among the clouds was a German flying-bomb, which had found its own way into Britain's air space and then, when its engine cut out, would crash and explode automatically on English soil. If the noise suddenly stopped before the bomb was overhead it was the time to head for cover.

When the bomb went silent near Lord's, the players on the field did the best they could, diving to the ground. The spectators – there were 3,100 of them – took up strange postures in positions they deemed safe. The bomb whistled as it came down and looked as though it would land in the practice-ground at Lord's. In fact it fell 200 yards (183m) short, in Albert Road, according to one source. *Wisden* describes the bomb's journey as from the south, and recounts that it dropped in Regent's Park.

The players stood up and restarted play. Two balls later came the second incident. Jack Robertson, the Middlesex player, hooked a ball from Bob Wyatt for six. The crowd cheered and morale was restored.

The Army left their declaration late – maybe they felt it

was safer in the pavilion – and the RAF were set 212 in 105 minutes. Charlie Barnett started as though he would score the bulk of the runs himself, but the middle-order batsmen failed. Walter Hammond, after three years in Africa and a recent back injury, wasn't yet at top form but he was unlucky to be dismissed by a brilliant catch. Les Ames and Wyatt got stuck in, and forced the draw.

After this flying-bomb incident, it was decided to move the forthcoming public-school games, customarily played at Lord's, to safer venues in the provinces.

THE ARMY

Lt J.D. Robertson b Wyatt	42
Cpl H. Halliday b Matthews	12
Sgt C.B. Harris c Oakes b Wyatt	12
Lt M. Leyland c Hammond b Oakes	28
Capt. C.H. Townsend c Wilson b Wyatt	52
Lt C.H. Palmer lbw b Matthews	11
L/Cpl W.L. Creese b Wyatt	10
Sgt T.G. Evans c Hammond b Wyatt	1
Lt/Col G.O. Allen not out	17
Bdr L.L. Wilkinson not out	13
Extras	13
(declared)	211–8

Bowling: Matthews 21–5–53–2, Edrich 6–0–24–0, Wyatt 19–2–81–5, Oakes 6–1–23–1. Warburton 5–0–17–0.

ROYAL AIR FORCE

Flt/Lt C.J. Barnett c Townsend b Pollard	18
F/O R.T. Simpson c Evans b Pollard	25
Sgt D. Brookes lbw b Allen	22
Flt/Lt W.R. Hammond c and b Wilkinson	3
Sqd./Ldr W.J. Edrich b Pollard	6
Sqd./Ldr L.E.G. Ames not out	24
F/O R.E.S. Wyatt c Wilkinson b Leyland	11
F/O E.W. Wilson c Evans b Creese	7
Sgt C. Oakes b Pollard	4
L/A/C L. Warburton not out	0
Extras	9
	129–8

Bowling: Pollard 12–4–33–4, Allen 7–1–25–1, Wilkinson 11–0–50–1, Creese 3–0–10–1, Leyland 1–0–1–1, Robertson 1–0–1–0.

THE BIGGEST STAND
BARODA, INDIA, MARCH 1947

In the final of the cricket championship of India, played for the Ranji Trophy, Baroda and Holkar had all the time in the world to complete their game, but Holkar started as though a rapid conclusion was required. They were 20 for four after 30 minutes, and 78 for six at lunch. Chandra Sarwate, famous in England for his last-wicket partnership of 249 with Shute Banerjee against Surrey in 1946, held the innings together and deserved a century. When the last wicket fell at 202, after only 248 minutes' batting, Sarwate had an unbeaten 94 to his credit. When Baroda batted, C.K. Nayudu, India's first-ever captain (in 1932), took three wickets and the game looked relatively well-balanced. Baroda were 91 for three, and, if Holkar could break through the fourth-wicket pair, Gul Mahomed and Vijay Hazare, they would be in control. However, a stand of 577, a world record in first-class cricket, obliterated any cause for optimism.

As one might expect of Gul Mahomed and Vijay Hazare, who batted throughout the third day, one was left-handed, the other right-handed. Poor Holkar fielders.

Vijay Hazare, who had taken six wickets in the Holkar first innings, helped to overhaul his own Indian partnership record, made with 'Ranga' Sohoni for Maharashtra against Bombay six years previously. His role in another major stand – 266 out of 300 with Vivek Hazare in 1943–4 – was also legendary. But this stand of 577, completed against a useful full-strength bowling attack, replaced the unbroken 574, made by Frank Worrell (255) and Clyde Walcott (314) for Barbados in February 1946, as the new world record for any wicket in first-class cricket. Curiously, both were fourth-wicket partnerships.

Gul Mahomed made 319 in 505 minutes, and Vijay Hazare scored 288. Both batsmen were out in the same way, caught at first slip by Jagdale off the bowling of Gaekwad. The last seven Baroda wickets tumbled for 116 runs. Had it not been for the mammoth stand, Holkar would have ended the first innings at something approaching parity. Instead they were spun to defeat by Amir Elahi, and the game was over by 15 minutes before the tea interval on the fifth day. The margin was an innings and 409 runs. Vijay Hazare had match bowling figures of eight for 137 to add to his innings of 288, and Gul Mahomed, scorer of 319, took two catches and bowled six tidy overs. Theirs is still the world record for a partnership of any wicket.

HOLKAR

Mushtaq Ali lbw b Hazare	8	run out ... 10
M. Jagdale c Nimbalkar b Ahmed Patel	0	c Ahmed Patel b Amir Elahi ... 21
C.T. Sarwate not out	94	c Gul Mahomed b Amir Elahi ... 1
B.B. Nimbalkar b Hazare	0	b Hazare ... 87
C.K. Nayudu c Nimbalkar b Hazare	0	c Vivek Hazare b Amir Elahi ... 0
C.S. Nayudu st Nimbalkar b Amir Elahi	20	c and b Adhikari ... 28
J.N. Bhaya c Nimbalkar b Hazare	0	c Nimbalkar b Amir Elahi ... 12
Gaekwad b Amir Elahi	27	b Amir Elahi ... 1
Kunzru st Nimbalkar b Amir Elahi	28	c Gul Mahomed b Amir Elahi ... 4
Surendra Singh b Hazare	5	c Vivek Hazare b Amir Elahi ... 1
O. Rawal b Hazare	4	not out ... 2
Extras	16	... 6
	202	173

Bowling: *First Innings*; Vijay Hazare 32.2–7–85–6, Ahmed Patel 11–4–30–1, Vivek Hazare 4–1–15–0, Amir Elahi 32–9–47–3, Vichare 2–1–3–0, Adhikari 2–0–6–0. *Second Innings*; Vijay Hazare 13–8–52–2, Ahmed Patel 3–0–10–0, Vivek Hazare 7–5–35–0, Amir Elahi 33–1–62–6, Adhikari 5–2–3–1, Gul Mahomed 6–2–5–0.

BARODA

S.G. Powar c Jadgale b Nayudu (C.K.)	14
Nimbalkar b Nayudu (C.K.)	43
H. Adhikari lbw b Nayudu (C.K.)	19
V.S. Hazare c Jagdale b Gaekwad	288
Gul Mahomed c Jagdale b Gaekwad	319
Yuvaraj of Baroda c Mushtaq Ali b Nayudu (C.K.)	1
M.M. Naidu lbw b Gaekwad	8
Amir Elahi run out	1
Vichare run out	24
Vivek Hazare not out	10
Ahmed Patel b Sarwate	17
Extras	40
	784

Bowling: Gaekwad 71–19–134–3, Jagdale 24–1–81–0, Nayudu (C.S.) 48–6–160–0, Nayudu (C.K.) 80–12–178–4, Sarwate 43–8–93–1, Mushtaq Ali 2–0–8–0, Surendra Singh 9–0–37–0, Rawal 12–4–50–0, Kunzru 2–0–3–0.

Fall of wickets: 60, 65, 91, 668, 671, 692, 693, 746, 754, 784

LAST MAN 163
CHESTERFIELD, AUGUST 1947

When Ray Smith was caught by Marsh off Pope, Essex were 199 for nine, still 24 behind Derbyshire's first-innings total of 223. On his walk back to the dressing-room Smith passed his cousin, Peter Smith, an unusual number-11 batsman if ever there was one.

The previous season Peter Smith was one of the five *Wisden* cricketers of the year, in the distinguished company of Laurie Fishlock, Vinoo Mankad, Cyril Washbrook and Alec Bedser, but his special talent lay in bowling leg-breaks, googlies and top-spinners rather than batting. Ipswich-born, Smith had had early pretensions as a batsman and quick bowler, but, when attending a trial with Essex, he bowled leg spinners by chance, just when the county were about to reject him. In his first season he played five games and picked up one wicket – a full toss landed on the top of Jupp's stumps – but one event of that season was recalled almost 20 years later. In his first county match, against Derbyshire, Peter Smith watched the opposition's opening bats, Storer and Bowden, put together a stand of 322. Whether or not he intended to pay back Derbyshire for this some day is a matter for conjecture, but he certainly did so on an August day in 1947.

Peter Smith could bat a bit, and he moved up and down the batting order. In 1936 he hit a century in 80 minutes against Hampshire, and, batting at three, he scored another century against Hampshire just after the war. In this 1947 season, however, his benefit year, Peter Smith's form had been erratic. In the last match, against Worcestershire, batting at ten, he had been bowled by Jackson for nought in both innings. On that form he deserved his place at number 11 against Derbyshire. On his form against Derbyshire, though, he made a mockery of it all.

In 140 minutes, Peter Smith scored 163 runs, surely the most devastating annihilation a number 11 has given first-class bowling. Vigar, the number-five Essex bat, offered support and steadily made his way to his own century. When Smith was finally bowled by Worthington, the two men had put on 218 for the last wicket. Peter Smith offered two hard chances while hitting three sixes and 22 fours in his scintillating innings.

In their second innings, Derbyshire lost eight wickets before they took the lead. Almost as intriguing as Essex's lower-order revival was that of Derbyshire. Cliff Gladwin, batting at ten, scored a 50 and was his county's second highest scorer for the second time in the match. Gothard, at nine, made runs for the second time. And, even more surprising was the 38 not out made by fast-bowler Bill Copson, who went in last for Derbyshire. Copson was a rustic bat who swung the bat hard and was never expected to stay long. In his career he averaged 6.81 in 279 matches. There is a story of him going out to bat against Glamorgan at Swansea and simply plonking the bat down in the block-hole.

'Don't you want a guard, Bill?' the umpire asked.

'No, I had one here last year.'

In Essex's second innings, when they were set 111 to win, Peter Smith was promoted in the order. He made four. But that year he did the 'double' of 100 wickets and 1,000 runs for the first time in his career, and his cousin Ray did the same.

DERBYSHIRE

A. Townsend b P. Smith	86	b R. Smith	1
C.S. Elliott b R. Smith	2	run out	68
T.S. Worthington c P. Smith b Bailey	0	b Bailey	9
D. Smith run out	10	b R. Smith	35
G.H. Pope c Insole b Bailey	5	c Dodds b Bailey	11
A. E. Alderman b Bailey	20	c Insole b Bailey	27
E. Marsh c Crabtree b P. Smith	24	c Horsfall b Bailey	4
A.E. Rhodes c Insole b P. Smith	4	c Horsfall b R. Smith	0
E.J. Gothard not out	24	b R. Smith	40
C. Gladwin c Insole b Bailey	27	c Wilcox b Bailey	52
W.H. Copson b Bailey	0	not out	38
Extras	21		19
	223		**304**

Bowling: *First Innings*; Bailey 24.2–1–83–5, R. Smith 18–3–50–1, T.P.B. Smith 18–2–59–3, Vigar 2–0–10–0. *Second Innings*; Bailey 30.5–6–92–5, R. Smith 49–14–122–4, T.P.B. Smith 22–6–53–0, Vigar 5–0–18–0.

ESSEX

T.C. Dodds lbw b Copson	20	c Townsend b Copson	23
S.J. Cray b Copson	11	b Pope	9
A.V. Avery c Pope b Copson	0	lbw b Pope	0
H.P. Crabtree lbw b Pope	2	c Worthington b Gladwin	30
F.H. Vigar not out	114	not out	40
R. Horsfall b Pope	8	not out	3
D.R. Wilcox b Gladwin	9		
T.E. Bailey b Worthington	19		
D.J. Insole b Copson	48		
R. Smith c Marsh b Pope	21		
T.P.B. Smith b Worthington	163	c Worthington b Copson	4
Extras	2		5
	417		**114–5**

Bowling: *First Innings*; Copson 36–8–117–4, Pope 27–8–73–3, Gladwin 13–3–54–1, Worthington 21.5–1–90–2, Rhodes 18–4–44–0, Marsh 11–3–37–0.
Second Innings; Copson 14–3–36–2, Pope 15–5–39–2, Gladwin 3.1–0–15–1, Rhodes 5–0–19–0.

LAKING AGAINST THE REST

BRADFORD, MAY 1950

In northern England, the verb 'to lake' means to play or
sport, and Jim Laker certainly lived up to his name. Although
he spent his career in the south, he was born in Yorkshire,
5 miles (8km) from the ground at Bradford, the setting for
the England-against-the-Rest Test trial on the last day of
May 1950. The slight fall of the Bradford ground was even
more suited to Laker's off-break bowling on a wicket that
was difficult for batsmen.

Norman Yardley, the England captain, won the toss and
gave the Rest first innings. It was an astonishing innings.
When Jim Laker came on to bowl, early in the game, the
Rest were ten for one. Virtually single-handed, Laker
bowled them out. The Rest reached their total of 27, made
in 110 minutes, only with the help of a spirited innings of
five from last-man Les Jackson. Even so, it was, at the time,
the record lowest total for a representative game.

Jim Laker ended with the sensational figures of 14–12–2–
8. The only runs in 14 overs were two singles, one by Bedser
in the fifth over, by when Laker had taken his first three
wickets, and one by Trueman in the eleventh, at which point
Laker had seven wickets. It was a performance which had
reporters searching for similar analyses where wickets had
dominated runs. Only Gideon Elliott of Victoria, who took
nine for two against Tasmania in 1858, had ever returned
an analysis in a first-class innings where wickets dominated

runs by more than five. However, Jim Laker later told the story of how one young reporter had asked him if they were his best-ever figures.

Seven of Laker's wickets came in succession. Doggart (caught at forward short-leg) and May (caught at backward short-leg) went in his first over. Carr was caught off a skier at mid-wicket and Kenyon went to a leg-side catch by wicket-keeper Godfrey Evans. Eric Bedser was leg-before and then Spooner and Berry went in the same over. Alec Bedser broke the spell by taking Trueman's wicket.

By the end of the day, the Rest were batting again, 202 behind on first innings. Coincidentally they reached 27 by the end of play. This time there were only two wickets down rather than ten, and only one had been claimed by Jim Laker. The next day Eric Hollies finished off the match, and England won by an innings and 89 runs after less than eight hours' play. The selectors had learned very little. The Test 12, announced soon after the trial, included all the 'England' team except Robertson and Dewes, plus two from the Rest, Doggart and Berry, and a choice between Compton and Dollery which was dependent on fitness.

THE REST

Kenyon c Evans b Laker 7	lbw b Hollies 9
Sheppard lbw b Bailey 4	b Laker 3
Doggart c Bailey b Laker 2	st Evans b Hollies 12
May c Hutton b Laker 0	b Laker 2
Carr c Bailey b Laker 0	st Evans b Hollies 2
Bedser (E.A.) lbw b Laker 3	c Evans b Hollies 30
Spooner b Laker 0	c Yardley b Bedser (A.V.) ...22
Jenkins not out 0	c Bedser (A.V.) b Hollies 3
Berry b Laker 0	c Yardley b Bedser (A.V.) ...16
Trueman st Evans b Bedser (A.V.) 1	not out 0
Jackson c and b Laker 5	st Evans b Hollies 1
Extras 5	 13
27	113

Bowling: *First Innings*; Bailey 6–4–3–1, Bedser (A.V.) 9–3–12–1, Laker 14–12–2–8, Hollies 7–5–5–0. *Second Innings*; Bailey 5–2–6–0, Bedser (A.V.) 9–2–22–2, Laker 18–4–44–2, Hollies 22.4–13–28–6.

ENGLAND

Hutton b Trueman 85
Simpson st Spooner b Berry 26
Edrich lbw b Jenkins 46
Robertson c Shepherd b Berry 0
Dewes c Doggart b Berry 34
Yardley c Trueman b Jenkins 13
Bailey c Spooner b Berry 7
Evans run out 1
Laker not out 6
Bedser (A.V.) c Jackson b Jenkins 5
Hollies st Spooner b Berry 4
Extras 2
                                                                    229

Bowling: Jackson 12–3–38–0, Bedser (E.A.) 13–0–60–0, Jenkins 10–0–38–3,
Berry 32–10–73–5, Trueman 9–3–18–1.

SLOW PROGRESS
NOTTINGHAM, JUNE AND JULY 1951

In those days Trent Bridge was a batting paradise, and the Nottingham crowd were quick to barrack any batsman not taking full advantage. Take Charlie Harris, for instance. The Nottinghamshire stalwart, a natural comedian who would hang a 'do not disturb' notice over his stumps or take a torch out of his pocket to signify the light was bad, was once batting on a perfect track at Trent Bridge, and the barrackers were booing angrily. Harris, scoring more slowly than his usual rate of 25 an hour, responded by swinging a ball to leg for four. He walked towards the Trent Bridge Hotel. 'Let me know when I get behind the clock again,' he shouted.

The barrackers had a big day out when Glamorgan visited Trent Bridge at the end of June 1951. What set them off was the attitude of Glamorgan captain Wilf Wooller, who had reasoned, with some sense, that the most a team could expect from Trent Bridge was four points from first innings. Wooller, a man of strong opinions who had captained a Glamorgan team without stars to the 1948 County Championship, was happy to see his batsmen slowly grind through the first day. The crowd were not.

Left-hander Emrys Davies made his 110 in four hours, but Jones and Wooller himself were far slower, scoring only 12 runs from 15 overs on a perfect afternoon, refusing to be tempted by Nottinghamshire's deep-set field. The crowd booed, frustrated in the hot sun, realising that

Nottinghamshire, bottom of the table, would gain nothing if Glamorgan simply occupied the crease. Eventually Nottinghamshire captain Reg Simpson could stand no more of it. He brought himself on to bowl and stood beside umpire Joe Hill, explaining how he was going to bowl. When he bowled his first ball, the crowd audibly gasped, and the press-box came alive. Simpson was bowling underarm lobs. Wooller, of course, played them back watchfully, but Simpson shouted loudly when one hit a pad. The over was worth two runs, no wickets, and plenty of column inches in the newspapers. Strangely, Glamorgan lost four wickets soon after this incident.

A reader of the *Nottingham Evening Post*, calling himself *No-ball*, summed up the mood of the crowd in a letter later that week: 'I was shocked at Simpson's falling into the trap of making as big a farce of county cricket as the Glamorgan side, but now I think more about it the visitors certainly asked for it.' Glamorgan, batting on the next day, crawled to 330 in seven and a half hours, only quickening the rate when Muncer and Haydn Davis added 46 in 55 minutes. It must be remembered that teams regularly scored over 400 on the first day at Trent Bridge in the post-war era, and toss-losers had to rely on a thunderstorm or a declaration to halt a team's progress.

When Nottinghamshire batted they did no better. They lost three quick wickets before Walter Keeton and Freddie Stocks made a stand. Then it was left to Charlie Harris, the man the crowd loved to hate. Harris batted 105 minutes for his 29 runs, and the barracking was at its loudest.

'That's a bat in yer hand, 'arris.'

Harris, never flustered, simply tucked his bat under his arm and simulated machine-gun fire. Wooller, meanwhile, bowling from one end, took a long time placing his field. The crowd booed him too, and Wooller responded by stopping as he ran in to bowl and refusing to continue unless the barracking subsided.

Nottinghamshire, following on, saved the game by lunch-time on the shortened third day, the left-handed Poole making 135 in three and a half hours to restore some normality to the game. Wilf Wooller's final retort was to try all his bowlers – all 11 of them, including wicket-keeper Haydn Davis, who handed over his pads and gloves to Wooller. Davis got a wicket too, the only one of a career of 423 first-class matches. In fact, seven Glamorgan bowlers took wickets, including irregular bowlers like Montgomery (six wickets in his career), Clift (11 wickets) and Parkhouse (two).

It was after this game that Nottinghamshire decided to do something about their wicket at Trent Bridge, while, the next month, Glamorgan became the only county to beat the touring South Africans that year.

GLAMORGAN

E. Davies b Stocks	110
P.B. Clift b Harvey	19
W.G.A. Parkhouse lbw b Jepson	36
W.E. Jones c Harvey b Farr	20
A.J. Watkins lbw b Jepson	24
W. Wooller c Meads b Harvey	13
S. Montgomery c Meads b Farr	0
B.L. Muncer not out	46
J. McConnon lbw b Farr	1
H.G. Davis c Simpson b Richardson	45
N.G. Hever lbw b Farr	1
Extras	15
	330

Bowling: Jepson 30–6–79–2, Richardson 30–11–58–1, Farr 19–2–65–4, Stocks 30–21–31–1, Harvey 35–13–71–2, Harris 13–8–9–0, Simpson 1–0–2–0.

NOTTINGHAMSHIRE

W.W. Keeton lbw b Watkins	40	lbw b Hever	0
R.T. Simpson c Clift b Wooller	8	b Watkins	30
C.J. Poole c Clift b Hever	1	c Watkins b Montgomery	135
R. Giles b Wooller	2	lbw b McConnon	7
F.W. Stocks b Watkins	51	lbw b Parkhouse	35
C.B. Harris c Davis (H.) b Watkins	29		
P.F. Harvey not out	29	not out	28
A. Jepson c and b Wooller	1	c Watkins b Clift	21
B.H. Farr b Hever	2		
E.A. Meads c Clift b Watkins	4	hit wkt b Davis (H.)	2
A. Richardson b Hever	1	not out	0
Extras	4		2
	172		**260–7**

Bowling: *First Innings*; Hever 17.3–4–37–3, Wooller 30–10–60–3, Watkins 25–6–62–4, Muncer 6–2–9–0. *Second Innings*; Hever 10–2–26–1, Wooller 10–4–27–0, Watkins 9–3–24–1, Muncer 4–0–31–0, McConnon 17–2–48–1, Davies (E.) 9–2–20–0, Jones 6–1–11–0, Parkhouse 3–0–22–1, Montgomery 4–0–11–1, Clift 5–1–18–1, Davis (H.) 3–0–20–1.

FLOODLIGHTS AT HIGHBURY

LONDON, AUGUST 1952

In the daytime Middlesex were skittled for 77 by Surrey. In the evening, in aid of Jack Young's benefit, they took a team to Highbury football stadium to play a team of Arsenal footballers – at cricket. The novelty of the game was the use of floodlights, used on occasions in the early days of cricket. A crowd of 8,000 turned up, while millions saw the last part of the action on television.

Instead of sight-screens there were goal-posts, while the centre-circle was partly covered by a black matting wicket. The rectangular shape of Highbury's football pitch necessitated short on and off boundaries, but fair-sized straight boundaries. The Bedser twins acted as umpires, the Compton brothers were the two captains, and the crowd knew they were in for a strange, entertaining evening when the Middlesex team of 13 players, having lost the toss, came out of the tunnel kicking footballs.

Taking advantage of the short boundaries, Arsenal rattled up an all-out score of 189, made in little more than an hour. Colin Grimshaw made 65, Freddie Cox scored 21 and big centre-forward Cliff Holton scored more easily than he usually did at Highbury. Les Compton, playing for Arsenal though he had an option on either team, mixed sports easily when he shoulder-charged Bill Edrich, the Middlesex fielder, in order to ensure a safer single.

The Arsenal innings ended in gloomy conditions. When

the floodlights were switched on, the crowd cheered. The tannoy announcer then communicated one of the strangest messages heard at a cricket ground: 'Keep your eye on the ball. When you see it coming, keep low. The batsmen will try to keep it down, but they can't promise.'

To make the spectators' task easier, the ball was white, constantly replaced when the paint chipped off. The cricketers said later that they had no trouble spotting the ball.

Bill Edrich scored 70, but Middlesex collapsed. At 187 for nine, they needed three to win with three wickets to fall, remembering that this was a 13-a-side game. At this critical point, out came Jack Young, the beneficiary, a bowler who would take 137 wickets that season despite a troublesome knee injury. Young came to the wicket wearing a miner's helmet and lamp. Middlesex scored the required runs, and were allowed to bat on until they were all out.

The floodlighting experiment received a good press, but there was little likelihood that it would enjoy the same popularity in cricket as it did in football towards the end of the 1950s. There were various cricketing experiments with luminous stumps in South Africa and lighting for schoolboys in Australia, but it was not until the late 1970s that the idea of floodlit cricket games was resurrected.

ARSENAL: 189 all out.
MIDDLESEX: 237 all out.

SUTCLIFFE'S MASTERLY INNINGS

CHRISTCHURCH, NEW ZEALAND, DECEMBER 1952

'In batting, much will depend on Bert Sutcliffe, who has been showing delightful form in club matches.'

That was how the *Christchurch Star-Sun* summarised Otago's chances against Canterbury in the first Plunket Shield match of the 1952–3 season. Canterbury were holders of the Shield, so Otago had an uphill task ... unless Sutcliffe came off.

It was 12.34p.m. on the second day when Sutcliffe and Watt opened the first and only Otago innings of the game. Canterbury, 233 for five overnight (Leggat 104 not out), had taken their score to 309 before the fall of the last wicket. News that Sutcliffe was batting brought in more spectators. The brilliant 29-year-old left-hander already had a stream of big scores in his career – 208 for North Island v South Island (1947–8), 243 for New Zealand against Essex (1949), 275 for Otago against Auckland (1950–1) and 355 for Otago v Auckland (1949–50).

Canterbury could have had Sutcliffe out before he had scored. The two opening batsmen sprinted an extremely risky single and Smith shied at the stumps. Had the ball hit, Sutcliffe was out. Instead it went for four overthrows.

Hayes picked up two wickets, Watt and Haig, but had to leave the field with a stomach-muscle injury before Otago had reached 100. Sutcliffe settled in to demonstrate his driving, pulling and hooking, stealing singles to keep the bowling whenever he could. He was utterly in charge. He dominated the bowlers and dominated his partners. He added 42 for the third wicket and Flaws scored four of them. He added 115 for the fourth wicket and Watson contributed a dozen. The fifth wicket raised 55 and Mills scored 12. At the close of the second day, Otago were 284 for five, and Sutcliffe, 215 not out, had given just one chance, very hard and very low to slip when on 189. It wasn't much to keep the fielders interested.

On the third day, Sutcliffe, unshaken by his not-out lunchtime score of 299, broke his own New Zealand individual scoring record and established a new record which still stands. His 385 was the record first-class score for a left-handed batsman.

With Gilbertson (29), Sutcliffe added 182 for the seventh wicket. By the time he was out, he had scored 385 out of the 471 that had come from the bat, 385 out of his team's 500. It was an astonishing innings that supporters of both provinces thoroughly enjoyed, recognising the quality of the play. He gave one more difficult 'hot chance' on that final day of the innings.

The statistics of the innings, which lasted less than eight hours, emphasised Sutcliffe's consistently fast run-getting pace: 50 in 72 minutes, 100 in 128 minutes, 200 in 247 minutes, 250 in 316 minutes, 300 in 379 minutes, 350 in 428 minutes and 385 in 460 minutes. He scored 46 fours and three sixes, and one over from Poore cost 30 runs.

The demoralised Canterbury team slumped heavily in the second innings, ending the day on 91 for nine with the injured Hayes as one of the not-out batsmen. Otago needed eight minutes of the fourth day to seal the game, winning by an innings and 93 runs. In two innings, Canterbury had scored 382 runs from the bat, three fewer than Bert Sutcliffe had managed on his own.

CANTERBURY

Leggat c Moir b Overton 110
Emery b Stanley 0
Harris c Mills b Overton 18
Chapple c Gilbertson b Smith 79
Poore c Watson b Moir 5
Smith b Moir 0
MacGibbon c Flaws b Overton 28
Britton b Smith 11
Burtt b Moir 29
Hayes b Sutcliffe 19
McNicholl not out 0
Extras 10
                                                                          309

c Mills b Stanley 14
c Haig b Overton 14
c Mills b Overton 0
c Sutcliffe b Smith 2
(6) c Flaws b Stanley 8
(5) c Flaws b Overton 11
c Flaws b Smith 5
b Moir 10
c Haig b Stanley 8
c Haig b Watson 5
not out 6
.... 15
                                       98

Bowling: *First Innings*; Overton 27–6–73–3, Stanley 18–5–54–1, Smith 25–9–41–2, Moir 27–2–97–3, Sutcliffe 7.3–1–34–1. *Second Innings*; Overton 14–8–25–3, Stanley 14–9–22–3, Smith 11–5–21–2, Moir 2–1–4–1, Sutcliffe 2–0–5–0, Watson 1.1–0–6–1.

Fall of wickets: *First Innings*; 4, 29, 175, 192, 192, 247, 258, 260, 307, 309. *Second Innings*; 16, 26, 29, 44, 60, 65, 67, 87, 87, 98.

OTAGO

Sutcliffe b Poore 385
Watt c Smith b Hayes 19
Haig lbw b Hayes 0
Flaws b Burtt 4
Watson c Smith b Burtt 12
Mills lbw b McNicholl 12
Smith lbw b McNicholl 8
Gilbertson c Leggat b Burtt 29
Moir b Poore 0
Stanley not out 2
Overton st Britton b Poore 0
Extras 29
                                                                          500

Bowling: Hayes 9–2–20–2, McNicholl 16–2–92–2, Chapple 28–6–81–0, MacGibbon 20–1–76–0, Burtt 43–10–88–3, Harris 9–2–37–0, Poore 13.5–7–48–3, Emery 4–0–29–0.

Fall of wickets: 61, 61, 103, 218, 273, 300, 482, 483, 500, 500.

THE LOWEST
COUNTY-CHAMPIONSHIP
AGGREGATE

THE OVAL, AUGUST 1954

In the 1950s Surrey won seven successive County
Championships. The game which sealed the third of these
titles, at home to Worcestershire, provides one of the
clearest examples of a team's confidence in the midst of a
successful run.

In the first over of the game, delayed until 2 o'clock,
Worcestershire opener Peter Richardson was brilliantly
caught low down by Peter May at slip off Alec Bedser's
bowling. It was a typical example of the magnificent fielding
that had contributed to much of Surrey's sustained success.
Although Kenyon and Outschoorn stayed for 45 minutes
until the second wicket fell, the innings crumbled. The last
eight Worcestershire wickets fell for only five runs in 35
minutes. The 105-minute innings produced only 25 runs,
the lowest first-class score since 1947. Bedser made the
occasional ball lift, while Jim Laker and Tony Lock, Surrey's
spin twins, made the most of the wicket's acceptance of the
turning ball. Lock took five for two in 33 balls.

First-innings points would ensure Surrey a share in
the Championship. This was achieved without too much
difficulty, although, in another game with more normal
scoring, they might have claimed to have lost two cheap
wickets. Peter May batted well, Bernard Constable was
steady, but the amazing thing was that captain Stuart
Surridge should choose to declare with less than 100 on the

board. Such was the confidence in his bowlers on the Oval wicket that he opted to have an extra shot at Worcestershire before 6.30p.m. Also, rain was forecast. Lock and Laker opened the bowling, and each produced an impossible delivery. At the close Worcestershire were 13 for two, still 54 behind.

Surrey needed only an hour the next day, aided by Devereux having to retire with a fractured finger. The last-wicket pair, Yarnold and Ashman, coming together at 26 for eight, managed to delay the end with a few lusty strokes. Yarnold hit two fours, the only boundaries of the innings, and the total struggled to 40. Lock had incredible match figures of six for five, Laker six for 30 and Bedser five for 19.

Surrey's eighth win in nine games was completed in only four hours and 50 minutes of playing time. The total score of 157 (for 22 wickets and one retired hurt) is the lowest aggregate for a completed County Championship match.

WORCESTERSHIRE

Kenyon c Surridge b Bedser (A.V.)	8	c Stewart b Lock 0
P.E. Richardson c May b Bedser (A.V.)	0	c McIntyre b Laker 9
Outschoorn b Laker	9	c Lock b Laker 3
Broadbent c Laker b Lock	3	c McIntyre b Laker 1
Hughes run out	0	hit wkt b Bedser (A.V.) 2
Devereux not out	2	retired hurt 1
Jenkins c Stewart b Lock	1	c Laker b Bedser (A.V.) 1
Yarnold b Barrington b Lock	1	not out 14
Perks c Barrington b Laker	0	b Bedser (A.V.) 2
Flavell c Constable b Lock	0	c Clark b Laker 3
Ashman c and b Lock	0	c Bedser (A.V.) b Loader 2
Extras	1	 2
	25	**40**

Bowling: *First Innings*; Bedser (A.V.) 9–4–12–2, Loader 6–3–5–0, Laker 8–3–5–2, Lock 5.3–4–2–5. *Second Innings*; Lock 10–7–3–1, Laker 17–9–25–4, Bedser (A.V.) 6–3–7–3, Loader 2.4–1–3–1.

Fall of wickets: *First Innings*; 1,16, 20, 20, 21, 23, 25, 25, 25, 25. *Second Innings*; 0, 5, 13, 16, 16, 18, 23, 26, 40.

SURREY

Clark c Richardson b Perks	10
Stewart c Flavell b Perks	11
P.B.H. May not out	31
Constable c and b Ashman	29
Barrington not out	10
Extras	1
(declared)	92–3

Bowling: Perks 12–1–43–2, Flavell 3–1–17–0, Ashman 8–3–29–1, Devereux 1–0–2–0.

Fall of wickets: 12, 31, 77.

POLITICIANS
AGAINST THE STAGE
EAST GRINSTEAD, SEPTEMBER 1955

Can you imagine the present government putting together a team of cricketers which includes the Foreign Secretary, the Home Secretary, the Lord Chancellor, the Employment Minister and an assortment of other Members of Parliament? Well, it happened in 1955, and surprisingly there was no place for Sir Alec Douglas-Home, who had once been a useful cricketer.

The team of Politicians included Harold Macmillan (Foreign Secretary) and Viscount Kilmuir (Lord Chancellor), both of whom hadn't played for 30 years. (Viscount Kilmuir cheated somewhat by using practice nets a few times before the game.) Sir Walter Monckton (Minister of Labour) had played as recently as nine years before, but Major Lloyd George (Home Secretary) was another whose cricket kit was difficult to find and even more difficult to fit into.

The Stage XI, captained by John Mills, included regular Lord's Taverner cricketers like Leo Genn, John Slater, Richard Attenborough and Mills himself, but Douglas Fairbanks and David Niven were late cry-offs. Each team was strengthened by the inclusion of county cricketers – Gerald Cogger (Sussex) and Hubert Doggart (Sussex) for the Politicians, Denis Compton, Reg Routledge and John Warr (all Middlesex) for the Stage team – and there were two strange rules. One rule was that a batsman reaching 50 would compulsorily retire. The other was that any bowler capturing a player's wicket before he had scored would be fined a guinea.

The Politicians' captain Earl De La Warr (Postmaster-General) won the toss and decided that his team would bat. Lord Hawke, nephew of the famous cricketing namesake, opened the innings with Lieutenant-Colonel Bromley-Davenport, the MP for Knutsford, Cheshire. Lord Hawke made a single before being bowled by Denis Compton's second ball. Bromley-Davenport (29) and Lloyd George (three fours in his 23) put together a substantial partnership, during which there occurred an accident. Leo Genn bowled a friendly full toss, and Bromley-Davenport hit it towards Dickie Attenborough in the deep. Attenborough ran 20 yards (18.3m) and misjudged the flight of the ball, which hit him on the forehead. He collapsed unconscious, blood poured out, and he was taken on a stretcher to the Queen Victoria Hospital, East Grinstead, where he stayed for two days before being discharged. The game continued in his absence.

After Hubert Doggart's quick 50, two Cabinet Minsters, Harold Macmillan and Sir Walter Monckton, found themselves batting together. The stand was broken during an especially strange over from Richard Hearne, well known to every child in the land as 'Mr Pastry', a man responsible for many a custard-pie war. Mr Pastry bamboozled Harold Macmillan; the future British Prime Minister played back so far that he hit his own wicket. Sir Walter Monckton was even more baffled by a ball from Rex Harrison which bounced four times and bowled him. Some good batting from the late-order peers took the total to 178 for eight, made in 100 minutes.

At the fall of the first Stage wicket, Dickie Hearne came out to bat dressed like an American football player, padded out with chest and elbow protectors. He hit two fours before being bowled.

Then came the big shock of the afternoon. Denis Compton,

whom many of the crowd had come to see bat, was bowled second ball by Gerald Cogger. As Compton had yet to score, Cogger was fined a guinea. He wasn't displeased.

The absence of the hospitalised Dickie Attenborough meant the Stage XI might have to bat a man short, but they had a better idea. A make-up artist got to work on Denis Compton, who created some kind of record by batting twice in the same innings. The tannoy announcer, John Snagge of the BBC, welcomed the number seven batsman as 'Denis Pastry'. Compton did better this time, but the Stage could not match their target, the game ending in a draw.

The beneficiary, incidentally, was the Sackville College Appeal.

POLITICIANS
Lord Hawke b Compton 1
Lt-Col Bromley-Davenport b Warr 29
Major Lloyd George b Mattingly 23
Hubert Doggart retired 53
Sir Walter Monckton b Harrison 6
Harold Macmillan hit wkt b Hearne 2
Lord Kilmuir b Compton 15
Earl De La Warr b Mills 16
Viscount Gage not out 10
Gerald Cogger did not bat
Mr J.B. Goudge did not bat
Extras 23
                                                                      178–8

STAGE
Leo Genn st Sub b Lord Hawke 16
Edward Underdown c Doggart b Lloyd George 10
Richard Hearne b Lloyd George 8
Denis Compton b Cogger 0
John Mills b Doggart 6
John Slater retired 50
'Denis Pastry' b Doggart 32
Rex Harrison c Sub b Bromley-Davenport 0
John Mattingly not out 18
Reg Routledge not out 14
John Warr did not bat
Extras 8
                                                                      162–8

HALF A THOUSAND ...
NEARLY
KARACHI, JANUARY 1959

In first-class cricket, individual scores don't come much bigger than that made by 24-year-old Hanif Mohammed for Karachi against Bahawalpur. His innings began after tea on a Thursday and ended with the last ball of the following Sunday. He batted for 10 hours 35 minutes and overhauled Don Bradman's unbeaten 453 for New South Wales against Queensland in 1929–30. Hanif's innings contained 64 fours.

Bahawalpur batted first and were bowled out for 185. By the end of the first day, Hanif Mohammed had reached 25, then, batting all the next day, he took his score to 255, sharing two century partnerships. The first (172 in 155 minutes) was with Waqar Husan for the second wicket, the second (103 in 95 minutes) was for the third wicket with Wazir Mohammed, one of three Mohammed brothers, the third being Mushtaq.

After a rest day on the Saturday, Hanif Mohammed continued to wear down the Bahawalpur bowlers, putting on 259 with Wallis Mathias for the fourth wicket, the runs being made in even time. Hanif's score eventually reached 499 and he was facing the last ball of the day. He set off for a short single and was run out.

People believed that he was out looking for his five hundredth run, but a later story suggested that he believed his score was 498 and he was trying to farm the bowling for the morning. As it happened, Karachi declared at their overnight total and won by an innings and 479 runs.

This sensational victory was marred by a tragic event in the final of the same competition, against Combined Services, a week later. Abdul Aziz, the 17-year-old Karachi wicket-keeper, was struck on the heart by the fifth ball from Dildar Awan, a slow off-break bowler. Aziz died 15 minutes later on the way to hospital. A wave of gloom came over the match, play was suspended for the day, and the two captains went to Aziz's house as a mark of respect. It was later confirmed that Aziz had a heart complaint.

BAHAWALPUR

Ijaz Hussain run out	24
Zulfiqar Ahmed c Aziz b Mahmood	0
Mohammed Iqbal b Ikram	20
Mohammed Ramzan c Wallis b Ikram	64
Ghiasuddin b Ikram	4
Jamil Khalid run out	12
Farrukh Salim c Aziz b Mahmood	3
Riaz Mahmood b Mahmood	4
Asad Bhatti st Aziz b Mushtaq	21
Tanvir Hussan not out	16
Aziz Ahmed b Ikram	8
Extras	9
	185

c Waqar b Mahmood	32
c Aziz b Mahmood	8
c Aziz b Munaf	0
lbw b Munaf	5
c Wazir b Ikram	12
b D'Souza	4
b Ikram	4
lbw b Mushtaq	10
b Ikram	4
c Aziz b D'Souza	7
not out	5
	17
	108

Bowling: *First Innings*; Mahmood 18–4–38–3, Ikram 17–3–48–4, Munaf 8–1–23–0, D'Souza 11–2–42–0, Mushtaq 4–0–19–1, Hanif 1–0–6–0. *Second Innings*; Mahmood 10–2–27–2, Ikram 8–2–10–3, Munaf 9–1–29–2, D'Souza 11–3–17–2, Mushtaq 1–0–8–1.

KARACHI

Hanif Mohammed run out	499
Alim-ud-din c Zulfiqar b Aziz	32
Waqar Hassan c Tanvir b Iqbal	37
Wazir Mohammed st Tanvir b Jamil	31
Wallis Mathias run out	103
Mushtaq Mohammed lbw b Aziz	21
Abdul Munaf b Iqbal	18
Abdul Aziz not out	9
Extras	22
(declared)	**772–7**

Bowling: Zulfiqar 34–5–95–0, Ramzan 19–0–83–0, Aziz 50–4–208–2, Riaz 9–0–44–0, Ghias 37–3–139–0, Jamil 23–1–93–1, Iqbal 25–3–81–2, Tanvir 3–0–7–0.

A BURNLEY BONANZA

BURNLEY, JUNE 1959

His real name was O'Neill Gordon Smith and he was raised as an orphan in Jamaica. After he had scored a century against the Australian touring team, in 1955, he hit another century on his Test debut for the West Indies, the first of his 26 Tests in four years. When Burnley signed 'Collie' Smith for their Lancashire League team in 1959, they were recruiting a player considered by many to be as good an all-rounder as his close friend Gary Sobers.

'Collie' Smith etched his name into the Lancashire League record books with his performance in the first round of the Worsley Cup, which was played over four evenings early in June. The two teams, Burnley and Lowerhouse, batted on each evening even though it was a one-innings game.

Smith, going in at the fall of the second Burnley wicket, batted on all four evenings. The West End ground was too small to permit sixes, but Smith hit 56 boundaries in his undefeated innings of 306, a record for all Lancashire Leagues. The biggest spell of hitting came on the third evening, when he repeatedly hit the ball into a nearby park. The Burnley last man stayed with him long enough for Smith's treble-century to be achieved. The innings forced the scorers to stick appendices into their scorebooks and made casual park-users take refuge. He was dropped five times, but such was the power of his hitting, staggering for a man of only 5ft 2in (1.6m), that all the chances were difficult, and none came before his first century.

His 306 comfortably beat the previous Lancashire League high scores, by men like Albert Rhodes (220 for Haslingden in 1925) and West Indies Test star Everton Weekes, who, playing for Bacup, hit unbeaten scores of 195 in 1949 and 225 in 1958. Such are the vagaries of cricket, however, that 'Collie' Smith's next innings ended quickly, bowled by Nelson's Johnny Wardle for six.

The Burnley total of 523 for nine declared was also a Lancashire League record. Over the same four evenings, Lowerhouse made their way to an all-out total of 147. This meant that Burnley won by 376 runs and one wicket.

'Collie' Smith was 26 at the time of his mammoth innings. Later that summer he was killed in a car crash. Cricket lost a bouncy character who was an exceptionally strong hitter and niggling off-break bowler. Smith made 1,331 Test runs at 31.69 and took 48 wickets at 33.85.

BURNLEY

E. Entwhistle b Wade	33
P. Stansfield st Foster b Salkeld	24
D.G. Ormerod run out	34
Smith not out	306
A. Miller c and b Salkeld	10
F.P. Kippax c Cheesebrough b Devon (R.)	20
J. Clare b Salkeld	55
C. Martindale c and b Lowe	7
J. Schofield b Salkeld	5
R. Haworth st Foster b Salkeld	2
J. Richardson not out	19
Extras	8
(declared)	523–9

Bowling: Lowe 22–3–134–1, Bartels 24–2–101–0, Salkeld 17–0–99–5, Wade 17–4–89–1, Cheesebrough 9–0–59–0, Devon (R.) 5–0–33–1.

LOWERHOUSE

R.A. Devon lbw b Schofield 7
R. Foster c Ormerod b Schofield 4
J.L. Devon lbw b Schofield 0
M. Mahmood c Richardson b Haworth 60
B. Smith c and b Smith 4
K. Tranter lbw b Schofield 4
Bartels c Richardson b Martindale 42
A. Lowe b Haworth 6
A Cheesebrough b Haworth 2
P. Wade c Kippax b Martindale 0
J. Salkeld not out 1
Extras 17
147

Bowling: Haworth 13–5–39–3, Stansfield 3–0–7–0, Schofield 16–4–42–4, Smith 15–2–41–1, Martindale 1–0–1–2.

118

BORDERING ON THE RIDICULOUS
EAST LONDON, SOUTH AFRICA, DECEMBER 1959

Border against Natal in the Currie Cup. Border, having a run of indifferent form and bad luck, hosted the game at the Jan Smuts Ground. They had a psychological lift from memories of the corresponding game the previous season, when they had forced Natal to follow-on 199 runs behind.

Natal batted first on a treacherous rain-affected wicket. Border struck immediately with the wicket of Jackie McGlew, appointed South Africa captain for the forthcoming tour to England. Had Border not dropped five catches, Natal would have been skittled out more cheaply, but they recovered from 50 for eight to reach a final total of 90, inspired by a bat-fling by Malcolm Smith which brought a six and five fours.

Border's reply was uninspired, to say the least. Only four batsmen scored runs. Trevor Goddard, bowling a good length, moving the ball both ways, did most of the damage. In 11 overs, Goddard conceded a two (in his sixth over) and a single (in his seventh), and the last three of his six wickets came in the form of a hat-trick – Griffith, Knott and During. The last, top score with nine, tried to club his team out of trouble. He achieved more than half of Border's 16 runs.

By the close of a rain-interrupted day, 23 wickets had fallen for 145 runs in four hours' play. Natal had made 90 in 110 minutes, Border 16 in 80 minutes, Natal 39 for three in 55 minutes.

Batting was easier on the second day – for Natal. Kim

Elgie's unbeaten 162 was the backbone of a big score. When Jackie McGlew declared, eight wickets down, Border were required to make 369 to win.

The Border batsmen did no better the second time around, but, with the help of a couple of extras, they forced their total up to 18 runs. Unlike the first innings, there could be no complaint about the difficulty of the wicket. Wicket-keeper Malcolm Smith took seven catches, and the bowling architect in chief was Geoff Griffin, who a few months later would find himself the central figure in a throwing controversy. John Cole finished with match figures of seven for 17, Goddard six for four, Griffin seven for 11. Natal won a game of 418 runs by the margin of 350.

Kevin Commins, promoted after his first-innings duck, bagged a pair, as did Peter Muzzell and Sid Knott. Peter Tainton batted for 57 minutes for his unbeaten seven. This time the innings lasted 97 minutes. Border's aggregate score of 34, made in less than three hours' total batting, is still the record lowest aggregate for a first-class match, and Neil During's first-innings boundary was the only four they hit in the whole game. In their next game, against Western Province, Border proved that it was a fluke by making 163 and 116.

NATAL

D.J. McGlew c Hagemann b Knott	0	(5) c During b Schreiber ..22
T. Goddard lbw b Knott	4	(1) lbw b Knott 0
M.K. Elgie b Hagemann	11	(3) not out 162
R. McLean b Knott	0	(6) c Hagemann b During ..23
C. Wesley c and b Hagemann	11	(7) b Schreiber 36
L. Morby-Smith c Muzzell b Hagemann	0	(8) c Griffith b Schreiber ..43
G. Griffin c Hagemann b Knott	22	(2) st Kirsten b Schreiber ...5
A. Tillim c Schreiber b Hagemann	0	
M. Smith c Griffith b Hagemann	33	(9) lbw b Schreiber 2
P. Dodds b Knott	8	(4) c Knott b Schreiber 0
J. Cole not out	0	
Extras	1	1
	90	(declared) 294–8

Bowling: *First Innings*; Knott 13.3–2–40–5, Hagemann 13–2–49–5. *Second Innings*; Knott 15–5–24–1, Hagemann 10–3–37–0, Schreiber 29–5–126–6, Tainton 3–0–13–0, Commins 4–1–16–0, Griffith 1–0–5–0, Muzzell 3–0–23–0, During 15–3–49–1.

Fall of wickets: *First Innings*; 0, 15, 15, 18, 21, 47, 47, 50, 90, 90. *Second Innings*; 0, 13, 13, 46, 80, 145, 267, 294.

BORDER

A. Hagemann b Cole	2	c Smith b Griffin	3
P. Muzzell lbw b Goddard	0	b Griffin	0
P. Fenix b Goddard	0	c Smith b Cole	1
K. Kirton b Elgie b Cole	4	c Smith b Griffin	3
N. During b Goddard	9	(8) c Smith b Cole	1
K. Commins c Tillim b Goddard	0	(5) c Smith b Griffin	0
P. Tainton c Elgie b Cole	0	(6) not out	7
M. Griffith lbw b Goddard	1	(7) b Griffin	0
S. Knott c Cole b Goddard	0	c Smith b Griffin	0
E. Schreiber c McLean b Cole	0	c Smith b Cole	1
N. Kirsten not out	0	c McLean b Griffin	0
Extras	0		2
	16		**18**

Bowling: *First Innings*; Griffin 1–1–0–0, Goddard 11–9–3–6, Cole 11–4–13–4. *Second Innings*; Griffin 13–6–11–7, Goddard 4–3–1–0, Cole 9–7–4–3.

Fall of Wckets: *First Innings*; 2, 2, 2, 8, 11, 11, 12, 16, 16, 16. *Second Innings*; 1, 5, 5, 5, 10, 10, 11, 12, 15, 18.

THE FIRST TIED TEST

BRISBANE, AUSTRALIA, DECEMBER 1960

After 83 years and 502 Tests, cricket produced equality between two Test teams in a match that had all the qualities of strangeness, particularly in the last hour when the game went out of control and into the realm of fantasy. This was the first match of the 1960–61 Australia–West Indies series, the sixteenth Test between the two countries.

The last Test played at Brisbane, against England two years previously, had brought only 518 runs in four days. West Indies, batting first, came within sight of that on the first day. Gary Sobers made a sensational century in 125 minutes. When he was finally out, to the day's worst ball, he had made 132 in 174 minutes. Frank Worrell batted almost as long for his 65 and by the end of the day West Indies were 359 for seven.

The next morning Wes Hall made a flamboyant 50, and the Australians replied to a total of 453, reaching 196 for three by the end of play.

The third day was dominated by Norman O'Neill, who had three fortunate escapes between 47 and 54 but went on to make 181. Nightwatchman Les Favell did well, Ken Mackay chewed gum and made a few, and Alan Davidson added 44 runs to his five wickets. Australia took a first-innings lead of 52.

O'Neill's innings swung the game back towards Australia. By the close of the fourth day, West Indies were 259 for nine, only 207 ahead. They were grateful for an innings by Joe Solomon which lasted 222 minutes. Fortunately, for the West

Indies (and all cricket fans who relished the game's eventual finish), Wes Hall and Alf Valentine took their last-wicket stand to 31. Most neutrals reckoned that the Australian target, 233 in 312 minutes, was certainly attainable.

Most neutrals, however, reckoned without the poor start to Australia's second innings. After being 28 for two at lunch on the final day, made in 70 minutes, they tumbled to 57 for five. At that point 176 were needed in 200 minutes. In those days runs per hour were what counted. There were no minimum overs to be bowled in the last hour.

Davidson and Mackay put on 35 in an hour. The target at tea, 123 in 120 minutes with four wickets remaining, looked increasingly beyond Australia's reach. That calculation reckoned without a stand between two quick-scoring batsmen – Alan Davidson and Richie Benaud, the Australian captain. They scored at the required rate, and the target came down accordingly – 80 needed in 75 minutes, 60 in 60 minutes, 27 in 30 minutes. When the West Indies took the new ball, Australia still had four wickets in hand. There was time for five eight-ball overs.

Wes Hall's first over, which took nine minutes to bowl and included a no-ball, had plenty of action. Four singles and a four from Davidson, hooked from a bouncer, brought the target down to 19. Benaud was almost caught, and, off another ball, Davidson ran almost to Benaud's end and back, just avoiding a run-out.

Gary Sobers, bowling the next over, conceded a leg-bye, two singles to Benaud, an on-driven four by the Australian captain, a single to Davidson and a no-ball. Ten needed in 15 minutes (24 balls).

Hall's next over brought one single, and Sobers conceded three in the penultimate over. More important was the run-out in that over. Benaud played the ball towards square-leg and Davidson failed to beat Solomon's direct hit. That ended Alan Davidson's sensational participation in the match – five for 135, 44 runs, six for 87 and 80 more runs.

A single by Wally Grout left him facing the first ball of the last over, to be bowled by Wes Hall with Australia needing six to win and three wickets left.

Ball One – hits Grout high on the leg, drops in front of him. Benaud reaches the ball almost before Grout, who scrambles the run.

Ball Two – is Hall's bouncer. Benaud edges his hook and wicket-keeper Alexander makes the catch.

Ball Three – is played for no run by new batsman Meckiff.

Ball Four – goes through to the wicket-keeper. The batsmen run, Hall runs, Grout reaches the striker's end, Hall throws at Meckiff's end and fails there too, overthrows being prevented. Four runs needed off four balls; two wickets to fall.

Ball Five – is hit into the air by Grout. Kanhai is under the ball at mid-wicket. Hall competes for the catch, the ball lands on the ground and Grout and Meckiff run. Three to win.

Ball Six – is hit by Meckiff towards the unattended square-leg boundary. Meckiff smells at least three runs and victory. Conrad Hunte reaches the ball just as the batsmen turn for the winning run. What a throw. Alexander lunges for the stumps and Grout is out. The scores are tied – 737 each.

Ball Seven – is clipped to leg by the last Australian batsman, left-hander Lindsay Kline. The Australians set off, Joe Solomon pounces on the ball and takes aim at the one stump he can see. His 15 yard (13.7m) throw hits. The game is tied.

The two captains, Frank Worrell and Richie Benaud, left the field arm in arm after this incredible finish. But this first Test match had far more than a great finish. It was a magnificent game which set alive a series and rejuvenated cricket. In the fourth Test, for instance, Lindsay Kline and Ken Mackay saved the match for Australia by putting on 66 for the last wicket.

The marvellous thing about a tied cricket match is that everyone contributes. Had groundstaff not taken four minutes to free a sightscreen on the first day, it might not have happened as it did.

WEST INDIES

	First Innings		Second Innings	
C. Hunte	c Benaud b Davidson	24	c Simpson b Mackay	39
C. Smith	c Grout b Davidson	7	c O'Neill b Davidson	6
R. Kanhai	c Grout b Davidson	15	c Grout b Davidson	54
G. Sobers	c Kline b Meckiff	132	b Davidson	14
F. Worrell	c Grout b Davidson	65	c Grout b Davidson	65
J. Solomon	hit wkt b Simpson	65	lbw b Simpson	47
P. Lashley	c Grout b Kline	19	b Davidson	0
G. Alexander	c Davidson b Kline	60	b Benaud	5
S. Ramadhin	c Harvey b Davidson	12	c Harvey b Simpson	6
W. Hall	st Grout b Kline	50	b Davidson	18
A. Valentine	not out	0	not out	7
Extras		4		23
		453		**284**

Bowling: *First Innings*; Davidson 30–2–135–5, Meckiff 18–0–129–1, Mackay 3–0–15–0, Benaud 24–3–93–0, Simpson 8–0–25–1, Kline 17.6–6–52–3. *Second Innings*; Davidson 24.6–4–87–6, Meckiff 4–1–19–0, Mackay 21–7–52–1, Benaud 31–6–69–1, Simpson 7–2–18–2, Kline 4–0–14–0, O'Neill 1–0–2–0.

Fall of Wickets; *First Innings*; 23, 42, 65, 239, 243, 283, 347, 366, 452, 453. *Second Innings*; 13, 88, 114, 127, 210, 210, 241, 250, 253, 284.

AUSTRALIA

	First Innings		Second Innings	
C. McDonald	c Hunte b Sobers	57	b Worrell	16
R. Simpson	b Ramadhin	92	c Sub b Hall	0
N. Harvey	b Valentine	15	c Sobers b Hall	5
N. O'Neill	c Valentine b Hall	181	c Alexander b Hall	26
L. Favell	run out	45	c Solomon b Hall	7
K. Mackay	b Sobers	35	b Ramadhin	28
A. Davidson	c Alexander b Hall	44	run out	80
R. Benaud	lbw b Hall	10	c Alexander b Hall	52
W. Grout	lbw b Hall	4	run out	2
I. Meckiff	run out	4	run out	2
L. Kline	not out	3	not out	0
Extras		15		14
		505		**232**

Bowling: *First Innings*; Hall 29.3–1–140–4, Worrell 30–0–93–0, Sobers 32–0–115–2, Valentine 24–6–82–1, Ramadhin 15–1–60–1. *Second Innings*; Hall 17.7–3–63–5, Worrell 16–3–41–4, Sobers 8–0–30–0, Valentine 10–4–27–0, Ramadhin 17–3–57–1.

Fall of wickets: *First Innings*; 84, 138, 194, 278, 381, 469, 484, 489, 496, 505. *Second Innings*; 1, 7, 49, 49, 57, 92, 226, 228, 232, 232.

LATE ARRIVALS
FOR THE BALL
TUNBRIDGE WELLS, JUNE 1963

Wisden called the events of the Monday morning, the second day of the game between Kent and Middlesex, 'a situation without parallel in the history of first-class cricket'. It is a cautionary tale for all cricketers who have ever travelled to a game.

On the Saturday, Middlesex played themselves into a winning position. The spinners bowled out Kent for 150, then, after losing two quick wickets, they batted to within 29 of the Kent total, seven wickets still standing. The not-out batsmen were White (43) and Hooker (13).

It was a Monday morning, and the traffic was heavy around the London Bridge area. The Middlesex players had stayed in a local Tunbridge Wells hotel for Friday night, but had spent Saturday and Sunday nights in their own beds. The traffic jams reduced them to a crawl, and the chances of the players in some cars arriving in time for the 11.30a.m. start lessened.

Three Middlesex players were punctual. White, one of the not-out batsmen, was ready to continue his innings, Russell (already dismissed) was present, and so was Clark, the Middlesex twelfth man. White changed, put on pads and gloves and waited on the boundary for someone to partner him. The Kent team took the field and waited … and waited … and waited.

Where were all the Middlesex players? Perhaps they had

met with accidents, or perhaps they had been scared off Tunbridge Wells by the stories of hand-grenade discoveries on the ground the previous year. Most likely, they were stuck in the traffic.

The big conundrum was how the umpires should react. What was the correct decision? Should they award the match to Kent? Could the three Middlesex players present declare in the absence of their captain and borrow eight players to take the field? Should the umpires rule out each batsman in turn if they failed to appear within the stipulated two minutes?

The solution was none of these. The umpires officially closed the Middlesex innings.

This unprecedented decision raised a few more confused questions for the compilers of averages. Was Hooker out or not out? Were the rest of the Middlesex players, excluding White, out? The answer to both these questions was no.

There followed a ten-minute interval before Middlesex took the field. Colin Cowdrey, the Kent captain, generously offered to loan players to Middlesex and allowed Clark, the Middlesex twelfth man, to keep wicket.

Three more Middlesex players arrived, which meant that only five substitutes were borrowed from Kent – Underwood, Catt, Prodger, Brown and Dye. Bennett and Price opened the bowling, and after three overs the whole of the Middlesex team was present and on the field. During that time, Prodger took an excellent catch at second slip to dismiss his team-mate Brian Luckhurst. Later in the innings, Prodger became one of the few players to score a 50 and take a catch in the same county-championship innings.

A swashbuckling innings by Peter Richardson – 95 out of 120 in 100 minutes – took Kent to a match-winning position. Middlesex, set 371 to win in 390 minutes, were 15 for one overnight. It had not been a good day for them.

Rain prevented much play on the Tuesday, and Middlesex escaped with a draw.

KENT

P.E. Richardson b Hooker	35	c Murray b Titmus	95
B.W. Luckhurst c Murray b Hooker	26	c Sub (Prodger) b Bennett	4
D. Nicholls c Parfitt b Titmus	15	lbw b Bennett	16
M.C. Cowdrey c and b Hooker	8	c Hooker b Moss	23
S.E. Leary c Moss b Hooker	6	not out	92
J. Prodger c Hooker b Titmus	30	c Drybrough b Hooker	74
A.W. Catt c Moss b Titmus	19	c Hooker b Price	25
A.L. Dixon c Titmus b Drybrough	0	c Moss b Price	5
D. Underwood not out	4	not out	6
A. Brown b Drybrough	0		
J. Dye lbw b Titmus	1		
Extras	6		1
	150	(declared)	**341–7**

Bowling: *First Innings*; Moss 8–2–12–0, Price 6–1–25–0, Hooker 21–6–57–4, Titmus 29.1–14–39–4, Drybrough 10–4–11–2. *Second Innings*; Bennett 9–1–48–2, Price 11–0–81–2, Moss 22–7–48–1, Titmus 28–6–82–1, Drybrough 19–7–50–0, Hooker 8–0–31–1.

Fall of wickets: *First Innings*; 53, 70, 79, 90, 91, 144, 145, 145, 145, 150. *Second Innings*; 5, 75, 120, 150, 270, 307, 317.

MIDDLESEX

W.E. Russell b Dixon	4	lbw b Dixon	4
S.E. Russell c Cowdrey b Brown	3	c Leary b Dixon	28
P.H. Parfitt run out	54	c Prodger b Brown	27
R.A. White not out	43	not out	19
R.W. Hooker not out	13	not out	2
Extras	4		2
	121–3		**82–3**

(declared closed by the umpires)

Bowling: *First Innings*; Brown 16–2–34–1, Dixon 18–7–26–1, Dye 2–0–10–0, Underwood 9–3–33–0, Leary 7–2–14–0. *Second Innings*; Brown 11–3–33–1, Dixon 8–4–15–2, Underwood 3.3–1–21–0, Dye 2–0–11–0.

Fall of wickets: *First Innings*; 5, 9, 106. *Second Innings*; 5, 51, 73.

A CLOSE FINISH

LORD'S, JUNE 1963

Enjoyment is often easier when expectations are low. On the final day of the second Test match between West Indies and England, there was little hope of play and less hope that play would start early enough for a competitive finish. Instead, when play began at 2.20p.m. it was the prelude to one of cricket's most exciting and dramatic finishes.

From the moment that Conrad Hunte set about the English bowling at the start of the game – he hit Trueman's first three balls for four – there was something enthralling about the contest. With Ted Dexter in full flow, scoring 70 in 81 minutes from 73 balls, England looked like building a big first innings lead, but they finished four short of the West Indies total of 301.

Basil Butcher's remarkable second innings – 133 in 270 minutes – rescued the West Indies and helped them set England 234 to win. England lost three wickets for 31, and Colin Cowdrey retired hurt with a broken left forearm after he had been struck by a ball from Wes Hall, probably the fastest bowler in the world at the time. England ended the fourth day on 116 for three.

After the delayed start on the final day, England began slowly, scoring only 18 in the first hour, Ken Barrington passing 45 minutes without scoring. The West Indian bowlers, bowling their overs slowly, were not helping. Barrington was finally out, and Parks followed him after a fighting innings. At tea, England needed 63 in 85 minutes with four wickets remaining … unless, of course, Cowdrey was to return to the wicket with his left arm in plaster. Then there were five wickets to fall.

Brian Close was batting heroically, and the next day his body would be bruised black and blue where he was hit by balls from Griffith and Hall. Close and Titmus scampered singles, Close late-cut, swept and hooked fours, and England's target reduced to 31 before two sudden setbacks altered the course of the game, Titmus and Trueman falling to Hall in successive balls. Close continued in his cavalier mood, advancing down the wicket to Hall, sweeping and hooking more fours until he edged a ball from Griffith to the wicket-keeper. Close was gone for 70, and England, needing 15 to win, were 219 for eight, with only Cowdrey to come if another wicket fell. Cowdrey, meanwhile, in the dressing-room, was practising batting left-handed with one fit arm.

When Wes Hall began the last over the target had been whittled down to eight runs. The two batsmen were David Allen, the Gloucestershire off-break bowler, and Derek Shackleton, the 38-year-old Hampshire seam bowler, who was playing his first Test match for 11 years.

The first ball swung away viciously. Shackleton swung his bat just as viciously and missed the ball.

The second ball was straighter and Shackleton stopped it dead. The batsmen ran, Hall ran, wicket-keeper Murray ran and all the fielders ran. One run was scored. Seven to win.

The third ball was played by Allen for a single on the on-side. Six to win.

The fourth ball went through to the wicket-keeper and the batsmen were off again, Shackleton starting much too slowly. Murray threw the ball to Worrell, who sprinted to the bowler's end ahead of Shackleton and ran him out.

Cowdrey, left arm in plaster from the elbow down, walked from the Lord's pavilion to the non-receiver's end, accompanied by a warm reception. Six runs were still needed for victory, but David Allen did the sensible thing, playing the last two balls with a straight bat to ensure the game finished as an honourable draw.

Cowdrey himself joked of the potential quiz question – 'What Test player started his career as a right-hander and finished it as a left-hander?' – but he would return to captain England.

WEST INDIES

C.C. Hunte c Close b Trueman	44	c Cowdrey b Shackleton	7
E.D. McMorris lbw b Trueman	16	c Cowdrey b Trueman	8
G.S. Sobers c Cowdrey b Allen	42	c Parks b Trueman	8
R.B. Kanhai c Edrich b Trueman	73	c Cowdrey b Shackleton	21
B.F. Butcher c Barrington b Trueman	14	lbw b Shackleton	133
J.S. Solomon lbw b Shackleton	56	c Stewart b Allen	5
F.M. Worrell b Trueman	0	c Stewart b Trueman	33
D.L. Murray c Cowdrey b Trueman	20	c Parks b Trueman	2
W.W. Hall not out	25	c Parks b Trueman	2
C.C. Griffith c Cowdrey b Shackleton	0	b Shackleton	1
L.R. Gibbs c Stewart b Shackleton	0	not out	1
Extras	11		8
	301		229

Bowling: *First Innings*; Trueman 44–16–100–6, Shackleton 50.2–22–93–3, Dexter 20–6–41–0, Close 9–3–21–0, Allen 10–3–35–1. *Second Innings*; Trueman 26–9–52–5, Shackleton 34–14–72–4, Titmus 17–3–47–0, Allen 21–7–50–1.

Fall of wickets: *First Innings*; 51, 64, 127, 145, 219, 219, 263, 297, 297, 301. *Second Innings*; 15, 15, 64, 84, 104, 214, 224, 226, 228, 229.

ENGLAND

M.J. Stewart c Kanhai b Griffith	2	c Solomon b Hall	17
J.H. Edrich c Murray b Griffith	0	c Murray b Hall	8
E.R. Dexter lbw b Sobers	70	b Gibbs	2
K.F. Barrington c Sobers b Worrell	80	c Murray b Griffith	60
M.C. Cowdrey b Gibbs	4	not out	19
D.B. Close c Murray b Griffith	9	c Murray b Griffith	70
J.M. Parks b Worrell	35	lbw b Griffith	17
F.J. Titmus not out	52	c McMorris b Hall	11
F.S. Trueman b Hall	10	c Murray b Hall	0
D.A. Allen lbw b Griffith	2	not out	4
D. Shackleton b Griffith	8	run out	4
Extras	25		16
	297		228–9

Bowling: *First Innings*; Hall 18–2–65–1, Griffith 26–6–91–5, Sobers 18–4–45–1, Gibbs 27–9–59–1, Worrell 13–6–12–2. *Second Innings*; Hall 40–9–93–4, Griffith 30–7–59–3, Gibbs 17–7–56–1, Sobers 4–1–4–0.

Fall of wickets: *First Innings*; 2, 20, 102, 115, 151, 206, 235, 271, 274, 297. *Second Innings*; 15, 27, 31, 130, 158, 203, 203, 219, 228.

ONE-A-SIDE
BY THE SEASIDE
SCARBOROUGH, SEPTEMBER 1963

The first single-wicket tournament of modern times took place at Scarborough. At stake was the Calling Trophy and a cash prize of £250. The runner-up would receive £100.

Sixteen players competed. The rules were that each player should bat for ten overs or until out. The fielding side consisted of club cricketers and a first-class wicket-keeper, Keith Andrew of Northants alternating with John Murray of Middlesex.

Eight games were scheduled for the first day, and they were all over by tea-time. Twelve wickets fell for 186 runs, and no player needed his full quota of ten overs. Only Jack van Geloven paced his innings, spending 49 balls over defeating Colin Milburn (34 runs). The quickest game was that between Derek Morgan and John Mortimore. Morgan was bowled first ball, Mortimore scored a single from the second.

Trevor Bailey was one famous all-rounder who went out at the first hurdle, while there were also surprise defeats for Yorkshiremen Freddie Trueman and Brian Close. Close lasted for three balls against West Indian Joe Solomon, whose first shy at the stumps came on the second ball and went for four overthrows. The second ran out Close on the third ball.

The first two quarter-final matches lasted a mere seven balls between them. David Allen reached five with the help of four overthrows, Peter Marner was out second ball. White's first-ball four was enough to beat Solomon.

The crowd had some consolation with Ken Palmer's one-run defeat of van Geloven. Again van Geloven paced his innings, leaving himself with seven to win from the last over. He stole a single, hit a four and then played on.

Ray Illingworth beat John Mortimore in the quarter-final and tied with Ken Palmer in the semi-final. He then lost the two-over tie-breaker.

The final was an anti-climax after a brilliant catch had dismissed White for seven. The trophy and £250 went to Somerset's Ken Palmer.

First Round: Trevor Bailey (Essex), 6 off 12 balls, lost to Peter Marner (Leicestershire), 7 not out off 15 balls; David Allen (Gloucestershire), 7 off 8 balls, beat C. Borde (India), 0 off 7 balls; W.A. White (West Indies), 31 off 37 balls, beat Fred Trueman (Yorkshire), 0 off 5 balls; Joe Solomon (West Indies), 18 off 26 balls, beat Brian Close (Yorkshire), 6 off 3 balls; Tom Cartwright (Warwickshire), 7 off 17 balls, lost to Ken Palmer, 8 not out off 15 balls; Colin Milburn (Northants), 34 off 36 balls, lost to Jack van Geloven (Leicestershire), 35 not out off 49 balls; Ray Illingworth (Yorkshire), 14 off 25 balls, beat Barry Knight (Essex), 12 off 19 balls; Derek Morgan (Derbyshire), 0 off 1 ball, lost to John Mortimore (Gloucestershire), 1 not out off 1 ball.

Second Round: Allen, 5 off 2 balls, beat Marner, 0 off 3 balls; Solomon, 0 off 1 ball, lost to White, 4 not out off 1 ball; Palmer, 28 off 39 balls, beat van Geloven, 27 off 57 balls; Mortimore, 16 off 11 balls, lost to Illingworth, 20 not out off 28 balls.

Semi-final: White, 50 off 44 balls, beat Allen, 36 off 53 balls; Illingworth, 11 off 23 balls, tied with Palmer, 11 off 24 balls, and Palmer, 21 not out off 12 balls, beat Illingworth, 4 off 4 balls, in the tie-break.

Final: White, 7 off 15 balls, lost to Palmer, 8 not out off 16 balls.

NOTHING TO LOSE
ELGIN, MAY 1964

In the North of Scotland League game at Elgin, the home team batted first and compiled a reasonable total of 145 for five declared. People thinking it might be a fair contest reckoned without the showing of the Ross County team, who batted a man short.

Elgin had a useful pace attack. Bernard Woolfson, from Beccles near Norwich, had twice played for Suffolk before moving to Scotland, where he worked as a Post Office sales representative. Dave Murray, employed by the Forestry Commission at Elgin, took the other end.

Up strode Woolfson for his first ball. A wicket. In came Woolfson to the new batsman. Bowled him. The number-four Ross County batsman, Oliver, survived the remaining four balls.

Now it was Murray's turn. He bowled a wicket-maiden and at the end of the second over Ross County were nought for three.

With the first ball of his new over Woolfson dismissed the stubborn Oliver. Hannant went to the fourth ball, Taylor to the sixth. Ross County were nought for six at the end of the third over.

Murray needed only one more over to finish the match. He claimed Niven's wicket with his third ball, bowled Northcliffe with his fourth and Frazer with his sixth. The ten-man Ross County team were all out for no runs. They had never really recovered from the bad start of losing two wickets with the first balls, although observers pointed out that they hadn't had much luck. One batsman had hit his own wicket, two others had played on to their stumps. They had no run of the ball ... and no run between the wickets.

Ross County won praise for their sportsmanship. Most of their away games involved travelling between 100 and 200 miles (161–322km). The home team were glad their opponents had turned up so they could play cricket, let alone beat the long-standing league records for low scoring. In 1896 Kinross had scored one against Auchtermuchty, while Arbroath United had amassed two against Aberdeen in 1868. It would be difficult to beat the Ross County record, although many teams have equalled it.

A writer in the *Cricketer* (June 1923), believed there were already about 70 instances of scores of nought at this stage of the sport's history, the first being a game at Hampton Green in Norfolk in 1815. 'Some years later an extraordinary game was played in Derbyshire between Kegworth and Diseworth,' the writer continues. 'The latter went in first and made only a single, the hero of the innings being the vicar's groom. An easy victory for Kegworth seemed assured, but, to everyone's amazement, the side collapsed without a run.' There is also mention of a game of dubious authenticity at Chiswick in April 1899, when both teams allegedly scored no runs.

One of the more interesting examples of a team being dismissed for nought was that of Fitzroy in a Victorian Scottish Cricket Association game in 1913. Replying to Williamstown's score of 98, they lost by 98 runs, and Davidson took ten for none. As with all such innings, the fall of wickets proves very easy to estimate.

ELGIN

Manley b Oliver 28
B. Woolfson b Hendry 0
J. Wright b Nevin 43
F. Muir lbw b Nevin 8
J. Leithead not out 36
W. Phimister b Nevin 6
R. Draggan not out 12
Extras 12

(declared) <u>45–5</u>

Bowling: Hendry 15–0–53–1, Northcliffe 7–1–20–0, Nevin 11–2–42–3, Oliver 4–1–18–1.

ROSS COUNTY

B. Kenny c Phimister b Woolfson 0
G. Shiels c Stewardson b Murray 0
J. Hendry b Woolfson 0
W. Oliver b Woolfson 0
J. Niven hit wkt b Murray 0
Hannant lbw b Woolfson 0
I. Taylor b Woolfson 0
Bull not out 0
J. Northcliffe b Murray 0
N. Frazer b Murray 0
Extras 0

<u>0</u>

Bowling: Woolfson 2–2–0–5, Murray 2–2–0–4.

A RECORD-WINNING MARGIN

LAHORE, DECEMBER 1964

The Moghalpura Institute provided a perfect batting surface and the team batting first, Pakistan Western Railways (PWR), certainly knew how to make the best of it. Their opposition for this Ayub Trophy fixture, Dera Ismail Khan (DIK), brought five stock bowlers who sportingly and obligingly trundled to and from the wickets for just over two days. The PWR batsmen lapped it up.

After a relatively early success – Anwar bowled Saeed Butt for 20 when the score was at 44 – the DIK bowlers were basically run-fodder. Javed Babar and Ijaz Hussain put on 244 runs for the second wicket before Mateen caught and bowled Ijaz Hussain for 124. At the end of the first day, PWR were 415 for two.

Javed Babar, unbeaten on 195 overnight, completed his double-century early the next day but was out soon afterwards. Parvez Akhtar, 63 overnight, batted all day and was 301 not out at the close. PWR were 825 for six after two days' batting. This was already a record for Pakistan.

The next morning, PWR went for quick runs. Sharif completed the fourth century of the innings, and the declaration finally came at 910 for six.

DIK, all out for 32, failed abysmally to avert the follow-on. To quote Scyld Berry's wonderful line in the *Observer* (27 November 1977), 'Railways then gambled on a lead of 878 and enforced the follow-on.'

Dera Ismail Khan did even worse, managing only 27 in the second innings, batting for only 28 overs in a total of two innings. They would have needed 31 innings at that rate to reach the Railways' total, so lost by an innings and 851 runs, the heaviest-ever defeat in a first-class match. It was the first and last first-class match for Dera Ismail Khan.

PAKISTAN WESTERN RAILWAYS: 910–6 declared (Parvez Akhtar 337 not out, Javed Baber 200, Ijaz Hussain 124, Mohd Sharif 106 not out, Anwar Husan 3–295, Inayet 1–279).

DERA ISMAIL KHAN: 32 (Afaq Khan 7–14) and 27 (Ahad Khan 9–7).

THE WICKET-KEEPER BOWLER

CLACTON, AUGUST 1965

Imagine you are both wicket-keeper and captain of a county
team. Your team starts a game without two main bowlers
who have been called up for the Test team. A deputy breaks
down during the game, leaving you with only one opening
bowler. Having taken 24 wickets in seven seasons yourself,
you decide you could do as well as anyone with the ball.
You hand over the pads and gloves to a team-mate and try
your brand of medium pace. Would you seriously expect
to emulate a regular bowler? When these circumstances
happened to Alan Smith of Warwickshire his performance
with the ball was astonishing by any bowler's standards.

Smith started the game against Essex by winning the toss,
but his Warwickshire batsmen did not respond especially
well. It was 90 minutes before the first boundary, and, as
wickets fell rapidly, Stewart was forced to dig in for an
untypically inconspicuous innings. A total of 160 seemed
too low to expect first-innings points.

However, Warwickshire's Jack Bannister took three
wickets in his first nine balls, Webster chipped in with one,
and Essex were soon four down for seven runs in their reply.
Bannister was in good form, having helped Tom Cartwright
to skittle Leicestershire for 80 in Warwickshire's last match.
At the end of the day Essex were 50 for five.

The left-handed Roger Wrightson batted for four hours to
help Essex to their first-innings lead, aided on the way by

late-order support from Stuart Turner and Robin Hobbs. When Warwickshire ended the day on 136 for five, 133 ahead, people were predicting the prospect of a good finish. In fact Essex were set 203 in 235 minutes.

In the absence of Webster, who had injured his back, Bannister and medium-pacer Billy Ibadulla opened the bowling, and the Essex openers sped along to 22 for no wicket. Alan Smith made his decision to bowl when Bannister needed resting. Dennis Amiss took over as wicket-keeper and Smith immediately produced lift and movement. His first over was a maiden.

Ibadulla bowled the next over – the score moved to 28 – before Smith collected a wicket with the fifth ball of his second over, Barker hooking him to Edmonds on the long-leg boundary. The batsmen crossed, so Essex's Geoff Smith faced the next ball, which he turned into the hands of Oakes at leg slip. Two wickets in two balls. Not bad for a wicket-keeper.

Ibadulla bowled a maiden to Steward, then Alan Smith bowled the first ball of a new over to Keith Fletcher, the Essex number four. Fletcher tried to pull him to mid-wicket and the ball flew off a top edge. Oakes took the catch to complete the hat-trick. Smith completed the over without conceding a run, bowled another maiden before lunch, then went in to enjoy the break with figures of 4–4–0–3.

Alan Smith bowled his fifth maiden after lunch, then took another wicket with the fourth ball of his sixth over, Bailey being caught behind by Amiss, the deputy wicket-keeper. At the end of that over Smith's figures were 6–6–0–4, probably the best analysis, even if temporary, ever recorded by a player who had started an innings as a wicket-keeper, along with Hon. Alfred Lyttelton's four for 19 at the 1884 Oval Test for England against Australia.

Knight broke Alan Smith's mesmerising effect by hitting a four and a two from his seventh over, but the wicket-keeper's spell ended with figures of 12–7–17–4. With Steward taking 50 minutes to score his first run, Essex were behind the clock and unable to recover. At 111 for eight, Warwickshire had the time for a comfortable victory, but it wasn't to be. The last pair held out for 15 minutes, and the game was drawn.

WARWICKSHIRE

K. Ibadulla c Taylor b Knight	26	c Fletcher b Bailey	17
B.A. Richardson c Taylor b Knight	4	c Turner b Smith	30
D.L. Amiss lbw b Turner	12	c Wrightson b Bailey	54
J.A. Jameson c Turner b Bailey	26	c Taylor b Turner	8
W.J. Stewart lbw b Knight	54	c Fletcher b Bailey	20
D.R. Oakes lbw b Bailey	3	c Taylor b Knight	0
A.C. Smith lbw b Turner	8	c Bailey b Knight	11
R. Miller c and b Knight	3	lbw b Hobbs	29
R.B. Edmonds lbw b Knight	19	lbw b Knight	1
R.V. Webster not out	2	c Steward b Hobbs	27
J.D. Bannister c Hobbs b Bailey	0	not out	2
Extras	3		6
	160		205

Bowling: *First Innings*; Knight 25–7–38–5, Bailey 29.2–6–47–3, Edmeades 21–6–29–0, Turner 17–5–28–2, Hobbs 6–2–13–0, Smith 1–0–2–0. S*econd Innings*; Knight 26–5–38–3, Bailey 27–6–65–3, Edmeades 8–0–26–0, Turner 12–0–33–1, Hobbs 7.1–2–20–2, Smith 5–0–17–1.

Fall of wickets: *First Innings*; 5, 38, 52, 83, 89, 102, 111, 156, 157, 160.
Second Innings; 22, 86, 98, 114, 115, 140, 150, 155, 202, 205.

ESSEX

G.E. Barker b Bannister	4	c Edmonds b Smith	12
G.J. Smith lbw b Webster	1	c Oakes b Smith	15
E.A. Steward lbw b Bannister	0	c Stewart b Miller	3
K. Fletcher c Smith b Bannister	2	c Oakes b Smith	0
B. Taylor c Smith b Webster	19	c Oakes b Bannister	3
R.W. Wrightson c and b Edmonds	84	lbw b Miller	18
B. Edmeades c Amiss b Bannister	5	not out	24
T.E. Bailey c Oakes b Webster	4	c Amiss b Smith	1
B.R. Knight c Stewart b Bannister	19	lbw b Miller	44
Turner lbw b Edmonds	12	c Ibadulla b Miller	13
R.N.S. Hobbs not out	12	not out	4
Extras	1		4
	163		141–9

Bowling: *First Innings*; Bannister 27–10–47–5, Webster 25–6–78–3, Ibadulla 12–2–24–0, Edmonds 7.1–2–13–2. *Second Innings*; Bannister 17–7–28–1, Ibadulla 7–3–12–0, Smith 21–10–36–4, Edmonds 13–10–6–0, Miller 23–9–55–4.

Fall of wickets: *First Innings*; 5, 5, 7, 7, 39, 58, 77, 111, 142, 163. *Second Innings*; 28, 28, 28, 29, 51, 60, 87, 112, 136.

WALKING OFF THE PITCH
CROMPTON, LANCASHIRE, AUGUST 1965

In his day, West Indian Roy Gilchrist was probably the fastest bowler of his era. In the late 1950s he played 13 Test matches, and it might have been more but for other things. His temperament, for one thing, was suspect.

An example of this came in a Central Lancashire League game in the mid-1960s, when Gilchrist was working as the professional at Crompton. Against Radcliffe, Gilchrist's team batted first and made 106 in 160 minutes. It was not a big score, but it could be enough if Gilchrist was in form.

Analysts of later events pointed to only one controversial incident during the Crompton innings. Marsh, the number-eight Crompton bat, popped up a catch immediately in front of him. Wicket-keeper Derek Bickley, the Radcliffe captain, dived forward to catch the ball but Marsh moved across him, probably accidentally. Bickley couldn't reach the ball, someone appealed and the umpire gave Marsh out.

The Radcliffe opening bats were Derek Bickley and Bill McDonald. Gilchrist opened the bowling to skipper Bickley. Not very tall, Gilchrist ran quickly to the wicket and was especially hostile. His first ball to Bickley was a beamer. The rest of the over was close to where a batsman might expect it to be. By the time of Gilchrist's second over, the Radcliffe score had moved on to four.

Up comes Gilchrist again, bowling to Bickley again. Another beamer. Here comes the second ball, and this one is a bumper. The atmosphere is tense now, Bickley points to his chin for some reason – one umpire later implied that Bickley was provoking Gilchrist – and the bowler, feeling as mad as he could ever be, goes back to his mark and runs in for the third ball of the over. This time Gilchrist runs past the wicket until he is 6 yards (5.5m) down the track. Then, rather than bowling the ball, he throws it at the other end. By this time, Bickley, sensing the danger, has retreated somewhere towards square leg. The ball flies over his head.

In protest, Bickley and McDonald walked off the pitch, and the game was abandoned. The crowd milled around the pavilion. Radcliffe supported their captain's actions, but the League ruled that Crompton should be awarded the points. They suspended Gilchrist and Bickley until the end of the season, which meant three games. It was perhaps surprising that the two men were treated with the same punishment, as Gilchrist already had a 'record'. Recently reprimanded by the League after two complaints about him, Gilchrist had been sent home from the West Indies' tour of India in 1959 after persistently bowling beamers at an Indian batsman when riled. He had also been at the centre of a walk-off incident in 1960 when playing for Middleton at Oldham, the home-team captain Bill Lawton calling off his team after one of his batsmen had been hit. Oldham were fined £5 and forfeited the points on that occasion.

CROMPTON

Grimshaw c Moores b Hilton 26
D. Shannon c Hilton b Whittle 4
S. Wales st Bickley b Hilton 20
D. Clarke st Bickley b Hilton 8
H. Jackson c Cockle b Hilton 5
R. Gilchrist c Hilton b Holt 2
B. Derbyshire c McDonald b Hilton 3
B. Marsh obstruction 5
B. Haley c Fletcher b Holt 6
G. Duckworth c Heaton b Hilton 16
P. Sutcliffe not out 4
Extras 7
106

Bowling: Whittle 6–0–13–1, Cockle 5–2–10–0, Tebay 3–0–13–0, Hilton 10.3–1–34–6, Holt 8–1–29–2.

RADCLIFFE
D. Bickley not out 3
W. McDonald not out 1
$\underline{4–0}$

Bowling: Gilchrist 1.3–0–3–0, Sutcliffe 1–0–1–0.

A FAST 50

NOTTINGHAM, AUGUST 1965

A 29-year-old Leicestershire batsman, born in Colombo, Ceylon (now Sri Lanka), engraved himself in cricket's record books in eight minutes' play on the third day of the game against Nottinghamshire. But there were some who thought Clive Inman's record was an insult to cricket.

It came on the final day of a game that was evenly balanced but running out of time. Despite Leicestershire's fast start – 75 in the first hour of the match and 161 in the 150 minutes before lunch – they needed to score quickly on the final morning if there was to be any chance of a finish. So they did. Jayasinghe thrashed the Nottinghamshire batsmen to various corners of the ground. Yes, batsmen. One of the tactics of the day was to use irregular bowlers in order to bring forward the declaration. When Jayasinghe was bowled for 99 by Brian Bolus, the Nottinghamshire opening bat, the fun really started. Clive Inman, the new batsman, took a single from Bolus to face the bowling of Norman Hill, the other Nottinghamshire opening bat. In the space of a further 12 balls (13 in total) Inman raced to the fastest 50 on record.

Norman Hill, bowling an inviting brand of 'donkey-drops', went for 4, 4, 0, 0, 6 and 4 in his first over and 4, 6, 6, 6, 6, 4 in his second. Inman, pulling strongly to mid-wicket, raced to his 50 in eight minutes, beating the 11-minute record by Jim Smith of Middlesex, against Gloucestershire at

Bristol in 1938. Leicestershire were now scoring almost too quickly, but the blitz could not be interrupted. The eventual declaration set Nottinghamshire 258 in 150 minutes, but it proved well beyond them. Umpire Syd Buller sent a report to the MCC.

LEICESTERSHIRE

M.R. Hallam c Millman b Davison	54	b Corran 22
B.J. Booth c Millman b Corran	20	b Davison 6
P. Marner c Smedley b Taylor	109	not out 71
S. Jayasinghe c Millman b Forbes	25	b Bolus 99
C.C. Inman b Forbes	8	not out 57
D. Constant not out	45	
J. van Geloven c Hill b Taylor	3	
R. Julian b Forbes	3	
R.J. Barratt c and b Corran	1	
J.S. Savage not out	9	
Extras	11	3
	(declared) 288–8	(declared) 258–3

Bowling: *First Innings*; Corran 20–4–61–2, Forbes 26–4–79–3, Davison 17–3–40–1, Taylor 21–7–56–2, Gillhouley 17–3–41–0. *Second Innings*; Corran 8–1–28–1, Davison 8–3–26–1, Taylor 6–1–18–0, Gillhouley 5–0–18–0, Whittingham 10–0–44–0, Moore 10–0–44–0, Bolus 8–3–27–1, Hill 2–0–50–0.

NOTTINGHAMSHIRE

N. Hill c and b Cotton	10	c Julian b Cotton 6
J.B. Bolus c Constant b Barratt	39	b van Geloven 46
B. Whittingham c Julian b Cotton	126	c Booth b van Geloven 43
I. Moore c Jayasinghe b Savage	10	not out 7
M.J. Smedley c Julian b Marner	58	not out 55
M. Taylor c Jayasinghe b van Geloven	13	
G. Millman b Marner	6	
K. Gillhouley not out	9	
A.J. Corran lbw b van Geloven	7	
I. Davison not out	0	
Extras	11	9
	(declared) 289–8	166–3

Bowling: *First Innings*; Cotton 24–2–62–2, Marner 29–6–86–2, van Geloven 24–6–45–2, Savage 21–7–40–1, Barratt 16–1–45–1. *Second Innings*; Cotton 6–0–23–1, Marner 3–0–6–0, van Geloven 10–1–47–2, Savage 12–1–58–0, Barratt 7–1–23–0.

A FARCICAL GAME
IN THE RAIN
CASTLEFORD, YORKSHIRE, MAY 1967

Three days had been set aside at Bradford for this 60-over Gillette Cup match between Yorkshire and Cambridgeshire, but no play was possible on any of the three days. The two counties agreed on one more date when the game would have to be completed. That date was 25 May. They met again, at Headingley.

It was soon obvious that the Headingley ground was under water and unfit for play. The ground held in reserve was that of Harrogate, which was also under water. Yorkshire officials hastily rang around the county to try to find a fit ground. They settled on Castleford, 12 miles (19.3km) from Headingley, which was expected to be fit by the afternoon. The itinerant cricketers headed for the game's fourth venue – and still no ball had been bowled.

Perfectly on cue, the rain fell heavily as soon as they arrived at Castleford. When it cleared up, temporarily it proved, the captains agreed to play a ten-over game and continue through any rain.

Yorkshire won the toss and put Cambridgeshire in. Fairey pulled Trueman for six and stuck manfully to his task, but wickets tumbled at the other end, an average of almost one per over.

Cambridgeshire scrambled to 43 for eight, and, by the time they took the field, it was raining heavily. Fairey and Johnny Wardle, the ex-Yorkshire player, opened the bowling, and they picked up a couple of quick wickets. Rain teemed down. The pitch cut up, water dripped off players' caps, and the bespectacled Geoff Boycott was held back in the order. The big hitters came in to finish the game before it became ultra-farcical, and the sole object was to get a result. Yorkshire won by six wickets. The man of the match was Cambridgeshire's Fairey, not only because he made the highest score of the match and took two good wickets, but perhaps because he was exposed to the rain longer than any other player.

CAMBRIDGESHIRE

D.H. Fairey c Close b Trueman	22
P.A. Shippey c Trueman b Nicholson	0
T. Hale c Trueman b Nicholson	1
R.A. Gautrey b Wilson	9
J.H. Wardle b Nicholson	0
E. Davis c Sharpe b Wilson	6
S.W. Shippey c Taylor b Close	0
A. Ponder c Sharpe b Close	0
C.B. Gadsby not out	2
D. Wing not out	2
Extras	1
	43–8

Bowling: Trueman 3–1–15–1, Nicholson 3–0–11–3, Close 2–0–8–2, Wilson 2–0–8–2.

Fall of wickets: 8, 15, 24, 24, 34, 38, 38, 40.

YORKSHIRE

J.H. Hampshire c Gadsby b Wardle	1
K. Taylor c Hale b Wardle	20
D.B. Close c and b Fairey	1
D. Wilson c Gadsby b Fairey	12
F.S. Trueman not out	11
R. Illingworth not out	1
	46–4

Bowling: Fairey 3–0–8–2, Wardle 3–0–32–2, Wing 0.5–0–6–0.

Fall of wickets: 7, 9, 26, 41.

NINE IN NINE BALLS

BLENHEIM, NEW ZEALAND, DECEMBER 1967

In a two-innings match between Marlborough College 'A' and Bohally Intermediate School, a 14-year-old Marlborough College bowler called Stephen Fleming achieved the phenomenal match figures of 1.1–1–0–9. Fleming bowled nine balls in the match and took a wicket with each ball.

Bohally, batting first, spluttered along to 17 for nine when Fleming first came into the attack. He took a wicket with his first ball to close the innings. The Marlborough College team replied with 45 for nine declared.

Fleming opened the bowling in the Bohally second innings. He bowled one eight-ball over and collected eight wickets, two caught and six bowled. Bohally were nought for eight, but, in the second over, they scrambled two byes and one run off the bat.

Fleming's reward for his scintillating bowling – nine wickets in nine balls – was to be taken off. Presumably, in the less ruthless world of schoolboy cricket, this was to give Bohally a bit more of a chance. In actuality, Graham Holdaway, who had taken a hat-trick in the first innings, took the remaining two Bohally wickets inside five balls. Bohally were all out for three in 21 balls, less than three eight-ball overs.

BOHALLY: 17 and 3 (Fleming 8–0).
MARLBOROUGH COLLEGE: 45–9 declared.

THE EMERALD GREEN WICKET

SION MILLS, LONDONDERRY, JULY 1969

The West Indian tourists, having achieved an honourable draw in an evenly balanced Test match at Lord's, travelled across to Northern Ireland to whip the Irish in a one-day game. It was an exhausting trip, but when Basil Butcher, the West Indies captain in the absence of the injured Sobers, told his opening bats to pad up, later-order players recognised that they had a chance to recover from the journey. It was better for the game that West Indies batted first and the crowd were able to see some runs.

The experienced Carew, on his third tour of England, opened the innings with Camacho, who had made 67 and 45 in the Lord's Test. They were warmly applauded when they walked to the wicket and courteously greeted when they returned. At one for two it was still anybody's game.

Foster was an unproven member of the touring party. The run-out didn't help him establish himself. Three for three.

The situation calling for a captain's innings, Basil Butcher then joined up with the prolific Clive Lloyd, whose excellent form included a scintillating 70 in 100 minutes in the second innings at Lord's. Sure enough, they put together the best stand of the innings so far. The score had been taken to six when they were both out. Six for five.

Clyde Walcott, the West Indies manager, in his prime a superb batsman who had hit 15 Test centuries, was able to lead the recovery. It also offered him an opportunity to study, at the relatively short distance of 22 yards (20.1m), why John Shepherd and Findlay were both caught for ducks. Walcott totally dominated the scoring while he was at the wicket – all six runs went to him – but all good things come to an end. Yet another catch went to hand. Twelve for eight.

A lot of responsibility rested with Roberts, the tenth West Indian batsman. When he went for nought, Ireland were in a confident position. West Indies were 12 for nine.

On a wet, green wicket, with the ball stopping and lifting, Ireland's steady medium-pacers, O'Riordan and captain Goodwin, had ripped through the West Indian batting in sensational style. This was no substandard touring team, as it included six of the previous day's Test team. Perhaps they were suffering from what Mike Brearley once referred to as 'post-Test letdown', the anti-climactic feeling after five days of adrenalin. Or perhaps the journey to Ireland had exhausted them. Or maybe Ireland were simply the better team on the day.

The West Indian quick bowlers, Shillingford and Blair, more than doubled the West Indies score with their last-wicket stand of 13. Ireland knocked off the runs for the loss of only one wicket to register an amazing victory.

In order to provide some entertainment for the crowd, Ireland batted on, then sportingly declared to give the West Indies a chance to redeem themselves. They did better in the second innings. The second wicket didn't fall until the score had reached two. Goodwin took two more wickets to record match figures of seven for seven. But a 50 by Basil Butcher restored some sense of normality.

West Indies, embarrassed by being caught on the emerald green wicket, agreed to play a two-day game while they were in Ireland. The home country, with scores of 126 and 165 for nine, held out for a draw after facing a West Indies score of 288 for five declared. The touring team's next game, in Glamorgan, saw Butcher and Lloyd stitch together a fifth-wicket partnership of 335.

West Indies, reorganising after the break-up of the early 1960s team of Worrell, Hall, Griffith, Hunte and Solomon, lost two and drew one of that three-Test series against England. Although the game against Ireland was not first class, it provided a first-class shock and a boost for Irish cricket.

WEST INDIES

G.S. Comacho c Dineen b Goodwin	1	c Dineen b Goodwin 1
M.C. Carew c Hughes b O'Riordan	0	c Pigot b Duffy 25
M.L.C. Foster run out	2	c Pigot b Goodwin 0
B.F. Butcher c Duffy b O'Riordan	2	c Waters b Duffy 50
C.H. Lloyd c Waters b Goodwin	1	not out 0
C.L. Walcott c Anderson b O'Riordan	6	not out 0
J.N. Shepherd c Duffy b Goodwin	0	
T.M. Findlay c Waters b Goodwin	0	
G.C. Shillingford not out	9	
P. Roberts c Colhoun b O'Riordan	0	
P.D. Blair b Goodwin	3	
Extras	1	 2
	25	**78–4**

Bowling: *First Innings*; O'Riordan 13–8–18–4, Goodwin 12.3–8–6–5. *Second Innings*; O'Riordan 6–1–21–0, Goodwin 2–1–1–2, Hughes 7–4–10–0, Duffy 12–8–12–2, Anderson 7–1–32–0.

Fall of wickets: *First Innings*; 1, 1, 3, 6, 6, 8, 12, 12, 12, 25. *Second Innings*; 1, 2, 73, 78.

IRELAND

R.H.C. Waters c Findlay b Blair	2
D.M. Pigot c Camacho b Shillingford	37
M. Reith lbw b Shepherd	10
J. Harrison lbw b Shepherd	0
I. Anderson c Shepherd b Roberts	7
P.J. Dineen b Shepherd	0
A.J. O'Riordan c and b Carew	35
G.A. Duffy not out	15
L.F. Hughes c Sub b Carew	13
Extras	6
(declared)	**125–8**

Bowling: Blair 8–4–14–1, Shillingford 7–2–19–1, Shepherd 13–4–20–3, Roberts 16–3–43–1, Carew 3.2–0–23–2.

Fall of wickets: 19, 30, 34, 51, 55, 69, 103, 125.

152

HITTING AT DUSK

MANCHESTER, JULY 1971

On the day that the editors of *Oz* were convicted of four obscenity charges and the Labour Party's National Executive voted for a policy opposing Britain's entry into the Common Market, a crowd of 23,520 watched a fascinating Gillette Cup semi-final duel between Lancashire and Gloucestershire at Old Trafford. They watched until just before 9 o'clock, the last few overs being played in desperately poor light.

Lancashire, the holders of the Gillette Cup, had a team of players who were committed to the one-day ethic. Gloucestershire perhaps relied more on specific individuals, particularly the all-round skills of Mike Procter. Batting first, Gloucestershire had the expected good innings from Procter, and support from the other batsmen led to a decent total of 229 for six.

More than an hour's play was lost through rain in the period after lunch, but at 7.30p.m., by which time the weather had cleared up, the umpires exercised their right to decide that the game should be played to a finish that evening. Naturally, Gloucestershire bowled their overs more and more slowly. On the other hand they were kept in the field for a four-hour stretch with no breaks and were undoubtedly weary towards the end. The light was bad for fielders as well as batsmen.

In the forty-sixth over, the game looked to have gone Gloucestershire's way. The freak dismissal of Farouk

Engineer, who slipped and touched his wicket with his foot while driving, meant that Lancashire, at 163 for six, needed 67 to win at almost five an over in poor light. Skipper Jack Bond acted as anchor while Jack Simmons hit as well as he could see, clouting one six over long-on off John Mortimore's off-spin. When Simmons was bowled by Mortimore, at 203, Lancashire needed 27 at much the same pace, about five an over, with the light even worse – street lights were shining through the dusk around Old Trafford – and only three wickets to fall.

A story is told of how David Hughes spent time in a dark dressing-room getting used to the bad light before going out to bat. Hughes was on strike at the start of the fifty-sixth over of the match, when Lancashire needed 25 from five overs, and the bowler, John Mortimore, had hitherto conceded 57 from his ten overs.

The onslaught launched by Hughes in that fifty-sixth over will never be erased from Lancashire folklore. Having decided, in consultation with Bond, that he must go after the slow bowler rather than Procter, he hit Mortimore for six, four, two, two, four and six – a total of 24 runs – and the scores were tied. Jack Bond scored the winning single from the fifth ball of Procter's next over, and, with Hughes, sprinted towards the lights of the pavilion to avoid the best of the back-slapping from the invading crowd.

David Hughes was acclaimed Man of the Match, almost solely for his innings in the dusk, and the cheering Lancashire crowd stayed until around 10 o'clock, providing novel, football-like scenes at Old Trafford. Elsewhere, there was some criticism of the fact that a big semi-final match had been settled in such poor conditions, but the partisan Lancashire crowd would not have had it any other way.

GLOUCESTERSHIRE

R.B. Nicholls b Simmons 53
D.M. Green run out 21
R.D.V. Knight c Simmons b Hughes 31
M.J. Procter c Engineer b Lever 65
D.R. Shepherd lbw b Simmons 6
M. Bissex not out 29
A.S. Brown c Engineer b Sullivan 6
H. Jarman not out 0
Extras 18
                              (60 overs) <u>229–6</u>

Bowling: Lever 12–3–40–1, Shuttleworth 12–3–33–0, Wood 12–3–39–0, Hughes 11–0–68–1, Simmons 12–3–25–2, Sullivan 1–0–6–1.

Fall of wickets: 57, 87, 113, 150, 201, 210.

LANCASHIRE

D. Lloyd lbw b Brown 31
B. Wood run out 50
H. Pilling b Brown 21
C.H. Lloyd b Mortimore 34
J. Sullivan b Davey 10
F.M. Engineer hit wkt b Mortimore 2
J.D. Bond not out 16
Simmons b Mortimore 25
D.P. Hughes not out 26
Extras 15
                            (56.5 overs) <u>230–7</u>

Bowling: Procter 10.5–3–38–0, Davey 11–1–22–1, Knight 12–2–42–0, Mortimore 11–0–81–3, Brown 12–0–32–2.

Fall of wickets: 61, 105, 136, 156, 160, 163, 203.

POCOCK'S DRAMATIC
LAST TWO OVERS
EASTBOURNE, AUGUST 1972

Considering only 13 overs were bowled on the first day of this match, Sussex and Surrey did remarkably well to conjure up a game of ebbs and flows that eventually produced an amazing climax and several world records.

On the Saturday, Surrey made 38 without loss from those 13 overs, and when play resumed they batted well, accumulating runs at a good rate. In fact 372 runs came on the Monday, Surrey declaring after reaching 300 and Sussex ending the day on 110 for three.

Two sporting declarations set the game alight on a final day which brought well over 400 runs. Sussex, left with a target of 205 in 135 minutes, looked totally in control when Geoffrey Greenidge and Roger Prideaux put together an excellent partnership for the second wicket. At the end of the seventeenth of the compulsory last 20 overs, Sussex were 187 for one. It seemed a foregone conclusion that they would make 18 runs from 18 balls, and probably either Greenidge (68 not out) or Prideaux (92 not out) would make the winning hit.

The next over was bowled by Pat Pocock, the Surrey off-break bowler who played 25 Tests for England between 1967 and 1985. His first ball bowled Greenidge, and Sussex were 187 for two. His third ball bowled Michael Buss, and Sussex were 187 for three. Jim Parks took two from the fourth ball of the over, but was caught and bowled from the last. Sussex, at 189 for four, still needed 16 to win from two overs.

Robin Jackman bowled the next over. Prideaux hit the first for four and took a single from the second, then Griffith hit the fifth ball clear of the boundary. At 200 for four, the Sussex target was down to a mere five runs and Prideaux, 97 not out, was on strike.

Prideaux hit the first ball of the last over, bowled by Pocock, into the air. Jackman took the catch – 200 for five. The batsmen had crossed, so Griffith faced Pocock's next ball with the bowler on a hat-trick. The catch went to Lewis, Pocock had his hat-trick and Sussex, 200 for six, still wanted five from four balls with four wickets standing. At this rate of tumbling wickets, Surrey could still win.

Morley charged out to Pocock's third ball, and wicket-keeper Arnold Long stumped him. Pocock had four wickets in four balls, six wickets in nine balls (a world record) and Sussex still wanted those five runs.

Spencer cut the target to four when he took a single from the fourth ball but Tony Buss was bowled by the next Pocock delivery and Sussex were 201 for eight with one ball remaining. Pocock had five wickets in six balls (equalling the world record) and seven in 11 (another world record).

When Pat Pocock bowled the last ball of the match, at Joshi, it meant he had bowled seven consecutive balls at seven different batsmen. Joshi put bat to ball and there were runs. They crossed for one, and tried for two. Joshi was run out. Sussex, 202 for nine, were still three short of victory, and the game was a draw. The fall of five wickets in an over was another world first.

Incredibly, Sussex had lost eight wickets in the last 18 balls while making 15 runs. Pat Pocock bowled his last two overs for the sensational analysis of 2–0–4–7, plus a run-out. It was the most dramatic burst of wicket-taking that first-class cricket has known, made all the more unbelievable by Pocock's analysis before the start of his penultimate over, which read 14–1–63–0.

SURREY

M.J. Edwards c Joshi b Buss (M.A.) 81	c Phillipson b Spencer 6
R.M. Lewis c Greenidge b Buss (M.A.) 72	st Parks b Spencer 28
D.R. Owen-Thomas c Parks b Spencer 31	c Griffith b Buss (M.A.) 32
Younis Admed c Parks b Phillipson 26	c Buss (A.) b Joshi 26
G.R.J. Roope not out 43	not out 21
M.J. Stewart not out 34	not out 1
Intikhab Alam c Spencer b Joshi 6	
Extras 13	10
(declared) <u>300–4</u>	(declared) <u>130–5</u>

Bowling: *First Innings*; Spencer 22.5–4–56–1, Buss (A.) 17–3–74–0, Phillipson 13–1–37–1, Buss (M.) 15–3–58–2, Joshi 15–5–62–0. *Second Innings*; Spencer 11–0–29–2, Buss (A.) 12–1–35–0, Buss (M.) 5–1–29–1, Joshi 6–0–27–2.

Fall of wickets: *First Innings*; 130, 167, 212, 232. *Second Innings*; 8, 61, 95, 101, 117.

SUSSEX

G.A. Greenidge c Long b Butcher 6	b Pocock 68
P.J. Graves b Pocock 35	c Roope b Jackman 14
R.M. Prideaux not out 106	c Jackman b Pocock 97
M.A. Buss c Long b Pocock 8	b Pocock 0
J.M. Parks c Roope b Intikhab 29	c and b Pocock 2
J. Spencer lbw b Intikhab 0	(8) not out 1
M.G. Griffith not out 29	(6) c Lewis b Pocock 6
J.D. Morley	(7) st Long b Pocock 0
A. Buss	b Pocock 0
U.C. Joshi	run out 1
Extras 13	13
(declared) <u>226–5</u>	<u>202–9</u>

Bowling: *First Innings*; Jackman 7–1–29–0, Butcher 15–4–33–1, Pocock 24–8–69–2, Intikhab 26.1–6–82–2. *Second Innings*; Jackman 13–1–62–1, Butcher 3–0–13–0, Pocock 16–1–67–7, Intikhab 12–2–47–0.

Fall of wickets: *First Innings*; 12, 80, 104, 117, 190. *Second Innings*; 27, 187, 187, 189, 200, 200, 200, 201, 202.

ALL AROUND THE CLOCK
CAMBRIDGE, JUNE 1973

There was a lot of cricket in Cambridgeshire that week. The local county team were playing Lincolnshire at Wisbech, the Queen Mother was shown a cricket match when she visited Leys school and the New Zealand tourists were in Cambridge, fashioning an exciting finish with a sporting declaration against the Combined Universities. Imran Khan inspired the Universities on their last-day chase of 211 to win. They finished 207 for nine.

The most unusual game that week took place on Parker's Piece, the open stretch of city-centre Cambridge land which divides 'gown' from 'town'. The cricket game was all 'gown'.

Members of the Cambridge University cricket society took the field at 5 o'clock on the afternoon of 14 June. Their mission was to create a record for non-stop cricket. They were helped in their challenge by the Fire Brigade, who pumped 1,500 gallons of water on to the wicket and also provided gas lamps for evening play, and by the sponsorship of various firms, including the cricket-ball manufacturer Alfred Reader, who provided special orange cricket balls. The students brought their own whisky and coffee to help them through the night.

The two captains agreed to suspend fast bowling during the darkness hours, and it was between 1a.m. and 4a.m. that Roger Coates scored the only century of the game, a feat which earned him the Haig prize for best batting. The Alfred Reader prize for best bowling went to Philip Cornes.

Each team had five innings. Altogether 1,395 runs were scored for the loss of 89 wickets in 367 overs. They played until 5 o'clock the following afternoon, 24 hours' cricket, non-stop apart from a lunch break. They raised £170 to help the mentally handicapped.

LANGLEY'S XI: 59, 179, 83 ,200 and 161.

SUCH'S XI: 126, 254–8 dec. 121, 142–8 dec and 70–3.

LANGLEY'S XI: T. Brown, A. Ave, R. Court, J. Brett, J. Chambers, D.J. Yeandle, T. Wald, J. Preston, N. Peace, M. Coultas, D. Langley.

SUCH'S XI: R. Coates, P. Such, P. Cornes, A. Radford, M. Williams, A.S.I. Berry, J. Burnett, P. Kinns, M. Shaw, R. Henson, M. Furneaux.

CAUGHT ON A
SNOW-AFFECTED WICKET

BUXTON, JUNE 1975

It was a game of three thirds: on the first day Lancashire made runs on a good wicket; the second day was ruled out by snow; and the third day saw Derbyshire lose wickets by the handful. Lancashire won the game by the incredible margin of an innings and 348 runs. 'I've never seen owt like it,' said Harold 'Dickie' Bird, one of the umpires.

It was a good toss to win. Only an early declaration stopped Lancashire reaching 500 on the first day. They were helped by the absence of Derbyshire's key pace bowlers, Mike Hendrick and Alan Ward. Also, Derbyshire's deputy quickies, Keith Stevenson and Mike Glenn, both adjusting badly to the altitude of Buxton, were below par with temperatures of over a hundred. Glenn went to hospital and took no further part in the match.

The Lancashire innings owed much to a superb century by Frank Hayes and even more to a sensational century, made in 130 minutes, by Clive Lloyd. After reaching 100, Lloyd hit out majestically, with seven sixes in his next 50. Lloyd and Simmons put on 171 in 72 minutes against tired bowling. When the declaration came, there was still time for two Derbyshire wickets to fall. The day brought 502 runs in 115 overs. It was the scoring pace of a previous era.

Two days later, on the Monday, there was 1in (2.5cm) of overnight snow on the ground at 9a.m. The weather forecasters for that day typically hedged their bets: 'sunny periods, scattered showers, sleet or snow on mountains; wind N, fresh or strong,' said one. It was quite understandable that forecasters should underestimate the extent of the bad weather – it was the worst summer's day of snow and sleet since 11 July 1888. There was 4in (10.2cm) of snow on the Scottish Highlands, 3in (7.6cm) on parts of Cumbria, and the County Championship game at Bradford was abandoned for the day without a ball being bowled. The start was delayed at Colchester.

Buxton had flurries of rain at the normal starting time, then heavy snow. At lunch time play was abandoned for the day. It was staggering that the wicket was fit to play on the following day, the Tuesday, although Derbyshire supporters must have questioned how fit it really was.

A snow-affected wicket proved to be no joke for the Derbyshire batsmen, although the weather was not in any way to blame for Morris's run-out in the first over of the day. Lancashire's Peter Lee was dangerously unplayable, making the ball lift awkwardly. He bowled 50 balls before conceding a run that day. 'Harvey-Walker, mindful of the degree of bounce, handed his false teeth to the umpire when he finally got down Lee's end,' reported Gerald Mortimer in the *Derby Evening Telegraph*. 'He was soon able to collect them again when he fended off and was comfortably caught by David Lloyd at short square-leg.'

On one of the most vicious pitches of recent history, Lee took four for four in the first hour of the day and Derbyshire, all out for 42, recorded the lowest total of the season. In their second innings, the Derbyshire batsmen experimented with different techniques and, although John Harvey-Walker and Alan Morris coped relatively well, Peter Lever mopped up the match with five wickets in 22 balls. Lancashire climbed into second place in the County Championship table, and Buxton moved into the annals of venues for strange matches.

LANCASHIRE

B. Wood b Russell 26
D. Lloyd c Swarbrook b Russell 69
F.C. Hayes c Page b Harvey-Walker 104
C.H. Lloyd not out 167
A. Kennedy c Sub b Miller 5
F.H. Engineer c Morris b Russell 18
J. Simmons not out 55
Extras 33

(declared) <u>477–5</u>

Bowling: Stevenson 14–3–50–0, Glenn 12–3–36–0, Russell 34–10–119–3, Swarbrook 17–1–111–0, Miller 14–0–94–1, Harvey-Walker 9–2–34–1.

Fall of wickets: 45, 175, 240, 261, 306.

DERBYSHIRE

A. Hill c Engineer b Lever 0	c Lloyd (D.) b Lee 2
J.B. Bolus c Engineer b Wood 11	c Shuttleworth b Hughes .. 14
M.H. Page c Simmons b Lee 13	c Engineer b Lee 15
A. Morris run out 4	c Simmons b Lever 26
A.J. Harvey-Walker c Lloyd (D.) b Lee 7	c Kennedy b Lever 26
F.W. Swarbrook not out 1	c Engineer b Lever 0
G. Miller c Lloyd (D.) b Hughes 2	b Lever 0
R.W. Taylor c Lloyd (C.) b Hughes 0	c Lloyd (D.) b Lever 4
P.E. Russell c Kennedy b Lee 1	c Hayes b Hughes 0
K. Stevenson c Engineer b Lee 0	not out 0
M. Glenn absent ill 0	absent ill 0
Extras 3	 0
<u>42</u>	<u>87</u>

<u>1̄63̄</u>

Bowling: *First Innings*; Lever 8–1–18–1, Lee 13.2–11–10–4, Wood 2–2–0–1, Hughes 9–5–11–2. *Second Innings*; Lever 5.2–2–16–5, Lee 17–9–26–2, Hughes 12–5–26–2, Shuttleworth 6–1–16–0, Simmons 4–1–3–0.

Fall of wickets: *First Innings*; 2, 20, 35, 35, 38, 41, 41, 42, 42. *Second Innings*; 7, 25, 39, 72, 72, 72, 85, 85, 87.

'G. DAVIS IS INNOCENT'

LEEDS, AUGUST 1975

'What does Headingley have in store this time, I wonder?' pondered John Woodcock in *The Times* on the morning of the third Test between England and Australia. 'Almost always this corresponding match has something unusual about it, whether it is Australia scoring 404 in a day to win, as in 1948, or Underwood running through the Australian batting on a controversial pitch, as in 1972.'

Neither spectators nor cricket correspondents could have foreseen the unusual controversy that struck Headingley on the final day. Nothing remotely like it had happened in living memory.

As a game, this Test was interesting and intriguing, edging further and further towards an England victory until Australia staged an excellent recovery on the fourth day. Australia were one up and held the Ashes, a strong position for a series of only four Tests.

David Steele plodded through the first day – during one 90-minute period his score moved by only ten runs – and there was some threat from Gary Gilmour's swing. On the second day, Australia slumped to 107 for eight when faced with the two English left-arm spin bowlers, the experienced Derek Underwood and the debutant Phil Edmonds. Edmonds, the 1973 Cambridge University captain, beat Ian Chappell's ungainly swing on the second ball of his second over, trapped Edwards not playing a shot next ball and added the wicket of Greg Chappell, caught at square-leg, in his next over. At tea Edmonds had three for four from 15 balls. At the end of the next session, cut short by rain, he had five for 17 from 12 overs. Another persevering innings by Steele on the third day – an unbeaten 59 in 210 minutes – provided the anchor for England's overnight lead of 337 and a match-winning position. Shortly before lunch on the fourth day, Australia went in for a second time needing 445 to win, but the ball wasn't turning as much and the wicket was more placid. At the close the game was beautifully poised. Australia needed another 225 with seven wickets remaining.

The storm broke the next morning, at 6.50a.m., when the Headingley groundsman rolled back the covers on the wicket. During the night, unseen by the police patrol, someone had climbed the wall, run on to the pitch and crawled under the covers, pouring oil over the wicket (right on a good length) and digging 3in (7.6cm) holes with kitchen knives and forks. On the outside wall were slogans proclaiming that George Davis was innocent. Until that day, few people were aware that George Davis, a 34-year-old London mini-cab driver, was serving a 17-year jail sentence for his alleged part in a robbery in which a policeman was shot. Within a week the name 'George Davis' was common knowledge.

The campaign to free George Davis had already been in action a year without being able to reopen the case. It was now stepped up: slogans at the Central Criminal Court, sit-down protests, a march to Downing Street, campaigners chained to the Monument and demonstrating on the dome of St Paul's Cathedral, and naked displays at an East London boating lake. The campaign leader, Peter Chappell (no relation to Ian, Greg or Trevor), was given an 18-month jail sentence at Birkenhead in January 1976 for his Leeds and London graffiti prose and for topping up the Headingley pitch with oil. When cricket fans now referred to the Chappells they had to define exactly who they were talking about.

Captains, managers and umpires converged on the Headingley wicket around 9 o'clock on the morning of the final day of the Third Test. The groundsman felt he could repair the holes in the wicket, but oil was a different matter. The only possible way of continuing the game was if the captains, Tony Greig and Ian Chappell, could agree on another strip of wicket of similar wear. Greig was happy to do this. Understandably, Chappell could not comply, and the game was abandoned. Loss of gate receipts and scorecard sales probably amounted to nearly £6,000, but it was unlikely that the game could have been finished anyway. At noon it rained.

Nine months later, after serving two years of his sentence, George Davis was released from jail by the Home Secretary. In July 1978 he was back in jail, sentenced to 15 years' imprisonment for an armed raid on a bank the previous September. He pleaded guilty to this offence, which helped reduce his sentence to 11 years on appeal. In January 1987, soon after his release from the bank-raid sentence, he was sent to prison for 18 months for an attempt to rob a mail-train. Again he pleaded guilty.

ENGLAND

J.H. Edrich c Mallett b Thomson	62	b Mallett 35
B. Wood lbw b Gilmour	9	lbw b Walker 25
D.S. Steele c Walters b Thomson	73	c Chappell (G.) b Gilmour 92
J.H. Hampshire lbw b Gilmour	14	(7) c Chappell (G.) b Thomson 0
K.W.R. Fletcher c Mallett b Lillee	8	(4) c Chappell (G.) b Lillee 14
A.W. Greig run out	51	(5) c and b Mallett 49
A.P.E. Knott lbw b Gilmour	14	(8) c Thomson b Lillee 31
P.H. Edmonds not out	13	(9) c Sub b Gilmour 8
C.M. Old b Gilmour	5	(6) st Marsh b Mallett 10
J.A. Snow c Walters b Gilmour	0	c Marsh b Gilmour 9
D.L. Underwood c Chappell (G.) b Gilmour	0	not out 0
Extras	39	 18
	288	**291**

Bowling: *First Innings*; Lillee 28–12–53–1, Thomson 22–8–53–2, Gilmour
31.2–10–85–6, Walker 18–4–54–0, Chappell (G.) 2–0–4–0. *Second Innings*;
Lillee 20–5–48–2, Thomson 20–6–67–1, Gilmour 20–5–72–3, Walker 15–4–36–1,
Mallett 19–4–50–3.

Fall of wickets: *First Innings*; 25, 137, 159, 189, 213, 268, 269, 284, 284, 288.
Second Innings; 55, 70, 103, 197, 209, 210, 272, 276, 285, 291.

AUSTRALIA

R.B. McCosker c Hampshire b Old	0	not out	95
R.W. Marsh b Snow	25	b Underwood	12
I.M. Chappell b Edmonds	35	lbw b Old	62
G.S. Chappell c Underwood b Edmonds	13	c Steele b Edmonds	12
R. Edwards lbw b Edmonds	0		
K.D. Walters lbw b Edmonds	19	(5) not out	27
G.J. Gilmour c Greig b Underwood	6		
M.H.N. Walker c Old b Edmonds	0		
J.R. Thomson c Steele b Snow	16		
D.K. Lillee b Snow	11		
A.A. Mallett not out	1		
Extras	9		12
	135		**220–3**

Bowling: *First Innings*; Snow 18.5–7–22–3, Old 11–3–30–1, Greig 3–0–14–0,
Wood 5–2–10–0, Underwood 19–12–22–1, Edmonds 20–7–28–5. *Second Innings*;
Snow 15–5–23–0, Old 17–5–61–1, Greig 9–3–20–0, Underwood 15–4–40–1,
Edmonds 17–4–64–1.

Fall of wickets: *First Innings*; 8, 53, 78, 78, 81, 96, 104, 107, 128, 135. *Second
Innings*; 51, 161, 174.

ON THE INJURED LIST
KINGSTON, JAMAICA, APRIL 1976

The series between West Indies and India was nicely balanced at one Test each with one to play. The fourth and final Test, however, would be remembered for reasons other than the West Indian victory which brought them the series. Indian captain Bishen Bedi later referred to the game as 'a war', and the scorecard bore testimony to the notion of a battlefield. India were forced to call on all 17 of their touring party to field at some stage of the match. The substitutes took almost as many catches as the original team.

The first day was fairly ordinary. India made a good start, and Gaekwad batted patiently to reach 60 in five and a half hours. When he continued his innings the next morning he found far more life in the wicket, particularly at the northern end.

Michael Holding, bowling on his home island for the first time in a Test match, was exceptionally dangerous. Viswanath, fending off a ball from Holding which fractured his finger, was caught at short-leg. Gaekwad, after two more hours' resistance, was hit on the left ear. He spent two days in hospital.

A ball from Holder reared up, and Patel deflected it from his glove to his mouth. He needed three stitches and took no further part in the game. Bedi, complaining about intimidating bowling, declared with six wickets down (and two others retired hurt). The Indian captain implied that he was protecting his two key bowlers – himself and Bhagwat Chandrasekhar – from injury. Those familiar with the Test batting averages of this pair could see a lot of sense in the declaration.

The next casualty, however, was indeed Bedi, who injured his left little finger when trying to catch Vivian Richards off his own bowling. Chandrasekhar kept India in the game with four wickets in 27 balls, but a stand of 107 between Deryck Murray and Michael Holding brought the West Indies a first-innings lead. A healthy last-wicket stand took the lead to 85 before lunch on the fourth day. By this time Chandrasekhar had injured a hand, and a substitute fielder, Surinder Amarnath, had been rushed to hospital for an emergency appendix operation.

The second Indian innings was amazingly depleted. Only six were able to bat. In effect, India slumped from 97 for two to 97 all out. Three wickets fell at that total, and then, with five wickets gone, Bedi called in Kirmani, the not-out batsman, and announced the innings closed. West Indies knocked off the required runs and won by ten wickets.

INDIA

S.M. Gavaskar b Holding	66	c Julien b Holding	2
A.D. Gaekwad retired hurt	81	absent injured	0
M. Amarnath c Julien b Holding	39	st Murray b Jumadeen	59
G.R. Viswanath c Julien b Holding	8	absent injured	0
D.B. Vengsarkar b Holding	39	lbw b Jumadeen	22
B.P. Patel retired hurt	14	absent injured	0
S. Madan Lal lbw b Daniel	5	b Holding	8
S. Venkataraghavan lbw b Daniel	9	b Holding	0
S.M.H. Kirmani not out	0	not out	0
B.S. Bedi	absent injured		0
B.S. Chandrasekhar	absent injured		0
Extras	45		6
(declared)	306–6		97

Bowling: *First Innings*; Holding 28–7–82–4, Daniel 20.2–7–52–2, Julien 23–10–53–0, Holder 27–4–58–0, Jumadeen 3–1–8–0, Fredericks 3–1–8–0.
Second Innings; Holding 7.1–0–35–3, Daniel 3–0–12–0, Julien 3–0–13–0, Holder 6–2–11–0, Jumadeen 7–2–20–2.

Fall of wickets: *First Innings*; 136, 205, 216, 280, 306, 306. *Second Innings*; 5, 68, 97, 97, 97.

WEST INDIES

R.C. Fredericks run out	82	not out ... 6
L.G. Rowe st Kirmani b Bedi	47	not out ... 6
I.V.A. Richards b Chandra	64	
A.I. Kallicharran b Chandra	12	
C.H. Lloyd c and b Chandra	0	
D.L. Murray c Sub (Solkar) b Chandra	71	
B.D. Julien b Chandra	5	
M.A. Holding c Sub (Sharma) b Bedi	55	
V.A. Holder not out	36	
R.R. Jumadeen c Gavaskar b Venkat	3	
W.W. Daniel c Amarnath b Venkat	11	
Extras	5	... 1
	391	**13–0**

Bowling: *First Innings*; Madan Lal 7–1–25–0, Amarnath 8–1–28–0, Chandrasekhar 42–7–153–5, Bedi 32–10–68–2, Venkataraghavan 51.3–12–112–2. *Second Innings*; Madan Lal 1–0–5–0, Vengsarkar 0.5–0–7–0.

A 'REMARKABLY CONTRADICTORY MATCH'

TAUNTON, MAY AND JUNE 1976

When the last two innings of the match contradict the first two, there is usually some sensible reason, such as injury, weather, a shift in confidence or some combination of these. That such a contradiction could occur at Taunton, where there is a notably reliable wicket, is particularly odd.

Somerset, playing Gloucestershire, had an excellent first day. A superb century from Brian Rose and steady all-round batting took them to 333 for seven before a declaration set up an entertaining start to the Gloucestershire innings – four down for only 43 in the 19 overs before the close. The game was going to form. Somerset were third in the County Championship table, Gloucestershire next to bottom. The only black mark for Somerset was that around Graham Burgess's eye, which closed after the ball hit him in the face while he was batting. Burgess, forced to retire, had stitches inserted.

Somerset were without two key bowlers, Tom Cartwright and Hallam Moseley, but a young swing bowler, 20-year-old Ian Botham, took a career-best six for 25, and Gloucestershire were forced to follow on, a massive 254 runs behind. Somerset captain Brian Close obviously assumed that his bowlers were not likely to be too tired to bowl out Gloucestershire a second time. He had a problem, however, when Clapp strained his side and was unfit to bowl in the second innings.

Botham bowled 37 overs on that second day, the wicket lively in the morning but soon settling down to its customary predictability. In his last, Botham picked up two wickets, Stovold and Brown, but Gloucestershire had recovered to reach 325 for six, 71 runs ahead. Zaheer Abbas had initiated this recovery, scoring 141 in 165 minutes, with 23 fours.

The next morning, Gloucestershire, at 327 for eight, still had little hope of turning round the game. They were grateful to the ninth-wicket pair, Julian Shackleton and Andy Brassington, who shared the wicket-keeping duties with Andy Stovold, for a partnership of 44. Somerset were left to make 119 in nearly four and a half hours.

Rose and Slocombe took the score to 43, and a mere 76 runs were needed for the expected victory. Then Slocombe was leg-before, Denning caught at leg-slip and Close spectacularly caught by the diving Shackleton at cover. This meant three wickets for Tony Brown, and Somerset were 73 for three. Kitchen and the persistent Rose worked their way to 97, so only 22 were needed and seven wickets were in hand.

It was then that Mike Procter produced a devastating spell of bowling, alternating slow off-breaks with quick balls, often using both types of bowling in the same over. Kitchen was caught at cover from an off-break (97 for four), Taylor caught at gully from a fast delivery (97 for five), Rose caught by a juggling Shepherd at mid-off (100 for six) and Botham bowled by an off-break after being hit in the face by a quicker ball (101 for seven).

Jennings hit a four, and Breakwell held out for 21 minutes. Eleven runs were wanted when Breakwell fell to Graveney (108 for eight). Almost immediately Jennings was caught behind (108 for nine), and Somerset still needed 11 with two injured players at the wicket. Burgess took a single, Clapp took a single, then Clapp edged a ball on to his pad and into the air. Sadiq pounced to take the catch and the game was over. Gloucestershire, 254 behind on first innings, had won by eight runs.

Ten Somerset wickets fell in 90 minutes for 67 runs. In his last 45 balls, Procter took six for 13, three wickets with off-breaks, three with fast balls. 'This remarkably contradictory match had an astonishing conclusion,' summarised *Wisden*. Perhaps a subliminal seed had been planted in the mind of Ian Botham, who took 11 for 150 and finished on the losing team: any team following-on still has a chance of victory, as would be demonstrated at Headingley five years later.

SOMERSET

B.C. Rose c Brassington b Graveney 104	c Shepherd b Procter 48
P.A. Slocombe lbw b Brown 36	lbw b Brown 17
P.W. Denning b Brown 41	c Sadiq b Brown 4
D.B. Close b Brown 0	c Shackleton b Brown 10
M.J. Kitchen c Davey b Graveney 69	c Shackleton b Procter 10
D.J.S. Taylor not out 41	c Sadiq b Procter 0
Burgess retired hurt 10	not out 1
I.T. Botham b Graveney 13	b Procter 3
D. Breakwell b Davey 0	c Shepherd b Graveney 0
K.F. Jennings not out 3	c Stovold b Procter 6
R.J. Clapp did not bat	c Sadiq b Procter 1
Extras 16	 10
(declared) 333-7	110

173

Bowling: *First Innings*; Davey 20–2–82–1, Shackleton 10–1–34–0, Procter 16–5–32–0, Brown 28–8–64–3, Graveney 24–4–94–3, Sadiq 2–0–11–0. *Second Innings*; Procter 14.3–4–35–6, Davey 5–0–20–0, Brown 9–2–27–3, Graveney 14–9–18–1.

Fall of wickets: *First Innings*; 58, 138, 138, 237, 290, 326, 327. *Second Innings*; 43, 47, 73, 97, 97, 100, 101, 108, 108, 110.

GLOUCESTERSHIRE

Sadiq Mohammed c Breakwell b Botham 2	c and b Jennings 8
N.H.C. Cooper b Botham 1	b Botham 38
Zaheer Abbas b Clapp 5	b Close 141
M.J. Procter c Taylor b Botham 7	c Breakwell b Close 32
A.W. Stovold c Close b Botham 18	b Botham 58
D.R. Shepherd b Clapp 27	lbw b Jennings 30
A.S. Brown lbw b Botham 0	b Botham 4
D.A. Graveney lbw b Jennings 2	b Botham 0
J.H. Shackleton c Close b Clapp 0	st Taylor b Breakwell 30
A.J. Brassington not out 4	not out 15
J. Davey b Botham 1	b Botham 0
Extras 12	 16
79	372

Bowling: *First Innings*; Clapp 13–6–18–3, Botham 16.1–6–25–6, Jennings 8–1–24–1, Close 1–1–0–0, Kitchen 1–1–0–0. *Second Innings*; Botham 37.1–6–125–5, Jennings 25–6–71–2, Close 27–9–90–2, Kitchen 3–0–21–0, Rose 4–0–9–0, Breakwell 24–12–40–1.

Fall of wickets: *First Innings*; 3, 9, 9, 29, 52, 52, 61, 68, 74, 79. *Second Innings*; 11, 126, 209, 236, 319, 325, 325, 327, 371, 372.

THE TEN-MINUTE GAME
WORCESTER, MAY 1979

The first thing to do, in order to understand this strange match, is to scrutinise the Benson & Hedges Group A Table on the morning of 24 May, the day of the match between Worcestershire and Somerset. Somerset captain Brian Rose and his team-mates certainly did so that Thursday morning. The table looked like this:

	Played	Won	Lost	Drawn	Points
Somerset	3	3	0	0	9
Worcestershire	3	2	1	0	6
Glamorgan	3	2	1	0	6
Gloucestershire	4	1	3	0	3
Minor Counties (South)	3	0	3	0	0

Two teams from the group would qualify for the quarter-final. Should any two teams finish level on points, the tie-breaker was their rate of wicket-taking. The statistics showed that Somerset were certain to qualify unless Worcestershire beat them that day AND Glamorgan beat the Minor Counties (South) in their final game AND both Worcester and Glamorgan significantly improved their wicket-taking rates so that they were superior to Somerset's.

The weather was poor that week. After Worcestershire's John Player Sunday League game had been washed out without a ball bowled, the groundstaff at New Road had been forced to work 12 hours a day in a bid to prepare a wicket while there was more rain. Extra work was caused by an accident with the roller damaging the first strip cut for the Cup game.

No play was possible on Wednesday 23 May, the day scheduled for the Worcestershire–Somerset Benson & Hedges game. The next morning, the weather was still unpredictable, and the start was delayed. Brian Rose was concerned about the weather. He was also concerned about guaranteeing Somerset's place in the quarter final. The 28-year-old left-handed opening bat was a shrewd captain who had seen Somerset to a Gillette Cup Final the previous year. Somerset were on the verge of great success – in 1979 they won the Gillette Cup and the John Player League – and Rose, who had already played five Test matches, was tipped as a possible future England captain.

In this match Brian Rose 'sacrificed all known cricketing principles', to use *Wisden*'s words. With the support of his team-mates, Rose declared after the first over, which produced one no-ball, thereby deliberately putting Somerset in a losing position. Worcestershire scored the required two runs without loss. The ten-minute game (not counting the ten minutes between innings) produced 3 runs from 17 balls.

Rose's decision was made to protect Somerset's wicket-taking rate in case they lost the game and all the other events worked out to their detriment. He recognised it was unusual practice, but he wasn't at fault, it was legal. There was nothing in the rules to prevent him declaring.

The 100 paying spectators were outraged, even when Worcestershire refunded their money. Some had been waiting around for a day and a half to see a game of cricket. Two farmers had travelled from Devon, a round trip of 300 miles (483km). A teacher had brought a party of 15 schoolchildren to reward them for their good work at school, and another man had spent two days of his holiday on the ground. The groundstaff had worked diligently to prepare the pitch for a day's use. The only humour came from those shocked spectators who tried to work out who would receive the gold medal. Vanburn Holder's maiden over was okay, and Glenn Turner's matchwinning two singles made him a strong candidate. In the event it was felt 'improper' to make a gold medal award.

Words like 'disgrace to cricket', 'farce' and 'not the spirit of the game' were bandied about, and the Test County Cricket board met to hold an inquiry. All the time Rose insisted his action was in accordance with the rules and his first duty was to Somerset. His committee supported him, although individuals made it clear that it wouldn't happen again.

On 1 June the Test & County Cricket Board ruled that Somerset should be expelled from that season's Benson & Hedges competition for not complying with the spirit of cricket. Worcestershire and Glamorgan, whose game with Minor Counties (South) was washed out, qualified for the quarter-final, but Essex won the trophy and the £6,500 prize money. The rules were amended to prevent declarations, and Somerset won two of the next three Benson & Hedges competitions.

SOMERSET

B.C. Rose not out 0
P.W. Denning not out 0
Extras 1
                                   (declared) <u>1–0</u>

Bowling: Holder 1–1–0–0.

WORCESTERSHIRE

G.M. Turner not out 2
J.A. Ormrod not out 0
Extras 0
                                                    <u>2–0</u>

Bowling: Dredge 1–0–1–0, Jennings 0.4–0–1–0.

The other players 'participating' were P.M. Roebuck, I.V.A. Richards, I.T. Botham, V.J. Marks, D. Breakwell, D.J.S. Taylor and H.R. Moseley (Somerset) and P.A. Neale, E.J.O. Hemsley, Younis Ahmed, D.N. Patel, D.J. Humphries, J.D. Inchmore, N. Gifford and A.P. Pridgeon (Worcestershire).

UNDERHAND BOWLING

MELBOURNE, AUSTRALIA,
FEBRUARY 1981

The World Series Final between Australia and New Zealand was the best of five 50-over games. This was the third, and the score stood at one each, New Zealand having won the first by 78 runs and Australia taking the second by seven wickets. This game would be remembered for two unsavoury incidents, the second of which, Greg Chappell's infamous 'underarm bowling' instruction, provoked opinions from virtually everybody interested in cricket.

The first incident, in the thirty-first over, also involved Greg Chappell, the Australian captain. The Australians were going well, 131 for one, when Chappell, whose score was on 52, pulled Cairns in the air towards mid-wicket. Snedden ran 30 yards (27.4m) full pelt, launched himself forward and caught the ball low down. Unfortunately, the umpires were not watching – they said later that they were studying the creases for run-outs and short runs – and when Chappell would not take Snedden's word that it was a clean catch, the umpires consulted and ruled 'not out'. As Adrian McGregor put it in his biography *Greg Chappell*, the umpires gave him 'the benefit of their ignorance'. The television replays showed that Snedden's word was pretty good.

When Chappell was caught for a second time, a brilliant piece of fielding by Edgar, he tucked his bat under his arm and walked off without hesitation. His innings of 90, made from 123 balls, together with Graeme Wood's 72, formed the backbone of Australia's total of 235 for four.

New Zealand's consistent openers, John Wright and Bruce Edgar, played solidly and kept their team in contention. At the start of the final over, New Zealand, 221 for six, needed 15 to win but Edgar was stranded at the non-striker's end with a century to his name. The crucial over was bowled by Trevor Chappell, brother of the Australian captain. Richard Hadlee hit the first ball for four but was out to the second. Eleven were needed from four balls. Ian Smith, the wicket-keeper, hit the third for two and the fourth for two. New Zealand wanted seven from two balls. Smith swung at the fifth ball of the over and was bowled by Trevor Chappell.

The number-ten batsman, Brian McKechnie, needed to hit a first-ball six to tie the game and force a replay. What were the chances? Well, McKechnie was an All-Black rugby player, a beefy bowler who might perhaps fluke a six-hit, so Greg Chappell came up with his controversial policy. He instructed his brother to bowl underarm, which was still permitted in Australian one-day games (until the following week) but was outlawed in England's one-day games. Greg Chappell obviously had a lot of confidence in his brother's ability to bowl a block-hole 'yorker' to a non-specialist batsman.

Chappell consulted with umpire Don Weser, and Weser checked with his colleague, Peter Cronin. McKechnie thought they were confirming it was the last ball. Then he was informed of what was about to happen.

Trevor Chappell bowled underarm, and the crowd of 53,000 roared as the ball bounced immediately in front of Chappell and ran along the ground to McKechnie. The New Zealand tail-ender simply blocked the ball and then threw his bat (overarm) in disgust. From the non-striker's end, Edgar raised two fingers. Australia won by six runs but their dressing-room was very quiet after the game.

The action was followed by outrage. New Zealand Prime Minister Robert Muldoon called it an act of cowardice appropriate to a team playing in yellow. Australian Prime

Minister Malcolm Fraser felt Chappell had made a mistake, and the skipper later regretted his decision.

The Australian Cricket Board made a clear statement: 'The Board deplores Greg Chappell's action and has advised him of the Board's strong feelings on this matter and of his responsibilities as Australia's captain to uphold the spirit of the game at all times. We acknowledge that his action was within the laws of the game, but that it was totally contrary to the spirit in which cricket has been, and should be, played.'

A couple of days later, after his innings of 87 had set up Australia's winning 3–1 margin, Greg Chappell was voted Man of the World Series.

AUSTRALIA
A.R. Border c Parker b Hadlee 5
G.M. Woods b McEwan 72
G.S. Chappell c Edgar b Snedden 90
M.F. Kent c Edgar b Snedden 33
R.W. Marsh not out 18
K.D. Walters not out 6
Extras 11
(50 overs) <u>235–4</u>

Bowling: Hadlee 10–0–41–1, Snedden 10–0–52–2, Cairns 10–0–34–0, McKechnie 10–0–54–0, McEwan 7–1–31–1, Howarth 3–0–12–0.

NEW ZEALAND
J.G. Wright c Kent b G. Chappell 42
B.A. Edgar not out 102
G.P. Howarth c Marsh b G. Chappell 18
B.L. Cairns b Beard 12
M.G. Burgess c T. Chappell b G. Chappell 2
P.E. McEwan c Wood b Beard 11
J.M. Parker c T. Chappell b Lillee 24
R.J. Hadlee lbw b T. Chappell 4
I.D.S. Smith b T. Chappell 4
B.J. McKechnie not out 0
Extras 10
(50 overs) <u>229–8</u>

Bowling: Lillee 10–1–34–1, Walker 10–0–35–0, Beard 10–0–50–2, G. Chappell 10–0–43–3, T. Chappell 10–0–57–2.

FOLLOWING-ON
AT HEADINGLEY
LEEDS, JULY 1981

England were losing one-nil to Australia, and this was the third of six Test matches in the series. Ian Botham had given way to Mike Brearley as England captain, but, at the end of the third day's play, having followed on 227 runs behind, England were staring defeat in the face, six for one in their second innings. At that point, Ladbroke's were offering 500–1 for an England victory.

On the first two days, England dropped catches, but Botham's six wickets ensured that Australia, progressing slowly, didn't get too far away. It looked far enough, especially when batting proved difficult on Saturday 18 July, the birthdate of W.G. Grace, Gary Sobers and Dennis Lillee, the last a key figure in the bowling out of England for 174.

The second innings was no better. The ball was still dodging about and Australia had ideal bowlers for the conditions in Lillee, Terry Alderman and Geoff Lawson. In sprite of resolute resistance from Geoff Boycott – 46 in 215 minutes – England slumped to 135 for seven, still 92 behind.

The next 35 overs saw England add 216 runs. Ian Botham and Graham Dilley agreed that they saw little point in trying to hang around for a couple of days. 'Let's give it some humpty,' Botham apparently said, in a famous mid-wicket conference. Dilley held his own with Botham, making 56 of their aggressive partnership of 117. This was a bit of a surprise. In the West Indies, the previous winter, Dilley had made 11 runs in seven innings. The Botham-Dilley stand came within eight of Hendren and Larwood's eighth-wicket England partnership against Australia. At the time, Botham and Dilley were just having a bit of fun.

England's number ten, Chris Old, was known to be suspect against fast bowling, but he pluckily kept the momentum going. Botham, now in full swing, using a bat borrowed from Graham Gooch, went from 36 to 100 by means of 14 fours, a six and two singles. When Old was out, for 29, Botham shielded Bob Willis, the last man, to the extent that Willis faced only five balls in the last 20 minutes of play that Monday. Willis made one of the 31 runs that came in that period.

The next morning, the stand ended at 37, with England 129 ahead. It had been a brave resurrection of the game – England players later confessed that they had checked out of their hotel rooms and had to rebook for Monday night – but Australia were still expected to make the 130 for victory. What shifted the mood England's way, however, was the psychological effect of Botham's innings.

An hour's play saw Australia at 56 for one. Seventy minutes later they were 75 for eight. The dramatic change had come from Bob Willis's second spell, bowled with the wind from the Kirkstall Lane end. Recognising that his England career was on the line, Willis put everything into that spell, and was rewarded with lift and life from the wicket. Chappell, Yallop and Hughes were all caught by close fielders after trying to fend off rising deliveries.

Lilley and Bright frustrated England with an eighth-wicket partnership of 35 in only four overs. Lillee hooked Willis, the ball bobbed up, Gatting ran 10 yards (9.1m) from mid-on and dived to hold the catch close to the ground. Bright was bowled by Willis, and England had won an unbelievable victory by 18 runs. It was only the second time in history that a Test had been won by a team following-on. The series was poised at one-one, and Brearley's team would recover enough to win it.

AUSTRALIA

J. Dyson b Dilley	102	(2) c Taylor b Willis	34
G.M. Wood lbw b Botham	34	(1) c Taylor b Botham	10
T.M. Chappell c Taylor b Willey	27	c Taylor b Willis	8
K.J. Hughes c and b Botham	89	c Botham b Willis	0
R.J. Bright b Dilley	7	(8) b Willis	19
G.N. Yallop c Taylor b Botham	58	(5) c Gatting b Willis	0
A.R. Border lbw b Botham	8	(6) b Old	0
R.W. Marsh b Botham	28	(7) c Dilley b Willis	4
G.F. Lawson c Taylor b Botham	13	c Taylor b Willis	1
D.K. Lillee not out	3	c Gatting b Willis	17
T.M. Alderman not out	0	not out	0
Extras	32		18
(declared)	401–9		111

Bowling: *First Innings*; Willis 30–8–72–0, Old 43–14–91–0, Dilley 27–4–78–2, Botham 39.2–11–95–6, Willey 13–2–31–1, Boycott 3–2–2–0. *Second Innings*; Botham 7–3–14–1, Dilley 2–0–11–0, Willis 15.1–3–43–8, Old 9–1–21–1, Willey 3–1–4–0.

Fall of Wickets; *First Innings*; 55, 149, 196, 220, 332, 354, 357, 396, 401. *Second Innings*; 13, 56, 58, 58, 65, 68, 74, 75, 110, 111.

ENGLAND

G.A. Gooch lbw b Alderman	2	c Alderman b Lillee	0
G. Boycott b Lawson	12	lbw b Alderman	46
J.M. Brearley c Marsh b Alderman	10	c Alderman b Lillee	14
D.I. Gower c Marsh b Lawson	24	c Border b Alderman	9
M.W. Gatting lbw b Lillee	15	lbw b Alderman	1
P. Willey b Lawson	8	c Dyson b Lillee	33
I.T. Botham c Marsh b Lillee	50	not out	149
R.W. Taylor c Marsh b Lillee	5	c Bright b Alderman	1
G.R. Dilley c and b Lillee	13	b Alderman	56
C.M. Old c Border b Alderman	0	b Lawson	29
R.G.D. Willis not out	1	c Border b Alderman	2
Extras	34		16
	174		356

Bowling: *First Innings*; Lillee 18.5–7–49–4, Alderman 19–4–59–3, Lawson 13–3–32–3. *Second Innings*; Lillee 25–6–94–3, Alderman 35.3–6–135–6, Lawson 23–4–96–1, Bright 4–0–15–0.

Fall of wickets: *First Innings*; 12, 40, 42, 84, 87, 112, 148, 166, 167, 174. *Second Innings*; 0, 18, 37, 41, 105, 133, 135, 252, 319, 356.

'A REMARKABLE MATCH OF MULTIPLE RECORDS'

SOUTHPORT, JULY 1982

When Lancashire and Warwickshire, two counties in the lower regions of the County Championship table, met at Southport, few could have imagined the incredible breadth of records that would be established. It was a game of the brilliant and the bizarre.

On the first day, Wednesday 28 July, Warwickshire were soon six for two, then 53 for three. At that point Geoff Humpage joined Alvin Kallicharran, and they put on 470 for the fourth wicket, beating the British record for this wicket, Abel and Hayward's 448 for Surrey against Yorkshire in 1899. Only three first-class partnerships in England had ever yielded more.

The bearded Humpage, 13 sixes and 24 fours in his career-best score of 254, equalled the English record for sixes in an innings and came within two of New Zealander John Reid's record for all countries. Kallicharran, 34 fours, completed his third double-century of the season. Amazingly, the two record-breakers gave only two chances of catches, Humpage on 185, Kallicharran on 177. When Dennis Amiss declared at 523 for four, Warwickshire looked in an invincible position, but 'looks' can be deceptive.

The second day was a Thursday, the starting day for England's first Test against Pakistan at Edgbaston, Warwickshire's home ground. As a precaution, to cover for injured players, England called up two men who were already playing in county games – Geoff Cook of Northamptonshire and Gladstone Small of Warwickshire. According to an appropriate regulation, confirmed during the day by Lord's, players called up for a Test match could be replaced, not only as fielders but also as batsmen and bowlers. Hence, Warwickshire's team manager, 40-year-old David Brown, a former England Test cricketer and Warwickshire captain, took Small's place on the Thursday morning. Brown became the first substitute to take a wicket in a match, trapping nightwatchman Scott, the Lancashire wicket-keeper, leg-before.

Small, not needed by England, drove rapidly up the motorway to rejoin his team at Southport in time for the afternoon session, and, that same day, Geoff Cook batted at number seven for Northants. Lancashire raced their way to within 109 of Warwickshire's total before declaring. Fowler made a century with the help of a runner, Cockbain failed by two to reach his maiden century, while Small and Brown, playing as one, took two for 85 between them.

Clive Lloyd's declaration allowed time for some more strange events by the end of the second day. Les McFarlane dismissed Dyer (for a pair) and bowled Lloyd next ball. On his hat-trick ball, fielders clustered round the bat, McFarlane must have created some kind of bizarre record by bowling a wide.

The next surprise was Warwickshire's batting on the final day. Kallicharran, having made a double-century on the first day, was out second ball on the third. Four wickets fell on 47, and no one made more than 24. McFarlane picked up the best figures of his career (six for 59) and Warwickshire were all out for 111, an innings which included five ducks. Lancashire needed 221 to win in 225 minutes.

In fact Lancashire won by ten wickets with seven overs to spare, and came within sight of Surrey's 1900 record of scoring 270 without loss, the highest-ever fourth-innings total without losing a wicket. Graeme Fowler completed his second century of the match. Batting with a strained thigh muscle, injured during the big stand on the first day, he used a runner (Ian Folley) in each innings, thus emulating the achievement of Warwickshire's Dennis Amiss against Derbyshire the previous season – a century in each innings with a runner. Oddly enough, Amiss dropped Fowler when he had made only two in his second innings. In recognition of the part played by Fowler's runner in the achievement, a Warwickshire fielder shook Folley's hand when Fowler reached his second century. Folley raised his bat.

A match that had started so well for Warwickshire, scoring 523 for four declared on the first day, ended with them being dismissed for the 'Nelson' figure of 111, appropriately enough on a ground called Trafalgar Road, and losing by ten wickets. Michael Austin, writing in *The Daily Telegraph*, described it as 'a remarkable match of multiple records'.

WARWICKSHIRE

D.L. Amiss c Abrahams b McFarlane	6	c. Scott b McFarlane 24
R.I.H.B. Dyer c Simmons b McFarlane	0	c Abrahams b McFarlane 0
T.A. Lloyd c Scott b Folley	23	b McFarlane 0
A.I. Kallicharran not out	230	(5) c Lloyd (D.) b O'Shaughnessy 0
G. Humpage b Lloyd (D.)	254	(6) c Lloyd (D.) b O'Shaughnessy 21
Asif Din		(4) c Abrahams b O'Shaughnessy 21
S. Wootton		b McFarlane 0
C. Lethbridge		c Hughes b Folley 18
P. Hartley		lbw b McFarlane 16
G.C. Small		c Scott b McFarlane 0
S.P. Sutcliffe		not out 7
Extras	10	4
(declared)	<u>523–4</u>	<u>111</u>

Bowling: *First Innings*; McFarlane 11–2–90–2, Folley 15–3–64–1, O'Shaughnessy 15–2–62–0, Simmons 20–2–97–0, Hughes 20–2–79–0, Abrahams 15–3–76–0, Lloyd 10.1–1–45–1. *Second Innings*; McFarlane 20–3–59–6, Folley 11–5–19–1, O'Shaughnessy 7.1–0–29–3, Simmons 1–1–0–0.

Fall of wickets: *First Innings*; 5, 6, 53, 523. *Second Innings*; 1, 1, 47, 47, 47, 47, 76, 81, 99, 111.

LANCASHIRE

G. Fowler b Asif Din	126	not out	128
D. Lloyd c Humpage b Small	10	not out	88
C.J. Scott lbw b Brown	9		
Cockbain c Amiss b Kallicharran	98		
C.H. Lloyd c Humpage b Kallicharran	45		
D.P. Hughes c Small b Kallicharran	14		
Abrahams not out	51		
S. O'Shaughnessy not out	26		
J. Simmons			
I. Folley			
L.L. McFarlane			
Extras	35		10
(declared)	<u>414–6</u>		<u>226–0</u>

Bowling: *First Innings*; Small 15–4–38–1, Hartley 14–0–66–0, Sutcliffe 38–9–103–0, Lethbridge 14–5–58–0, Brown 13–3–47–1, Asif Din 6–1–35–1, Kallicharran 13–3–32–3. *Second Innings*; Small 11–2–30–0, Hartley 9–1–38–0, Sutcliffe 19–5–60–0, Lethbridge 9–2–27–0, Asif Din 5–0–25–0, Kallicharran 6–0–35–0, Lloyd 1–0–1–0.

Fall of wickets: *First Innings*; 34, 109, 194, 305, 327,358.

THE LOWEST TOTAL OF MODERN TIMES

CHELMSFORD, MAY 1983

That section of *Wisden* listing 'lowest totals', including only innings of less than 20 runs, had stayed the same for more than 20 years. There had been no British contribution since Hampshire's infamous 15 at Edgbaston in 1922, although West Indies' 25 in Ireland (in 1969) threatened inclusion and Yorkshire's 23 at Middlesbrough (against Hampshire in 1965) gave a hint that anything could still happen. Yorkshire were the team of the 1960s ... but not during that hour.

In the Essex–Surrey fixture at Chelmsford, time was lost on the first day. On the Monday, a Bank Holiday, Essex worked their way to a total of 287, thanks to a flawless century by Keith Fletcher and support from almost everyone. The Surrey bowlers had to work hard for their wickets.

Surrey had time for 65 minutes' batting. It was a sensational spell. Norbert Philip and Neil Foster bowled 87 balls and took ten wickets between them. Butcher was caught behind down the leg side. Needham, Knight and Lynch went to ordinary-looking defensive shots. Clinton, top-scoring with six, was caught behind down the leg side and Richards was caught in the gully. Thomas and Payne soon followed and Surrey were eight for eight.

Monkhouse then edged the ball awkwardly through the slips and ran two to take Surrey to double figures. Sylvester Clarke clobbered a four to mid-wicket and 14 was on the board. Then Clarke was yorked, Monkhouse was out, and

Surrey had achieved a modern-day record by registering their lowest total in history. It was a phenomenal success for the two Essex bowlers, who swung the ball menacingly and didn't meet much decent batting resistance. Philip's staggering figures of 7.3–4–4–6 speak for themselves, but Essex perhaps derived more satisfaction from the performance of 21-year-old Foster, who had spent the summer of 1982 in a plaster-cast after suffering a spinal stress-fracture. Now he was back to the form that had won him acclaim when, still a schoolboy, he took three good Kent wickets on his debut in 1980.

The next day was, in its own way, relatively strange. Following heavy rain, the start was delayed until 12.30p.m., but Surrey were 20 for two at lunch and still in deep trouble. Then, out of all proportion with what had gone before, Clinton and Knight batted through the remaining three and a half hours and the game petered out into a draw. Essex had seven bonus points, Surrey four. The latter were for bowling.

ESSEX

G.A. Gooch b Thomas	1
B.R. Hardie b Clarke	16
K.W.R. Fletcher c Lynch b Monkhouse	110
K.S. McEwan c Lynch b Knight	45
K.R. Pont b Pocock	12
N. Philip b Pocock	8
S. Turner c and b Knight	20
R.E. East c Lynch c Clarke	19
D.E. East c Butcher b Pocock	17
N.A. Foster not out	19
D.L. Acfield run out	0
Extras	20
	287

Bowling: Clarke 20–3–58–2, Thomas 20–2–78–1, Monkhouse 13–2–49–1, Knight 17–6–33–2, Pocock 19.5–6–49–3.

Fall of wickets: 1, 27, 113, 156, 179, 222, 238, 252, 276, 287.

SURREY

A.R. Butcher c East (D.) b Phillip	2	c Gooch b Foster 5
G.S. Clinton c East (D.) b Foster	6	not out 61
A. Needham b Foster	0	lbw b Philip 4
R.D.V. Knight lbw b Philip	0	not out 101
M.A. Lynch lbw b Philip	0	
C.J. Richards c Turner b Philip	0	
D.J. Thomas lbw b Foster	0	
I.R. Payne b Philip	0	
Monkhouse lbw b Philip	2	
S.T. Clarke b Foster	4	
P. Pocock not out	0	
Extras	0	 14
	14	**185–2**

Bowling: *First Innings*; Philip 7.3–4–4–6, Foster 7–3–10–4. *Second Innings*; Philip 13–2–39–1, Foster 13–2–33–1, Turner 7–3–16–0, Gooch 22–6–45–0, Acfield 17–7–23–0, East (R.) 1–0–5–0. Pont 5–1–10–0.

Fall of wickets: *First Innings*; 2, 5, 6, 8, 8, 8, 8, 14, 14. *Second Innings*; 5,18.

AN END-OF-SEASON GAME

MANCHESTER, SEPTEMBER 1983

The weather delayed the start of the game between Lancashire and Leicestershire until 3.30p.m. on the second day. When Roger Tolchard won the toss for Leicestershire he elected to field first, one of his problems being the threat of a £1,000 fine, to be shared by the club and the players, for his county not bowling their overs quickly enough during the course of the season. From the moment that Graeme Fowler (28) and Steve O'Shaughnessy (3) began their opening stand of 31 in an environment of Leicestershire fielders running into position, this game was an odd one.

Fowler, a good player in matches strange and stable, went on to make 85 of the first 103, hitting two sixes and ten fours in 64 minutes (but plenty of overs). Paddy Clift broke the back of the batting with three wickets in seven balls, and Lancashire ended the second day on 187 for seven.

When Leicestershire batted they calculated that one batting point would ensure them fourth place in the County Championship table, the last of the prize-money places, worth £1,750. A win against Lancashire, though, could take them to third place and even more money, provided, of course, the inadequate over-rate was rectified. This was statistical training at its best.

Simmons and Stanworth took their unbeaten overnight stand to 79 before Leicestershire gained their breakthrough. Leicestershire, facing a total of 236, ensured fourth place on reaching 150 for four. Roger Tolchard declared 86 behind and started looking for a result.

In the second Lancashire innings, the new ball was taken by an unlikely duo, star batsmen Gower and Whitaker, who showed an excellent variety of length (full tosses and long hops). It was obvious that Leicestershire were trying to 'buy' a declaration and at first Fowler and O'Shaughnessy blocked the deliveries in protest. Then they decided to hit out, not sure whether to hit Gower and Whitaker for fours or sixes. On a cold Manchester day, the spectators in the pavilion, near the shortest boundary, were soon warming up, dodging the ball as it kept coming their way. Leicestershire, meanwhile, hurried through their overs in rapid fashion to add to the comic spectacle.

Steve O'Shaughnessy scored his century in 35 minutes, equalling the record fastest time (by Percy Fender in 1920 for Surrey against Northants) but taking 54 balls (at least eight more than Fender). The opening partnership, 201 in 43 minutes, was the fastest double-century partnership on record, helped by Leicestershire's need to sustain a lightning over-rate. Fowler hit ten sixes and five fours, and O'Shaughnessy's five sixes and 17 fours brought him 98 of his runs in boundaries.

There never was a declaration. After a serious spell of bowling and batting, the game was called off. Leicestershire, guaranteed fourth place, earned a reprieve from their possible over-rate fine, and Lancashire had some new records, but most outsiders saw it as a dismal end to the season. A few days later the *Manchester Evening News* took Steve O'Shaughnessy to see Percy Fender, who was then 91 years old.

LANCASHIRE

G. Fowler b Steele	85	b Balderstone 100
S.J. O'Shaughnessy c Steele b Cook	3	st Tolchard
		b Balderstone 105
F. C. Hayes b Clift	11	
C.H. Lloyd c Tolchard b Clift	24	
J. Abrahams c and b Clift	7	(4) not out 3
D.P. Hughes c Cook b Clift	0	
N.H. Fairbrother c Davison b Cook	4	(5) not out 1
J. Simmons b Clift	57	
J. Stanworth c Balderstone b Cook	29	(3) b Taylor 4
P.J.W. Allott c and b Taylor	4	
M. Watkinson not out	1	
Extras	11	 1
	236	214–3

Bowling: *First Innings*; Ferris 8–1–29–0, Taylor 4–0–14–1, Cook 28–10–74–3, Clift 31–5–73–5, Steele 16–3–35–1. *Second Innings*; Gower 9–0–102–0 Whitaker 8–1–87–0, Balderstone 4–0–10–2, Steele 5–2–13–0, Taylor 1.2–0–1–1.

Fall of wickets: *First Innings*; 31, 97, 103, 136, 136, 139, 145, 224, 231, 236. *Second Innings*; 201, 206, 213.

LEICESTERSHIRE

J.C. Balderstone c O'Shaughnessy	
b Simmons	33
I.P. Butcher lbw b Allott	4
D.I. Gower not out	56
B.F. Davison c Lloyd b Watkinson	2
J.J. Whitaker lbw b Simmons	24
P.B. Clift not out	26
Extras	5
(declared)	150–4

Bowling: Allott 7–2–15–1, Simmons 15–3–51–2, Watkinson 14–3–35–1, Hughes 7.5–1–44–0.

Fall of wickets: 31, 46, 51, 114.

THE REVIVAL
OF THE FAMILY GAME
HUISH CHAMPFLOWER,
SOMERSET, APRIL 1984

From cricket's earliest times, there have been strange games where one or more of the teams is composed of members of a single family. In 1867, for instance, 11 of Lord Lyttelton's family played Bromsgrove Grammar School. The family team won by ten wickets, or, if you prefer, by ten Lytteltons.

Alfred Gaston, writing a short piece on cricket curiosities in J.H. Lester's *Bat v Ball*, gives over 30 examples of family teams in the last century. There are probably far more.

The most famous family team was that of the Robinson family, based around Bakewell House, near Flax Bourton in Somerset, the home of Sidney Robinson, MP. Between 1878 and 1914, the Robinson family played 105 games, winning 53, losing 43 and drawing nine, the highlight of the season being the annual game against the Flax Bourton team. The first one resulted in an exciting one-wicket win for the Robinsons.

The family's games were usually watched by another 50 Robinsons. The early cornerstone of the team was Arthur Robinson, who was captain for 26 years. He was succeeded by Theodore Robinson, who played in all 105 Robinson games up to the First World War.

The most bizarre scorecards are those resulting from games between two family teams. Very occasionally the two teams are related by marriage, as was the case with the *Grace v Robinson* game of 13 August 1891. Annie Robinson, daughter of Alfred Robinson, had married Dr E.M. Grace.

The Graces batted first, and the details of their innings are shown here.

```
Dr E.M. Grace b Robinson (C.J.) .............................................. 81
Mr W. G. Grace, jun, b Robinson (W.) ...................................... 36
Mr A.H. Grace, b Robinson (T.) ................................................ 10
Mr Arthur Grace bw b Robinson (W.) ......................................... 6
Mr G.H. Grace c Robinson (E.) b Robinson (W.) ................... 25
Dr W.G. Grace b Robinson (T.) ................................................. 12
Dr A. Grace run out ....................................................................... 0
Dr M. Grace b Robinson (T.) ....................................................... 0
Mr Gerald Grace c Robinson (A) b Robinson (W.) ................... 1
Mr E.S.H. Grace not out ............................................................... 1
Mr Francis Grace c and b Robinson (W.) .................................... 0
Extras ........................................................................................... 12
                                                                                              184
```

The two most famous Graces, E.M. and Dr W.G., had opened the innings for Gloucestershire earlier that week, but W.G. was not having a particularly good season. The total of 184 meant that the Robinsons were more than a match for the Graces. At 101 for one, they looked set for an easy victory but a collapse led to them losing by 37 runs. By the end of that 1891 season, the Robinsons had played 44 games over a 13-year period, winning 30 and losing 13. They could call on half a dozen first-class cricketers, such as Cres Robinson of Somerset, who topped the Robinson batting averages. Theodore himself played a few games for Somerset.

To show how long the idea of the family game endured, let's move on to the 1930s, past the peak of the Robinson era. In August 1931, for instance, there was a game played at Knockholt, in Kent, between 11 of the Smithers family and 11 Streatfeilds, members of a well-known Kent cricket family. Like all these events, the scorecard was an oddity itself.

SMITHERS

P.W. Smithers b Streatfeild (H.G.C.) 0
R.L. Smithers st Streatfeild (G.E.S.) b Streatfeild (H.G.C.) .. 46
Smithers c Streatfeild (G.) b Streatfeild (G.G.C.) 36
P.W. Smithers b Streatfeild (G.) 0
J.F. Smithers run out. 4
M. Smithers b Streatfeild (G.G.C.) 18
D.W. Smithers not out 62
B.L. Smithers b Streatfeild (G.G.C.) 1
W. Smithers st Streatfeild (G.E.S.) b Streatfeild (H.G.C.) 14
L. Smithers c Streatfeild (A.H.O.) b Streatfeild (G.) 4
A.J.L. Smithers c Streatfeild (H.G.C.) b Streatfeild (G.) 3
Extras 11
                                                                                                         199

STREATFEILD

H.G.C. Streatfeild b Smithers (R.L.) 4
J.C. Streatfeild lbw Smithers (W.) 0
A.H.O. Streatfeild st Smithers (D.W.) b Smithers (W.) 57
G.G.C. Streatfeild b Smithers (R.L.) 88
G.H. Streatfeild st Smithers (D.W.) b Smithers (R.L.) 4
G.H.M. Streatfeild c Smithers (L.) b Smithers (W.) 3
H.C. Streatfeild b Smithers (R.L.) 6
G.E.S. Streatfeild b Smithers (W.) 2
G. Streatfeild c Smithers (J.F.) b Smithers (P.) 5
E. Streatfeild c Smithers (R.L.) b Smithers (W.) 0
Streatfeild not out 5
Extras 18
                                                                                                         192

Since the 1930s, family games have continued to appear sporadically on fixture lists – the Edrich family team has been able to call on generations of professional cricketers, and the Snowdon family played games in Cornwall in the 1970s – but a more formal revival of the formula has taken place in the 1980s.

In November 1983, a family called Buckingham, five of whom played for Huish Champflower in the West Somerset League, claimed they would be more than a match for any other cricketing family. They could field a team from the father, Stan Buckingham, seven sons and three cousins, most of whom lived in the hills near Exmoor. Eric Coombes of the *Somerset County Gazette* felt that if the Buckinghams could get another family to play them, then his newspaper might put up a trophy. A fellow from Cutcomb called Matravers said he had enough brothers to make a game of it. The Cup was purchased and on a cold day late in April 1984 the Buckingham family met the Matravers family at Huish Champflower.

The Buckingham–Matravers game is now played alternately at Cutcomb and Huish Champflower. It revives a tradition in an area with a rich history of family games. Says Eric Coombes: 'The next thing would be *Buckingham v Buckingham*.'

That would be a really strange scorecard. In the meantime, here is the historic scorecard, kindly supplied by Mary Elworthy, from the Buckingham–Matravers game played on Sunday 29 April, 1984, the first game of the series.

BUCKINGHAM

Buckingham ct Matravers (E.) b Matravers (C.)	31
S. Buckingham ct Matravers (F.) b Matravers (B.)	84
P. Buckingham lbw Matravers (C.)	2
T. Buckingham ct Matravers (C.) b Matravers (P.)	3
B. Buckingham ct Matravers (An.) b Matravers (P.)	7
D. Buckingham not out	31
R. Buckingham ct Matravers (K.) b Matravers (B.)	0
J. Buckingham b Matravers (F.)	9
N. Buckingham ct Matravers (D.) b Matravers (Ad.)	0
St. Buckingham b Matravers (Ad.)	0
M. Buckingham b Matravers (Ad.)	0
Extras	9
	176

Bowling: Matravers (C.) 8–0–40–2, Matravers (F.) 10–1–34–1, Matravers (P.) 7–1–34–2, Matravers (J.) 4–0–30–0, Matravers (B.) 2–0–13–2, Matravers (Ad.) 3.2–0–16–3.

Fall of wickets: 59, 65, 85, 99, 146, 146, 171, 172, 172, 176.

MATRAVERS

Matravers lbw b Buckingham (D.) 12
D. Matravers ct Buckingham (J.) b Buckingham (P.) 1
C. Matravers ct Buckingham (P.) b Buckingham (S.) 49
J. Matravers ct Buckingham (T.) b Buckingham (R.) 43
F. Matravers run out 11
E. Matravers c Buckingham (A.) b Buckingham (D.) 15
P. Matravers lbw b Buckingham (D.) 1
G. Matravers b Buckingham (P.) 3
K. Matravers c Buckingham (R.) b Buckingham (D.) 8
An. Matravers b Buckingham (D.) 1
Ad. Matravers not out 1
Extras 14
                                                    159

Bowling: Buckingham (D.) 11.3–3–21–5, Buckingham (P.) 10–2–26–2, Buckingham (R.) 8–0–48–1, Buckingham (S.) 7–0–37–1, Buckingham (N.) 1–0–9–0, Buckingham (J.) 1–0–4–0.

Fall of wickets: 3, 19, 93, 118, 125, 132, 143, 149, 150, 159.

THE BRAMBLE
BANK GAME
THE SOLENT, SEPTEMBER 1984

Twice a year, for about an hour on each occasion, a sandbar surfaces in the middle of the Solent, the stretch of water between Hampshire and the Isle of Wight. The sandbar is Bramble Bank, which generally hides under the water and provides a treacherous navigation hazard for ocean-going vessels. Many have run aground on Bramble Bank.

At the spring equinox and autumn equinox, when the water is at its lowest, Bramble Bank appears, bubbling through, slowly exposing itself, creating an island of about two acres. Those two separate hours, one in March, one in September, are the best times of the year for a cricket game, unless someone would like to devise an underwater game between two teams of divers.

Small-island cricket games have often been played to establish British sovereignty – the Goodwin Sands has a long history of games, and, in February 1988, two boys launched a British claim for a new island of washed-up shingle off the Isle of Wight coast – but they have also been played by lovers of the absurd for a bit of fun.

The Bramble Bank game has a lengthy history, albeit intermittent, dating back to the early part of the century. When yachtsman Uffa Fox organised a game in 1954, he was reviving an idea which had been dormant for 32 years since the previous game. Fox's team, using oars as bats, scored 29 and beat a team from Parkhurst Prison (mainly officers and their relatives) by seven runs. The winners had a slight advantage as only seven of the Parkhurst team were able to land.

In 1966 an air-cushion craft took the players to the sandbank, and Uffa Fox's team beat Cowes Cricket Club by three runs. The venue will always be a more natural habitat for a sailor than a landlubberly fast bowler. There haven't been too many green wickets at Bramble Bank over the years, but nor have runs been very easy to come by.

After Uffa Fox's 1972 game against Colin Cowdrey's XI, there was a gap of 12 years. Then the Royal Southern Yacht Club (Hamble) challenged the Island Sailing Club (Cowes). The two teams waited around in a flotilla of small boats until the island emerged from the water. They landed and took the field wearing wellingtons and whites. The Island Sailing Club batted first and made 24 all out – good sailors, poor cricketers. The mainland club knocked off the required runs, the winning hit being a six and lost ball.

ISLAND SAILING CLUB: 24
ROYAL SOUTHERN YACHT CLUB: 25 for 2.

A TIGHT FINISH

MADRAS, SEPTEMBER 1986

Australia dominated the first four days of the Test against India, the first of the series, but a sporting declaration by Australian captain Allan Border, setting India 348 to win in 87 overs, acted as a catalyst for a spectacular finish.

Over the first two and bit days, Australia accumulated their highest Test score in India – 574 for seven declared. David Boon, 21 fours in 122, provided an excellent example, Dean Jones became the first Australian to score a Test double-century in India, nightwatchman Bright did well, and Border himself chipped in with a century after taking 44 minutes to make his first run.

India, in trouble at 245–7, when they were still 129 short of avoiding the follow-on, were grateful for a sparkling century from their captain, Kapil Dev. The follow-on was avoided, and Australia ended the fourth day on 170 for five.

Border surprised many people by declaring at that overnight score, and even more were questioning his wisdom at lunch (India 94 for one) and at tea (India 193 for two). Only 155 were needed from 30 overs, and eight wickets still to fall. The odds had shifted towards India, and Border was responsible.

Although Kapil Dev fell quickly this time, the target was whittled down. Another 17 with four wickets in hand was well within range. Then Sharma was caught on the boundary, and More and Yadav were dismissed playing attacking shots against Bright, the slow left-armer. Eight balls left, four runs to win, and in came the turban-clad figure of 21-year-old Maninder Singh, the last man, a slow left-arm bowler whose major career batting success had been an innings of six, not out, against Worcestershire.

Bright had two balls of an over to bowl. Maninder Singh kept them out. The truculent Greg Matthews bounced up to bowl his off-breaks, the last over of the match. Ravi Shastri, unbeaten on 45, faced the first three balls. He put one away for two, another for a single. The scores were tied, but Shastri was at the wrong end.

Matthews to Maninder Singh. Bat on ball. No run. Two balls to come. Matthews to Maninder Singh again. Ball on pad. Bat on pad. Noise. The loudest appeal the throaty Aussies could muster. The umpire's finger was raised, and the game was a tie.

AUSTRALIA

D.C. Boon c Kapil Dev b Sharma	122	lbw b Maninder	49
G.R. Marsh c Kapil Dev b Yadav	22	b Shastri	11
D.M. Jones b Yadav	210	c Azharuddin b Maninder	24
R.J. Bright c Shastri b Yadav	30		
A.R. Border c Gavaskar b Shastri	106	b Maninder	27
G.M. Ritchie run out	3	c Pandit b Shastri	28
G.R.J. Matthews c Pandit b Yadav	44	not out	27
S.R. Waugh not out	12	not out	2
Extras	15		2
(declared)	574–7	(declared)	170–5

Bowling: *First Innings*; Kapil Dev 18–5–52–0, Sharma 16–1–70–1, Maninder Singh 39–8–135–0, Yadav 49.5–9–142–4, Shastri 47–8–161–1, Srikkanth 1–0–6–0. *Second Innings*; Kapil Dev 1–0–5–0, Sharma 6–0–19–0, Maninder Singh 19–2–60–3, Yadav 9–0–35–0, Shastri 14–2–50–2

Fall of wickets: *First Innings*; 48, 206, 282, 460, 481, 544, 574. *Second Innings*; 21, 81, 94, 125, 155.

INDIA

S.M. Gavaskar c and b Matthews 8	c Jones b Bright 90
K Srikkanth c Ritchie b Matthews 53	c Waugh b Matthews 39
M. Amarnath run out 1	c Boon b Matthews 51
M. Azharuddin c and b Bright 50	c Ritchie b Bright 42
R.J. Shastri c Zoehrer b Matthews 62	(7) not out 48
C.S. Pandit c Waugh b Matthews 35	(5) b Matthews 39
Kapil Dev c Border b Matthews 119	(6) c Bright b Matthews 1
K.S. More c Zoehrer b Waugh 4	(9) lbw b Bright 0
C. Sharma c Zoehrer b Reid 30	(8) c McDermott b Bright 23
N.S. Yadav c Border b Bright 19	b Bright 8
Maninder Singh not out 0	lbw b Matthews 0
Extras 16	 6
397	**347**

Bowling: *First Innings*; McDermott 14–2–59–0, Reid 18–4–93–1, Matthews 28.2–3–103–5, Bright 23–3–88–2, Waugh 11–2–44–1. *Second Innings*; McDermott 5–0–27–0, Reid 10–2–48–0, Matthews 39.5–7–146–5, Bright 25–3–94–5, Waugh 4–1–16–0, Border 3–0–12–0.

Fall of wickets: *First Innings*; 62, 65, 65, 142, 206, 220, 245, 330, 387, 397. *Second Innings*; 55, 158, 204, 251, 253, 291, 331, 334, 344, 347.

HICK'S INNINGS
TAUNTON, MAY 1988

A new format for the County Championship, including a number of four-day matches, paved the way for a dominating performance by Worcestershire's 21-year-old Zimbabwe-born batsman Graeme Hick. It came in the third match of the season, at Taunton against Somerset, after Worcestershire had won their first two Championship games.

On paper, the most interesting feature of this game was the return to Taunton of Ian Botham, who had moved from Somerset to Worcestershire in time for the 1988 season. In practice, the spectators spent the first five sessions admiring the punishment administered by the young Hick. He came in at 78 for one and scored 405 of the next 550 scored by Worcestershire. He was still unbeaten when Phil Neale declared at tea on the second day.

It was hard going at first. Hick started in a hurry but slowed down after he saw four wickets fall for 20 runs in nine overs shortly after lunch. One of them was Botham, bowled by Rose for seven. At 132 for five, there seemed little chance of anything sensational happening.

By the end of the first day, however, Hick (179 not out) and Steve Rhodes (40 not out) had taken the score to 312. Hick, who reached his century out of 120, had done the bulk of the scoring, and it proved the same on the second day. He hit 197 out of 265 for the sixth wicket (with Rhodes) and 137 out of 177 for the eighth wicket (with Richard Illingworth). Both stands were Worcestershire records.

Worcester captain Phil Neale declared at tea, having warned the batsmen that he would do so. Hick completed his fourth century in the last over before the declaration. In nine and a quarter hours, he had faced 469 balls, and his 405 contained 98 singles, 40 twos, seven threes, 35 fours and 11 sixes (mainly straight driven). His innings lasted 552 minutes. There were a couple of difficult chances in the middle of his first century, and a chance went to hand (and out again) when he'd made 391. It was only the second-ever County Championship score of over 400, following Archie MacLaren's innings of 424 (made out of 792) for Lancashire against Somerset in 1895, also at Taunton. It came when Hick was racing his way towards 1,000 runs in May, and this massive score took his tally to 815 in only six innings (one not out).

Worcestershire needed less than five sessions to bowl out Somerset twice and win by an innings and 214 runs. Strangely, Worcestershire's two new and famous recruits, Ian Botham and Graham Dilley, did not get a wicket between them. The damage was done by Phil Newport and Neil Radford, while a 21-year-old Zimbabwe-born off-break bowler took three for 33. It was a memorable match for Graeme Hick.

WORCESTERSHIRE

T.S. Curtis b Rose	27
G.J. Lord c Mallender b Dredge	49
G.A. Hick not out	405
D.B. D'Oliveira c Roebuck b Rose	0
P.A. Neale c Marks b Mallender	0
I.T. Botham b Rose	7
S.J. Rhodes c Felton b Dredge	56
P.J. Newport b Marks	27
R.K. Illingworth not out	31
Extras	26
(declared)	628–7

Bowling: Jones 32–4–97–0, Mallender 32–9–86–1, Marks 50–6–141–1, Rose 31–8–101–3, Dredge 34.5–8–133–2, Roebuck 10–0–48–0.

Fall of wickets: 78, 112, 112, 119, 132, 396, 451.

SOMERSET

N.A. Felton c Radford b Hick	24	c Rhodes b Newport	36
P.M. Roebuck lbw b Radford	0	lbw b Radford	17
J.J.E. Hardy c Rhodes b Radford	39	b Newport	0
M.D. Crowe c Rhodes b Newport	28	c Lord b Radford	53
R.J. Harden lbw b Hick	2	lbw b Newport	3
V.J. Marks c Botham b Newport	42	c Hick b Newport	7
N.D. Burns c Botham b Radford	32	c Illingworth b Hick	11
G.D. Rose c Curtis b Newport	12	c Rhodes b Newport	30
N.A. Mallender c Rhodes b Newport	3	lbw b Radford	1
C.H. Dredge b Radford	16	c Curtis b Newport	17
A.N. Jones not out	8	not out	3
Extras	16		14
	222		**192**

Bowling: *First Innings*; Dilley 12–0–40–0, Radford 23.5–1–77–4, Newport 17–4–59–4, Hick 8–3–18–2, Illingworth 1–0–4–0, Botham 9–3–18–0. *Second Innings*; Dilley 14–2–40–0, Radford 17–6–39–3, Newport 15.3–3–50–6, Hick 11–4–15–1, Illingworth 11–4–20–0, Botham 6–2–25–0.

Fall of wickets: *First Innings*; 1, 70, 70, 75, 147, 152, 166, 173, 203, 222. *Second Innings*; 49, 59, 62, 74, 90, 111, 154, 167, 185, 192.

SIXTY FROM ONE OVER

SHERBORNE, DORSET, JULY AND AUGUST, 1988

Eleven overs of the compulsory last 20 remained to be bowled. The two-day Minor Counties game between Dorset and Cheshire looked destined for a dull draw as Geoff Blackburn and Neil Smith had settled into a solid seventh-wicket partnership for Cheshire. Coming together with the score on 49 for six, they had added 43 runs and looked unlikely to be shifted, but Cheshire's target of 201 to win also looked completely out of range.

It was then that the Dorset captain, the Reverend Andrew Wingfield Digby, put his enterprising plan into action.

Wingfield Digby, author of a book called *A Loud Appeal*, subtitled *Playing by God's Rules*, scattered his field, including the wicket-keeper. He instructed seam-bowler Graeme Calway to bowl wides. The field was set so that Calway's wides travelled to the boundary without interruption.

Calway bowled 14 wides, each counting four runs. As Calway had already conceded one boundary off the bat, it meant his over cost 60 runs, 56 of them in wides.

Suddenly, both teams were interested in victory. Cheshire needed 53 to win in ten overs, Dorset needed four wickets. Cheshire took up the challenge and lost by 18 runs with two overs to play. It was Dorset's first victory of the season, but, morale restored, they won the next game, against Berkshire, by two wickets after an exciting finish, Wingfield

Digby scoring the winning run and racing jubilantly to the pavilion.

Wingfield Digby's decision to bring Cheshire back into the game met a mixed reception. Most players in the game seemed to support the decision, although it was uncertain whether Cheshire captain Neil O'Brien approved. The Test & County Cricket Board, meeting later, certainly didn't. They felt it wasn't in the spirit of the game.

The Dorset-Cheshire game, incidentally, had a number of other strange features worth mentioning. There was leg-spinner Simon Dyson's five-for-four spell in Dorset's first innings, the extension of play to about 8 o'clock on the rain-affected first day, former England opener Barry Wood's pair for Cheshire, an exciting duel for first-innings points (won for Cheshire by Blackburn's four with the last man at the wicket) and Neil Taylor's uncanny dismissal of the two O'Briens in consecutive balls.

Nothing, however, could compare for strangeness with Calway's over of 60 runs.

DORSET

Merriman b Dyson 21	c Varey b Dyson 5
Calway b O'Brien (N.) 15	c Varey b Dyson 0
Morgan lbw b O'Brien (N.) 10	(6) lbw b Dyson 0
Rintoul c Tansley b Dyson 45	c Smith b Fox 12
Sawney c Varey b Dyson 0	(8) c Blackburn b O'Brien (J.) 13
Wingfield Digby b O'Brien (N.) 23	(10) st Smith b O'Brien (J.) 3
Lewis lbw b Dyson 3	(9) not out 23
Taylor st Smith b Dyson 2	(11) b O'Brien (J.) 0
Stone b Dyson 1	(7) c Hitchmough b Blackburn 38
Stuart not out 0	(5) run out 62
Wagstaffe lbw Dyson 0	(3) c and b O'Brien (J.) 34
Extras 13	12
133	202

Bowling: (wicket-takers only) *First Innings*; Dyson 7–39, O'Brien (N) 3–56; *Second Innings*; Dyson 3–56, Fox 1–36, O'Brien (J) 4–56, Blackburn 1–47.

CHESHIRE

Wood b Stuart 0	c Lewis b Taylor 0
Varey c Wagstaffe b Taylor 28	lbw b Taylor 3
Hitchmough c Calway b Stuart 1	(5) c Merriman b Sawney 17
Tansley c Lewis b Stuart 24	c Morgan b Wingfield Digby 0
Crawley lbw b Stuart 11	(6) c Rintoul b Taylor 4
N. O'Brien b Taylor 29	(3) lbw b Wingfield Digby 13
Blackburn not out 32	b Taylor 29
Smith lbw b Wingfield Digby 0	c Calway b Taylor 36
Fox b Stone 0	(10) st Lewis b Stone 10
J. O'Brien lbw b Taylor 0	(9) lbw b Taylor 1
Dyson not out 0	not out 0
Extras 10	69
(declared) <u>135–9</u>	<u>182</u>

Bowling: (wicket-takers only) *First Innings*; Wingfield Digby 1–35, Stuart 4–44, Taylor 3–34, Stone 1–12. *Second Innings*; Stone 1–16, Taylor 6–38, Sawney 1–14, Wingfield Digby 2–38.

THROUGH AMERICAN EYES
MORETON-IN-MARSH, AUGUST 1989

'The first cricket game I saw was in Bermuda,' she told me. 'They were all dressed in white, and I didn't know what it was. But I knew it had to be something British because they were dressed for it.'

I knew I had some work to do.

Knowing Americans like definite outcomes to their sporting fixtures and hate drawn games, I decided to take my friend to a Sunday game between Gloucestershire and Northamptonshire. I explained the concept of 'limited overs'.

'Is that like how many hits off so many pitches?'

'Well, sort of.'

She could see it wasn't.

'In cricket there are 11 a side,' I started, realising I had to start somewhere. 'Two go out to bat together, until one is out and a third player bats.'

'Doesn't cricket have those sticks in the ground?' she asked.

'At each end, there are three sticks in the ground, known as "stumps".'

'No. You're kidding. Why would they call that a "stump"?' There was a long pause as I considered possible answers. 'Okay,' she added, recognising the need to bail me out of trouble, 'so there are two guys up at stump.'

'One batsman at one end,' I began. 'The bowler …'

'What about the ball? Is it a hard ball? Do they call it a "ball"?'

'Yes, they call it a ball ... so a bowler comes in from one end and bowls six balls, sorry, one ball six times.'

'Stop!'

'I'm going too quickly?'

'The number "six" is important in this game, isn't it?' my friend deduced. 'It's the number of balls you can throw from one end and it's the big macho thing that clears the boundary. Right?'

I sighed.

We set off for Moreton-in-Marsh in Gloucestershire, where an annual Refuge Assurance League game would be played in a rural, tree-lined setting with temporary sightscreens. I thought it would be 'very English'. We arrived near the end of the Gloucestershire innings – the induction course had taken longer than I anticipated – and spent a few minutes debating whether it should be an 'inning' or an 'innings'.

We were interrupted by Bill Athey swinging the ball square on the leg side. It landed in the crowd about 10 yards (9.1m) away. Two overs and two wickets later, after my treatise on deflections to the wicket-keeper, my defence of the several meanings of 'wickets' and my attempt to explain how runs were scored, the innings was over.

'What happens when they hit the ball?' my friend asked next. 'Do they just start running?'

'No, they need an understanding of whether to run.'

'Oh, I like this. It's a game about relationships. How very British.'

'There are three basic calls – "yes", "no" and "wait".'

'Why should he say "wait"?'

'He doesn't know what's happening.'

'Yes, that's just like relationships.' While I was pondering this, she asked another question: 'Is there a catcher?'

'He's called a wicket-keeper.'

'Oh, isn't that cute? That's the kind of nomenclature I would expect. "Stump" is a mistake.'

The Gloucestershire innings ended on 195 for five after 40

overs. During the 'tea interval' (hearty laughter at the idea of an interval for 'tea'), I explained more about the etiquette – no walking behind the bowler's arm by spectators, batsmen raising a bat and doffing a cap to greet applause. Through the rest of the afternoon, it was the polite British clapping that surprised her most, the uniformity of hands coming together as the ball hit the boundary fence or a batsman walked back to the pavilion. I explained that it wasn't always that polite.

Wayne Larkins, Northamptonshire's captain and opening bat, received the most applause, after his innings of 101 off 82 balls had been ended by a brave Athey catch from a skier off the bowling of Kevin Curran. I was grateful to Larkins for providing something so spectacular at American pace.

'You see that man fourth in the queue at the ice-cream van,' I asked, and she nodded. 'That's Nick Cook, the England left-arm orthodox spin bowler.'

I could see she was impressed. Moments before, when Jeremy Lloyds came on to bowl, I had tried to explain the art of spinning the ball. 'It's what we call "putting a little English" on the ball,' she remarked casually.

At the end we walked across to look at the wicket and study the pitch markings. 'If I could sit and watch one more game, I reckon I could figure it out,' she said. I didn't speak.

I say all this as a simple reminder. Cricket, for all its internal strangeness, can itself be seen as a strange game, and that is part of its charm.

GLOUCESTERSHIRE

J.W. Lloyds b Robinson	32
G.D. Hodgson run out	39
C.W.J. Athey c Robinson b Thomas	65
P. Bainbridge c Cook b Capel	0
K.M. Curran c Ripley b Ambrose	36
M.W. Alleyne not out	5
A.J. Wright not out	1
Extras	17
(40 overs)	195–5

Bowling: Robinson 8–1–22–1, Ambrose 8–0–48–1, Cook 8–0–40–0, Larkins 1–0–6–0, Capel 8–1–33–1, Thomas 7–1–32–1.

Fall of wickets: 63, 90,92, 186, 193

NORTHAMPTONSHIRE

W. Larkins c Athey b Curran	101
A. Fordham c Russell b Curran	10
R.J. Bailey c Wright b Bainbridge	46
D.J. Capel not out	25
N.A. Felton not out	5
Extras	11
(36.2 overs)	198–3

Bowling: Walsh 6.2–0–36–0, Curran 8–0–35–2, Jarvis 6–1–36–0, Pooley 8–0–33–0, Bainbridge 5–0–36–1, Lloyds 3–0–18–0.

Fall of wickets: 42, 144, 185.

NATWEST BOWL-OUT
BISHOP'S STORTFORD, JUNE 1991

Football Cup ties are sometimes decided by penalty shoot-outs. Tennis sets regularly go the way of tie-breaks. But what can cricket do about abandoned games that need a quick decision?

Administrators have contemplated all kinds of ways of settling knock-out games in minutes rather than hours. Hence the bowl-out, which arrived at senior level one Thursday in June 1991, when two first-round NatWest Trophy ties were decided by five players from each side, each bowling two balls at unguarded stumps.

The principle behind shoot-outs, tie-breaks and bowl-outs is that it is better to decide a match by some activity associated with the game rather than by the random act of tossing a coin (as happened to decide the 1983 Middlesex–Gloucestershire Benson & Hedges Cup match). Of course, people argue cogently that many cricket matches are decided by the toss of a coin anyway: 'On the notorious Worsening Wicket Ground at Crumbling-on-Sea, there was an air of inevitability about the result from the moment Muggins lost the toss on the first morning.'

The other principle behind shoot-outs and tie-breaks is that they are nerve-racking, exciting and therefore compulsively entertaining. Bowl-outs, however, have yet to attract large audiences, and even the players are sometimes too tense to watch what is happening.

The one-day game between Hertfordshire and Derbyshire provided two days of worry. Heavy rain prevented play on the Wednesday and by 2p.m. on the Thursday play was again abandoned without a ball being bowled. In previous years three days had been set aside for NatWest fixtures. In 1991 the time allotted was reduced to two days in order to accommodate the four-day County Championship games due to start on the Friday.

At Bishop's Stortford everybody thought hard about how a bowl-out might be avoided. Could the game be switched to another nearby ground that was fit for play? Why not play it on a first-class ground where facilities for draining might be better? Or how about a game of cards in the dressing-room to decide which team goes through?

After a number of telephone calls to the Test & County Cricket Board at Lord's, the inevitable arrived – a bowl-out.

The next decision was whether to hold this 'match within a match' indoors or outdoors. A break in the rain offered the opportunity to compete outside. Carefully choosing footwear to cope with the slippery grass and sweaters to accommodate the damp atmosphere, the players took the field. There were no batsmen, and the only fielder used was the wicket-keeper, who took up his usual position. All eyes were on the bowlers and the umpires, Alan Whitehead and Brian Harrison, who watched from normal enough positions – one behind a single stump at the bowler's end, the other at square-leg. There was no need to get the sightscreens correctly positioned, so, at 4.15p.m., the bowl-out began and another little divot in NatWest Trophy history was unearthed.

Derbyshire went first. Mortensen failed with his two attempts, as did Warner and Griffith and Base. The fifth and final bowler, Goldsmith, hit the unguarded stumps with his first attempt and missed with his second. Derbyshire had scored one.

Next came Hertfordshire. Needham equalised the scores

by hitting the stumps with his first attempt, but missed with his second. Carr missed with both. Merry missed with his first attempt and then knocked back the middle stump with his second. Hertfordshire had won … with four balls to spare.

A few hours later another NatWest Trophy tie was settled by a bowl-out in the Oval's Ken Barrington Sports Hall. Surrey and Oxfordshire had already had two games abandoned. On the Wednesday, Oxfordshire had won the toss and inserted Surrey, who sped to 142 for 1 before rain halted play in the thirty-third over. On the second day, a late start restricted play to a 20-over game. Surrey won the toss, and Oxfordshire, batting first, made 91 for six. Surrey were in some trouble at 39 for three when the next downpour came at 5.35p.m. Both sides had 45 minutes of bowl-out practice before the competition began. Oxfordshire had some experience of bowl-outs. Earlier that month they had lost 3–2 to Staffordshire in a Minor Counties Holt Cup match. This one against Surrey was a real thriller. Oxfordshire's third and fourth bowlers each hit the stumps once for a total of two. When Waqar Younis replied with a direct hit on Surrey's first attempt, it looked ominous for the Minor Counties team, but Surrey struggled from then on. Monte Lynch, Martin Bicknell and James Boiling all failed with two out of two. Up stepped medium-pacer Tony Murphy for two of the most dramatic balls of his career. His first made the score 2–2 and ensured a sudden-death bowl-out at the least. His second also hit the stumps, and Surrey were through.

That evening two NatWest Trophy cricket scores read more like football results:

HERTFORDSHIRE: 2 (Needham, Merry), DERBYSHIRE 1 (Goldsmith).
SURREY: 3 (Waqar Younis, Murphy 2), OXFORDSHIRE 2 (Curtis, Laudat).

RUNS, RUNS
AND MORE RUNS
HOVE, SUSSEX, SEPTEMBER 1993

Sussex (twelfth) and Essex (sixteenth) were two lower-table County Championship teams when they met in a four-day match towards the end of the 1993 season. Sussex won the toss and batted. What else would they do when the wicket at Hove was a beauty?

At the end of the first day Sussex were 392 for four and all the wickets had fallen to errors by the batsmen. Greenfield made a maiden century and helped to put on 183 with skipper Wells, who chalked up a century of his own. The day ended with Speight unbeaten on 75.

The next morning John North went on to complete his maiden Championship century and Speight would have been a fourth centurion but for a mistake in his nineties. Sussex were all out for 591 and there was time for Paul Prichard to make a 94-ball century as Essex raced to 256 for three at the close. That made 847 runs in two days.

The third day was more of the same. Prichard went on to make a double-century and even nightwatchman Ilott made a career-best score (51). Graham Gooch was able to declare 98 runs behind without having to bat himself. Sussex extended the lead to 326 by the end of the third day. They had lost two wickets, and one of those was Bill Athey to a catch in the deep off the penultimate over of the day. Three days had now seen 1312 runs.

Timing the Sussex declaration was a tricky business. Sussex

added 67 in the first 25 minutes of the day and the declaration set Essex 411 in 84 overs. Well, it was straightforward enough for Essex. This time the centuries came from Stephenson (122 off 206 balls) and Hussain (118 off 138 balls). At 269 for three, poor Sussex faced the prospect of Graham Gooch coming out to join Salim Malik on a pitch that had so far produced 1,665 runs. This aggregate was already a new Championship record, beating the 1,650 when Surrey played Lancashire in 1990, and soon the previous English record – 1723 for England v Australia in 1948 – was overhauled. Salim Malik and Gooch stayed together to ensure victory by seven wickets with almost eight overs to spare.

Sussex went straight from this game to the NatWest Final against Warwickshire. Sussex again batted first and again created a new record. Their 321 for six was the highest score in a final. Unfortunately for them, by the end of the day it was only the second highest. Warwickshire won by five wickets from the last ball, helped by a tremendous fifth-wicket stand of 142 by Asif Din and Dermot Reeve.

Having scored 312 and lost a 50-over game the previous Sunday, and 903 and lost a County Championship game during the week, Sussex had now scored 321 and lost a 60-over final. That's 1,536 runs but three lost games.

SUSSEX

Lenham c Lewis b Boden	52	c Stephenson b Salim Malik 149
Athey c Lewis b Boden	26	c sub b Salim Malik 96
Greenfield b Ilott	107	c Stephenson b Ilott 0
Wells c Rollins b Childs	106	not out 50
Speight c Gooch b Ilott	95	not out 3
North c Prichard b Stephenson	114	
Moores c Stephenson b Ilott	1	
Salisbury st Rollins b Childs	6	
Donelan not out	36	
Pigott c Salim Malik b Stephenson	18	
Giddins b Ilott	0	
Extras	30	14
	<u>591</u>	(declared) <u>312–3</u>

Bowling: *First Innings*; Ilott 38.3–11–119–4, Boden 25–3–118–2, Stephenson 33–8–111–2, Childs 34–12–104–2, Such 26–4–87–0, Salim Malik 7–0–37–0, Gooch 1–0–5–0; *Second Innings*; Ilott 7.5–0–23–1, Boden 10–0–62–0, Childs 17–4–47–0, Such 3–1–11–0, Stephenson 9–1–42–0, Salim Malik 18.1–1–88–2, Hussain 4.1–0–33–0.

ESSEX

Prichard not out	225	lbw b Giddins 24
Stephenson c Wells b Pigott	9	c Salisbury b Greenfield 122
Lewis c Salisbury b Lenham	43	
Salim Malik b Giddins	73	(4) not out 63
Ilott b Salisbury	51	
Hussain not out	70	(3) c Athey b Greenfield 118
Gooch		(5) not out 74
Extras	22	 11
(declared)	493–4	412–3

Bowling: *First Innings*; Pigott 23–0–127–1, Giddins 21.4–2–99–1, North 10–0–52–0, Donelan 14–2–64–0, Lenham 7–1–27–1, Salisbury 24–2–94–1, Athey 5–2–22–0; *Second Innings*; Giddins 10–0–37–1, Pigott 12–2–43–0, Salisbury 23–4–102–0, Donelan 12–1–66–0, Athey 3–0–31–0, North 13–0–87–0, Greenfield 11–0–40–2.

MORE RECORDS
FOR LARA

BIRMINGHAM, JUNE 1994

Warwickshire entertained Durham in a four-day County Championship game that started on a Thursday. Durham batted first and dominated the first day. At the close they were 365 for 3 with John Morris unbeaten on 204, an innings of five sixes and 24 fours.

Morris was out first thing the next morning but Durham continued to amass runs. A county record eighth-wicket stand of 134 between David Graveney and Anderson Cummins took the score past 500. The declaration came when the stand was broken.

Cummins then took an early wicket in the Warwickshire innings, wicket-keeper Chris Scott holding the catch to dismiss Dominic Ostler with the score on eight. That brought in 25-year-old Brian Lara. The West Indian left-hander had been having a sensational year.

The highlight of Lara's year – indeed the highlight of the year for many cricket followers – was his world record Test score of 375 against England in March. It came in the fifth Test at St John's Recreation Ground, Antigua, an innings played with barely a blemish. He was dropped only once and made only a handful of other false shots. When he broke the Gary Sobers record (365) with a pull off Chris Lewis, Sobers himself walked out to congratulate Lara at the crease.

Lara was in his first season with Warwickshire, and a fine season it was proving to be. He had started with five centuries in six innings – 147 against Glamorgan, 106 and 120 not out against Leicestershire, 136 against Somerset, and 26 and 140 against Middlesex. A century in the first innings against Durham would bring him a world record seven centuries in eight innings (including the 375 against England).

Lara received his first ball from fellow West Indian Anderson Cummins. The bowler dropped it short, suspecting that Lara would go for the shot. Meanwhile Lara was looking for the hook because he suspected that Cummins would bowl short. Everybody was correct. But Lara mistimed his hook and the ball looped up towards the bowler off the end of his bat. Cummins lunged for the catch. The ball was just out of his reach.

When Lara had made ten, Cummins produced a beautiful yorker. Lara played round the ball and his leg stump went over. Lara admitted later that he hadn't heard the call of 'No-ball'.

On 18, facing Simon Brown, Lara edged a straightforward catch to wicket-keeper Scott. The ball went down.

'Jeez, I hope he doesn't go on and get a hundred,' Lara heard the wicket-keeper say.

In his book, *Beating the Field*, Lara describes this shaky start: 'The period before tea was one of my sketchiest at the crease in my year with Warwickshire. My feet simply would not go to the right places.'

During the tea interval, Lara went to the indoor school with wicket-keeper Keith Piper in an attempt to sort out his footwork.

Durham had bowled well at Lara during the early part of his innings but their chance had now almost disappeared. The pitch was perfect for batting, the outfield was fast, and there were plenty of runs to come. Lara ended that Friday not out on 111, having achieved his first world record of the match – seven centuries in eight innings. It was his eleventh century of the year.

Saturday was rained out.

On the Sunday David Graveney got Lara's wicket after he had scored six but it didn't halt Lara's progress because it happened in a Sunday League game.

On the Monday Durham refused the offer of a double-declaration followed by a Warwickshire run-chase. Their captain, Phil Bainbridge, was aware that the Edgbaston pitch was easy-paced and he was also aware that one of his key bowlers, David Graveney, was out of action with a thigh strain. Maybe he was also thinking about Brian Lara in the fourth innings.

The match was virtually dead when Lara resumed his innings on the Monday morning. He brought it back to life with a scintillating performance that took his score to 285 at lunch. During the break the Warwickshire captain agreed to delay the declaration to give Lara a chance at the county record, which had been held by Frank Foster (305 not out) since 1914. Lara overtook Foster's score soon after lunch. His third century had taken only 58 balls but he had survived a chance to Cummins at mid-off when 238. Trevor Penney's dismissal ended a stand of 314. Penney had scored 44.

When he reached 325 Lara passed 1,000 runs for the season (an average of 200), equalling Don Bradman's 1938 feat of 1,000 runs in seven innings. He brought up his 400 with an all-run four and was then dropped on 413 by a substitute fielder at square-leg. He was unbeaten on 418 when tea was taken.

The next target was Archie McLaren's 424, the highest score made in England. Dermot Reeve decided that he would not declare while Lara was still batting, so the McLaren record fell soon after tea. Another record to fall was Charlie Macartney's 345 runs in a day, which Lara passed when he reached 457. Four successive fours off Bainbridge took Lara into the 470s.

Lara was tiring now but his stand with Keith Piper was growing towards 300 and the crowd was swelling as the news spread. Lara reached 494 with his sixty-ninth boundary (including ten sixes), thus overtaking Percy Perrin's 1904 record of 68 boundaries in an innings. There was only one more individual record outstanding – Hanif's record first-class score of 499.

Play was scheduled to finish at 5.30 and the last over was bowled by John Morris. Lara faced the third ball with 497 to his name. He was beaten by it. The next ball, the fourth of the over, was a bouncer which hit Lara on the helmet. Keith Piper walked down the pitch to make sure Lara knew that this was probably the last over. Two more balls to score the three needed to beat Hanif's world record 499.

Lara drove the next ball for four. 501 not out.

Lara scored his 501 from 427 balls in 474 minutes. He helped set two other county records – the unbroken sixth-wicket partnership of 322 and the total score of 810 for four. Scoring 390 runs in a day was yet another record for Lara.

Brian Lara went on to score 3,828 runs in 1994 at an average of 79.75. He made 14 hundreds, including one double-hundred, one triple-hundred and, of course, one quintuple-hundred.

223

DURHAM

Larkins c Penney b Munton	13
Saxelby b Small	19
Morris c Lara b P.A. Smith	204
Hutton b Davis	61
Bainbridge c Reeve b N. Smith	67
Longley lbw b N. Smith	24
Scott lbw b Small	13
Cummins lbw b Twose	62
Graveney not out	65
Extras	28
(declared)	556–8

Bowling: Small 22–8–80–2, Munton 28–4–103–1. Reeve 5–2–12–0, PA Smith 15–5–51–1, Davis 36–12–105–1, N Smith 32–6–97–2, Twose 9.5–1–42–1, Lara 11–1–47–0.

WARWICKSHIRE

Ostler c Scott b Cummins 8
Twose c Cox b Brown 51
Lara not out 501
Penney c Hutton b Bainbridge 44
P.A. Smith lbw b Cummins 12
Piper not out 116
Extras 78
                                                         <u>810–4</u>

Bowling: Cummins 28–1–158–2, Brown 27–1–164–1, Bainbridge 33–6–169–1
Graveney 7–1–34–0, Cox, 30–5–163–0, Larkins 5–0–39–0, Morris 5.5–1–33–0.

ABANDONED
AFTER 62 BALLS

KINGSTON, JAMAICA, JANUARY 1998

The wicket at Sabina Park was cracked and uneven. England captain Mike Atherton thought it would deteriorate over the five days. He won the toss and elected to bat. Brian Lara led the West Indies team on to the field and Courtney Walsh measured his run-up. The fielders dispersed, Atherton took guard and the umpire signalled 'Play'.

Walsh's first ball was a loosener and Atherton steered it for two runs. The second ball kept low. The third was a vicious leg-cutter that speared towards Atherton's ribs. The fourth rolled along the ground.

Atherton was out to the first ball of Walsh's second over. He tried to take his bat away but was caught at gully. Mark Butcher's first ball lifted dangerously and he gloved it to third slip. England were four for two and now everybody suspected that this relaid wicket was not suitable for a Test match.

During the first hour England physiotherapist Wayne Morton was out in the middle for longer than most of the batsmen. He came on to treat injuries on six occasions – once for Nasser Hussain, twice for Graham Thorpe and three times for Alec Stewart, who was hit twice on the hands and once on the shoulder. Another time a ball from Curtly Ambrose bounced over Stewart and over the wicket-keeper's head for four byes. Stewart must have played on worse pitches, but he was probably playing football at the time.

The umpires, local-man Steve Buckner and Srini Venkataraghavan from India, became very aware that the batsmen could be seriously injured, especially when Thorpe was hit on the hand by a ball which reared up from a good length. After the umpires had conferred twice they called over the two captains. The teams went off after playing for 66 minutes and 62 balls (including one no-ball). Stewart had made a courageous nine from 26 balls.

There followed an hour's negotiation with the International Cricket Conference before the match was formally abandoned. Thankfully, no one had been seriously injured.

It was the first-ever Test match to have been abandoned for a dangerous wicket but the India–Sri Lanka one-day match, on Christmas Day 1997, was called off after 18 balls in similar circumstances. The three previous Test match abandonments – Karachi (1968–9), Jamaica (1977–8) and Bangalore (1978–9) – had been provoked by crowd rioting.

ENGLAND

Atherton c Campbell b Walsh	2
Stewart not out	9
Butcher c S.C. Williams b Walsh	0
Hussain c Hooper b Ambrose	1
Thorpe not out	0
Extras	5
	17–3

Bowling: Walsh 5.1–1–10–2, Ambrose 5–3–3–1.

TEN FOR 73
DELHI, INDIA, FEBRUARY 1999

The two-match India–Pakistan Test series broke new ground in many ways. It brought the first Test match in India between the two countries for 12 years, but only after right-wing Shiv Sena Hindu extremists had threatened to disrupt the tour. Late negotiations with the Indian government stopped the protesters after they had dug up the Delhi wicket and caused the first Test to be switched to Chennai. The cricket took place against a background of heavy security.

The first Test was a captivating thriller. There was little between the two teams on first innings – Pakistan made 238 and India 254 – and the match continued to swing one way and then the other. Shahid Afridi's magnificent 141 put Pakistan in a winning position at 275 for four but the last six wickets fell for 13 runs. Then Pakistan bowled India to 82 for five and gave themselves a strong position. Only one thing was wrong for Pakistan – Indian captain Sachin Tendulkar was still batting.

Tendulkar went on to play one of the all-time great Test innings. He put on 136 with wicket-keeper Nayan Mongia before the 'keeper departed for 52. Despite suffering from a back injury, Tendulkar continued to fight by attacking the bowlers. When he was out, for 136, India needed 17 to win with three wickets left. Off-spinner Saqlain Mushtaq mopped up the tail to give Pakistan victory by 12 runs and take his tally to ten wickets in the match.

Tight security was still in operation when the teams prepared for the final Test. The Pakistani players were given escorts, spectators were asked to remove nationalistic clothing on arrival at the ground, and snake-charmers stood by in case extremists set loose snakes. This time India won the toss and batted.

India built on their 80-run first-innings lead with an innings of 96 by Sadagopan Ramesh and good support from Ganguly and Srinath. Wasim Akram became Pakistan's highest wicket-taker when Mongia became his three hundred and sixty-third victim. In the end, though, Pakistan were left to make 420 to win on a pitch that was increasingly helping the spin bowlers.

The Pakistani innings started with a century stand by Saeed Anwar and Shahid Afridi. But once Afridi had departed, caught behind off a debatable thin edge, the stage was open for Anil Kumble. The Indian leg-spinner dismissed Ijaz Ahmed (leg before to a full toss), Inzamam (bowled from an inside edge), Yousuf (leg before), Moin Khan (caught low at slip) and the stubborn Saeed Anwar (caught at short leg). Six of the side were out for 128 and hopes of a Pakistani victory had now disappeared.

Salim Malik added 58 with Wasim Akram but left to a Kumble top-spinner, and he was soon followed by Mushtaq Ahmed (caught at slip) and Saqlain Mushtaq (leg before).

Now Anil Kumble had nine wickets out of nine.

Play switched to the other end and Javagal Srinath deliberately bowled wide so as not to interfere with the perfect figures. Kumble needed only three more balls to dismiss Wasim Akram, caught at short leg.

The crowd went wild and Kumble was carried back to the pavilion. His figures of 26.3–9–74–10 (including two no-balls) were second only to Jim Laker's ten for 53 in the 1956 Old Trafford Test against Australia. In the contemporary climate, however, it was perhaps a more astonishing performance. Even more strange was that 53-year-old

Richard Stokes from Surrey had seen both Laker's ten for 53 and Kumble's ten for 74. Stokes had been in New Delhi on business on 7 February.

Kumble was declared man of the match and Saqlain man of the series for his four five-wicket hauls. The 1–1 result was a victory for both teams.

INDIA

Ramesh b Saqlain	60	c and b Mushtaq 96
Laxman b Wasim	35	b Wasim 8
Dravid lbw b Saqlain	33	c Ijaz b Saqlain 29
Tendulkar lbw b Saqlain	6	c Wasim b Mushtaq 29
Azharuddin c Ijaz b Mushtaq	67	b Wasim 14
Ganguly lbw b Mushtaq	13	not out 62
Mongia run out	10	lbw b Wasim 0
Kumble c Yousuf b Saqlain	0	c Ijaz b Saqlain 15
Srinath lbw b Saqlain	0	c Ijaz b Saqlain 49
Prasad not out	1	b Saqlain 6
Harbhajan Singh run out	1	b Saqlain 0
Extras	26	 31
	252	339

Bowling: *First Innings*; Wasim 13–3–23–1, Waqar 13–5–37–0, Mushtaq 26–5–64–2, Saqlain 35.5–9–94–5, Afridi 4–1–14–0. *Second Innings*; Wasim 21–3–43–3, Waqar 12–2–42–0, Mushtaq 26–4–86–2, Saqlain 46.4–13–122–5, Afridi 8–1–24–0.

PAKISTAN

Saeed Anwar c Mongia b Prasad	1	c Laxman b Kumble 69
Shahid Afridi b Harbhajan	32	c Mongia b Kumble 41
Ijaz Ahmed c Dravid b Kumble	17	lbw b Kumble 0
Inzamam-ul-Haq b Kumble	26	b Kumble 6
Yousuf Youhana c and b Kumble	3	lbw b Kumble 0
Salim Malik c Azharuddin b Prasad	31	(7) b Kumble 15
Moin Khan lbw b Srinath	14	(6) c Ganguly b Kumble 3
Wasim Akram lbw b Harbhajan	15	c Laxman b Kumble 37
Mushtaq Ahmed c Laxman b Harbhajan	12	c Dravid b Kumble 1
Saqlain Mushtaq lbw b Kumble	2	lbw b Kumble 0
Waqar Younis not out	1	not out 6
Extras	18	 29
	172	207

Bowling: *First Innings*; Srinath 12–1–38–1, Prasad 11–2–20–2, Harbhajan 17–5–30–3, Kumble 24.3–4–74–4. *Second Innings*; Srinath 12–2–50–0, Prasad 4–1–15–0, Harbhajan 18–5–51–0, Kumble 26.3–9–74–10.

THE END OF THE RUN
KOLKATA, INDIA, MARCH 2001

The second Test between India and Australia was an early candidate for match of the century. It was one of the most entertaining and amazing of all time.

Australia were one up in the three-match series and had won their last 16 Tests. Captained by the legendary Steve Waugh, Australia had scintillating batting from the likes of Mark Waugh and Michael Slater, and two of the best bowlers of any era in Glenn McGrath and leg-spinner Shane Warne.

The setting for the occasion was Eden Gardens, Kolkata, home to 75,000 fanatical spectators.

Australia won the toss and chose to bat. Matthew Hayden and Michael Slater gave them a good start. At lunch they were 88 without loss. When Slater was out, Justin Langer took over and tea came with the score at 193 for one.

The final session of the first day belonged to India. Hayden became Harbhajan Singh's first victim, the excellent Zaheer Khan picked up Langer's wicket, and Mark Waugh went just as he looked set for a big score. Harbhajan Singh, 20, then became India's first player to take a hat-trick (and the second youngest in Test cricket). He dismissed Ricky Ponting with the second ball of his sixteenth over, Adam Gilchrist with one that kept low, and Shane Warne when Sadagoppan Ramesh took a brilliant catch at forward short leg. The appeal against Warne was dramatically referred to the third umpire.

Having ended the first day on 291 for eight, Australia's position was strengthened by Steve Waugh's twenty-fifth Test century. Waugh and Jason Gillespie put on 113 runs for the ninth wicket, an Australian record against India, and Waugh passed Javed Miandad's total of 8,832 Test runs.

India ended the day on 128 for eight. An early Australian win seemed likely.

The third day did little to change that prediction. India followed on and ended the day trailing by 20 runs with six second-innings wickets in hand. When Tendulkar was out for only ten, most Indians gave up hope of a rescue act. At the close Vangipurappu Venkata Sai Laxman was undefeated on 109 and Rahul Dravid had seven to his name. Their fifth-wicket stand amounted to 22 ... so far.

Laxman's first-innings 59 had been made from 83 balls with 12 fours, ending only when he was given out caught from a ball that may have hit his forearm. Promoted to number three for the second innings, Laxman dominated the Australian attack with a sweetly struck century off 166 balls (17 fours). He scored 14 from one Kasprowicz over and took 11 from the next (by Warne). When journalists sought quotes from Laxman at the end of the day's play, his first response was to congratulate Pullela Gopichand for winning the all-England open badminton tournament.

V.V.S. Laxman and Rahul Dravid batted through the fourth day and added another 337 runs. On the fifth morning they took their stand to 376 off 625 balls. Laxman made 281 off 452 balls (44 fours), surpassing Sunil Gavaskar's Indian record for an individual score (236), and Dravid scored 180 from 353 balls (20 fours).

The quality of the batting made hardened journalists purr with pleasure and cheer like fans. Laxman played every stroke in the book and some of his own invention. Dravid was reliable and solid. They went through each session with the aim of not losing a wicket.

India bowled out Australia on the final day and won with

33 balls to spare. At one point it looked as though the top-order Australians could get close to the winning target. At tea, Australia looked in little danger of losing – 161 for three with Hayden on 59 and Steve Waugh 23 – but they lost five wickets for eight runs in only 32 balls.

V.V.S. Laxman was man of the match, while Harbhajan Singh took 13 for 196 (including a hat-trick). It was the first time India had followed on and won a Test. Indeed, in Test history, only England – in 1894 and again in 1981 – had achieved victory after a follow-on. Australia had been the losing team on those occasions too.

India's victory at Eden Gardens ended Australia's record of 16 successive wins – against West Indies (five), India (four), New Zealand (three), Pakistan (three) and Zimbabwe (one).

The series was set up perfectly for the Third and final Test. This was another wonderful spectacle. India won by two wickets to clinch the series 2–1, and Harbhajan Singh took his wicket tally to 32 in the three Tests. Australia made 391 (Hayden 203, Mark Waugh 70, Harbhajan Singh 7–133) and 264 (Mark Waugh 57, Harbhajan Singh 8–84), India scored 501 (Tendulkar 126, Das 84, Dravid 81, Laxman 65, Ramesh 61) and 155–8 (Laxman 66).

AUSTRALIA

Slater c Mongia b Khan	42	c Gaguly b Harbhajan Singh 96
Hayden c sub b Harbhajan Singh	97	lbw b Tendulkar 67
Langer c Mongia b Khan	58	c Ramesh b Harbhajan Singh 28
Waugh (M.) c Mongia b Harbhajan Singh	22	lbw b Raju 0
Waugh (S.) lbw b Harbhajan Singh	110	c sub b Harbhajan Singh ...24
Ponting lbw b Harbhajan Singh	6	c Das b Harbhajan Singh 0
Gilchrist lbw b Harbhajan Singh	0	lbw b Tendulkar 0
Warne c Ramesh b Harbhajan Singh	0	lbw b Tendulkar 0
Kasprowicz lbw b Ganguly	7	not out 13
Gillespie c Ramesh b Harbhajan Singh	7	(8) c Das b Harbhajan Singh 6
McGrath not out	21	lbw b Harbhajan Singh 0
Extras	36	19
	445	212

Bowling: *First Innings*; Khan 28.4–6–89–2, Prasad 30–5–95–0, Ganguly 13.2–3–44–1, Raju 20–2–58–0, Harbhajan Singh 37.5–7–123–7, Tendulkar 2–0–7–0. *Second Innings;* Khan 8–4–30–0, Prasad 3–1–7–0, Harbhajan Singh 30.3–8–73–6, Raju 15–3–58–1, Tendulkar 11–3–31–3, Ganguly 1–0–2–0.

Fall of wickets: *First Innings*; 103, 193, 214, 236, 252, 252, 252, 269, 402, 445. *Second Innings;* 74, 106, 116, 166, 166, 167, 173, 174, 191, 212.

INDIA

Das c Gilchrist b McGrath	20	hit wicket by Gillespie	39
Ramesh c Ponting b Gillespie	0	c Waugh (M.) b Warne	30
Dravid b Warne	25	(6) run out	180
Tendulkar lbw b McGrath	10	c Gilchrist b Gillespie	10
Ganguly c Waugh (S.) b Kasprowicz	23	c Gilchrist b McGrath	48
Laxman c Hayden b Warne	31	(3) c Ponting b McGrath	281
Mongia c Gilchrist b Kasprowicz	2	b McGrath	4
Harbhajan Singh c Ponting b Gillespie	4	(9) not out	8
Khan b McGrath	3	(8) not out	23
Raju lbw b McGrath	4		
Prasad not out	7		
Extras	14		34
	171	(declared)	657–7

Bowling: *First Innings*; McGrath 14–8–18–4, Gillespie 11–0–47–2, Kasprowicz 13–2–39–2, Warne 20.1–3–65–2. *Second Innings*; McGrath 39–12–103–3, Gillespie 31–6–115–2, Warne 34–3–152–1, Waugh (M) 18–1–58–0, Kasprowicz 35–6–139–0, Ponting 12–1–41–0, Hayden 6–0–24–0, Slater 2–1–4–0, Langer 1–0–3–0.

Fall of wickets: *First Innings;* 0, 34, 48, 88, 88, 92, 97, 113, 129, 171. *Second Innings;* 52, 97, 115, 232, 608, 624, 629

BURGLARY STOPS PLAY
EYNSHAM, OXFORDSHIRE, JULY 2001

With three overs remaining, the home team, Eynsham 2nd XI, looked set for a victory against Wantage 1st XI. Then their concentration was disturbed by events beyond the boundary.

An Eynsham fielder saw two strangers jump out of a sports-car and act suspiciously. The home captain, Phil Brown, asked the umpire for permission to leave the field.

The players sprinted towards the changing-rooms and Wantage players joined in. They caught two young men in the act of riffling through changing-room possessions. One suspect escaped through the clubhouse door and ran off towards the village. The other man was pinned to the floor by a bunch of cricketers representing both teams. One Wantage player was bitten by the suspect in the fracas and had to go to hospital for a tetanus injection and tests.

A mobile-phone call brought five police-cars to the Eynsham clubhouse, and a man was arrested on suspicion of attempted theft and assault. A Thames Valley Police helicopter circled above in a search for the second suspect.

Play resumed after a delay of 40 minutes. The remaining three overs of the Oxfordshire Cricket Association Division Five match were completed. According to some observers, the interlude had been more exciting than the match.

EYNSHAM 2nd XI: 186 for 8 (Brown 45, Harris 35 not out, Frost 33).
WANTAGE: 163–8 (Berryman 59, O'Dimbylow 44).

CAUGHT FOR NOUGHT
DISHFORTH, NORTH YORKSHIRE, JULY 2006

It had rained on the morning of Saturday, 22 July, so Dishforth captain Steve Wilson thought there might be a bit in the wicket for his bowlers. He won the toss and asked Goldsborough 2nd XI to bat. On paper it was a 45-over match. In fact the match lasted only 78 balls.

The match involved two North Yorkshire teams: Dishforth, based near Ripon, were top of the Nidderdale & District League Division Four; Goldsborough 2nds, from near Knaresborough, were bottom. The venue was a classic village ground just off the A1 (M). The wicket was cut at the edge of the square with a short boundary on one side. The boundary looked inviting but it proved elusive until the very last shot of the day. Dishforth players still refer to the track at the edge of the square as 'the Goldsborough wicket'.

Asked to bat, Goldsborough were soon nought for two and then four leg-side byes got the team off the mark. At four for two the scorebook showed no sign of what was to come. But Goldsborough added only one more run to their total and that came from a leg-bye. They were all out for five with one ball remaining in the twelfth over.

When Goldsborough were four for four their captain Peter Horseman jokingly said that it would be strange if they were all out for ducks. He certainly didn't plan it that way though. He couldn't believe that no one even edged a run. There was one golden chance for a single but the batsman turned the opportunity down because he'd been hit on the foot the previous ball and was still recovering. The only batsman not culpable was last man John Tomlinson, who held up his end for nought not out.

Two things were astonishing about the Goldsborough innings – all ten dismissed batsmen made ducks and all ten were out caught. Some of the batsmen were out playing attacking shots and only one catch went to the wicket-keeper. How is it possible that all ten dismissed players could hit the ball well enough to be caught and yet not hit the ball well enough to score a run?

A whole team caught for nought.

'It was very surreal,' Dishforth captain Steve Wilson said later. 'We knew that no one had ever done anything like it before. It was certainly a rarity in this part of the world. We couldn't believe it and then it kept getting closer and closer to the end of the innings. Surreal, it was.'

Nothing remotely like it had happened in the 112-year history of the Nidderdale & District League. The innings also produced three bowlers who took more wickets than they conceded runs. Gavin Hardisty took seven for none, Craig Costello two for none and Anthony Addison one for none.

When Dishforth batted Wilson sent in numbers ten and 11 first. They were both out for ducks, and they were both caught too. Twelve wickets fell in the match before there was a run off the bat. A big cheer went up when Dan Bettles-Hall forced a single. Fifteen men batted that day but Bettles-Hall was the only one of them to have a run against his name.

The Goldsborough team were left ruing two dropped catches at a time when Dishforth were nought for two. Had they had them nought for four then maybe …

The match finished at 2.57p.m. It had lasted three minutes less than an hour. Normally the two teams would go to the local village pub. On this occasion, however, the pub had only just shut after lunch. It would be a few hours before it was open again.

The Dishforth players stayed in their kit while they had a photograph taken with their manual black scoreboard – RUNS 5, WKTS 10, OVERS 12 – and then, after changing, they tidied up the pavilion. It was still only 4 o'clock and there was plenty of cricket left in the day, so they wandered a couple of miles up the road to see how their league rivals, Rainton, were doing. At 5 o'clock it was a bright and sunny day but it started raining during the next hour. The rained-off Rainton team had to settle for two points while Dishforth had chalked up six points before the rain came. Dishforth eventually won the league.

GOLDSBOROUGH 2ND XI

Brackenbury c Gillespie b Costello	0
Page c Addison b Hardisty	0
Evans c Potts b Hardisty	0
Wilson c Addison b Hardisty	0
Horseman c Gillespie b Costello	0
Mackrill c Lawson b Hardisty	0
Morgan c Burnett b Hardisty	0
Mace c Reed b Hardisty	0
Morris c Costello b Addison	0
Clayton c and b Hardisty	0
Tomkinson not out	0
Extras	5
	5

Bowling: Costello 5–5–0–2, Hardisty 5.5–5–0–7, Addison 1–1–0–1.

Fall of wickets: 0, 0, 4, 4, 4, 4, 5, 5, 5, 5.

DISHFORTH

Wintersgill c off Morgan	0
Lawson c off Morgan	0
Bettles-Hall not out	5
Reed not out	0
Extra	1
	6–2

Bowling: Morgan 1–0–1–2, Evans 0.1–0–4–0.

Fall of wickets: 0, 0.

A RECORD TEST-MATCH STAND OF 624

COLOMBO, SRI LANKA, JULY 2006

A world record for first-class and Test cricket was achieved at the Sinhalese Sports Club, Colombo, when Mahele Jayawardene and Kumar Sangakarra put on 624 for Sri Lanka against South Africa in the first Test of the series. Naturally the record stand involved a right-hander (Jayawardene) and a left-hander (Sangakarra).

South Africa won the toss, batted first and were all out for 169 by tea. Sri Lanka's reply started badly. After only 21 balls they were 14 for two, having lost both openers to the bowling of Dale Steyn. That brought together Jayawardene, the Sri Lankan captain, and Sangakarra, who was dropped at gully on seven and bowled by a Steyn no-ball. After that, however, the partnership got better and better for the Sri Lankans. By the end of the first day Jayawardene and Sangakarra had both made fifties and the score was 128 for two.

Jayawardene and Sangakkara batted through the whole of the next day giving no further chances, although Sangakarra was close to being caught on 99. Sangakarra was first to his century (116 balls) and Jayawardene, 99 at lunch, completed his century in 162 balls. Later that day Jayawardene brought up his 200 with a six and the day ended with him on 229 and Jayawardene on 224. That evening the two not-out batsmen went out to dinner together with their wives and relaxed before resuming their Test-match partnership the following morning.

The runs stacked up. Lunch on the third day arrived with

the stand worth 570 runs, only six away from the existing Test record of 576, which had been achieved in 1998 by Sanath Jayasuriya (340 runs) and Roshan Mahanama (225) of Sri Lanka, and seven away from the first-class record of 577. It was a tense lunch-break and then two records were broken with four byes. Fireworks greeted the achievement.

The stand lasted 157 overs. Sangakkara made a career best of 287 in 454 balls before he was caught by wicket-keeper Mark Boucher off Andrew Hall. The Sri Lankan batsman left the field smiling. Well, he had helped to put on 624 runs.

Tillakaratne Dilshan, who had sat padded up for 11 hours on three separate days, came in and scored 45 from 67 balls. Then Jayawardene went on to reach 374 (in 572 balls) before Andre Nel bowled him with a delivery that kept low and came back a bit. The Sri Lankan skipper declared immediately with his team's score on 756 for five. The first-innings lead of 587 was a record, and Jayawardene's 374 was the fourth highest individual score in Test history, behind Brian Lara (400 not out and 375) and Matthew Hayden (380).

At the end of the third day, South Africa had made 43 without loss. They were still 554 runs behind. The following day South Africa took their second-innings total to 434 all out and lost by an innings and 153 runs.

The second Test in the two-match series was much closer. Sri Lanka (321 and 351 for nine) beat South Africa (361 and 311) by one wicket.

Another example of a left-handed batsman combining with a right-hander in a long stand came in August 2011, when Michael Carberry (300 not out) and Neil McKenzie (237) put on 523 runs in 135 overs for Hampshire in a County Championship match against Yorkshire. This was only Carberry's third match after missing nine months with a serious illness with blood clots on the lungs. Only 14 wickets fell in a match of 1,171 runs. It would have needed another week to get a result other than a draw.

THE FIRST
FORFEITED TEST
THE OVAL, AUGUST 2006

In the history of Test cricket – 1,814 matches in 129 years – there had never been a Test match decided by forfeit. Then along came the fourth day of the fourth Test of an England–Pakistan series and an Australian umpire called Darrell Hair.

England had already won the four-match series – they led 2–0 with one to play – and the Tests had been relatively free of controversy. At the Oval Inzamam-ul-Haq won the toss and decided to field first. England were dismissed for 170 with Marcus Trescothick looking out of sorts and Kevin Pietersen out first ball. A century by Mohammad Yousuf helped Pakistan to a 334-run first-innings lead.

At 2.30p.m. on the fourth day, England were 250 for three after 56 overs, still 84 short of avoiding an innings defeat. But Pietersen was batting so well that some punters hadn't discarded the possibility of a Bothamesque England revival.

Then came the turning-point. Senior umpire Darrell Hair decided that Pakistan had somehow tampered with the ball. The fourth umpire, Trevor Jesty, arrived at the wicket with a box of six used balls. Pietersen chose one from the box.

Pundits later guessed that Hair might have started suspecting the ball when Umar Gul trapped Alastair Cook lbw with a massive in-swinger. But the Pakistanis pointed to a history of ill-feeling between Hair and Asian teams. Hair had previously called Sri Lanka bowler Muttiah

Muralitharan for throwing and Pakistan had not wished Hair to stand in this series after other incidents.

Hair penalised Pakistan five runs for ball-tampering and the Pakistanis were deeply offended. The charge cut at their religious beliefs and what is known in Urdu as *izzat* (honour). But they went about their business on the field professionally. Inzamam's astute bowling change accounted for Pietersen while the batsman was in full flow.

The problems came when bad light forced off the players at 3.47p.m. After a delay of 53 minutes the bell went and the umpires took to the field. Hair and his colleague Billy Doctrove waited in the middle. England's two not-out batsmen, Ian Bell and Paul Collingwood, watched from the dressing-room balcony. But the fielding side did not appear. The umpires spent four minutes on the field and then returned to the pavilion.

According to one report the Pakistan dressing-room was a confused and angry place. People were shouting advice at Inzamam but the captain was still trying to understand the ball-tampering charge. Pakistan coach Bob Woolmer advised Inzamam to take the field with his team – if they wanted to protest a five-minute sit-down was a better idea – but Inzamam was shocked and hurt. The Pakistani players swore under oath to Woolmer that they had not tampered with the ball.

At 4.55p.m. the umpires went out again, accompanied by Bell and Collingwood. But the Pakistan players stayed indoors. Bell and Collingwood were ready to play but Pakistan were not, so Hair melodramatically removed the bails. The umpires and batsmen left the field.

At this point it was unclear what was happening. There had been no announcement. Even the journalists were baffled. Almost everybody thought that it was just another delay. If the match was over, the stumps would have been pulled from the ground, wouldn't they?

There had been previous Test matches where a forfeit had

been a brief possibility. In 1981, during the third Test in an Australia–India series, India captain Sunil Gavaskar was given out lbw to Dennis Lillee by umpire Rex Whitehead. Gavaskar thought the ball had gone from bat to pad so he stood his ground. After Lillee had baited Gavaskar with some choice words Gavaskar led his opening partner Chetan Chauhan off the field in protest. But Chauhan was met at the boundary by the India team manager, Wing Commander S.K. Durrani, and told to continue.

The negotiations took much longer when New Zealand played West Indies at Christchurch in February 1980. West Indies fast bowler Colin Croft took umbrage at decisions by umpire Goodall, and the West Indies demanded that Goodall be replaced or the team wouldn't come out for the third session on the third day. There was a delay of 11 minutes before play resumed, and then much of the next day, a rest day, was spent in dispute before the match continued.

Here, at the Oval, the Pakistan players eventually abandoned their protest. At 5.23p.m. Inzamam took his players on to the field. Spectators booed and jeered. No one came out to join the Pakistan players so they left the field again. At 6.13p.m. there was an announcement that play had been called off for the day.

Almost four hours later, at 10.12p.m., the result was finally announced – England had won by a forfeit.

Most people were shocked that the matter had not been resolved more subtly, especially as there was a capacity crowd of 23,000 waiting to see some cricket and 12,000 tickets had been sold for the Sunday. Inzamam later apologised for not leading out his team and was suspended for four one-day matches on a charge of 'bringing the game into disrepute'.

Some people argued that Darrell Hair could have had a quiet word with the Pakistan captain about the ball-tampering and the ball could have been switched without penalty. Twenty-six television cameras had failed to pick up any ball-tampering offence, but one senior umpire sided with Hair by saying that a charge of ball-tampering was just a judgment call like any other umpiring decision and didn't need proof. Other experts said that the ball could have been scuffed by a shot that hit the boundary boards or a six from Pietersen that landed in the stand. A charge of ball-tampering, later brought by the International Cricket Council (ICC), was found not proven. The ICC banned Hair from umpiring in Test matches from November 2006. He returned briefly to top-level umpiring in 2008 but retired later that year to take a cricket job in Australia.

The fourth Test, decided by a forfeit, was a sad and strange tale. An editorial in *The Times* suggested that 'the rash of ill-judgments ... should be packaged into a corporate training video about how not to manage a crisis'.

VATICAN CITY AWAY

VATICAN CITY, SEPTEMBER 2008

Any cricket club with 'Fairly Odd' as its middle name is an obvious candidate for a book on strange matches. That is certainly true of the Dutch Fellowship of Fairly Odd Places (FFOP). Their once-a-year match is developed around some outrageous geographical concepts.

Formed in 2005, the team's inaugural match took place on a pitch located in two countries. The *ad hoc* ground had the Holland–Belgium border running across the square and, for once, it didn't take a wild slog to send the ball into another country. A batsman could take guard in Holland, play a forward defensive stroke and jab the ball into Belgium. FFOP lost by 68 runs to Rood en Wit Zami 2.

The following year's annual match was a revival of Manor House cricket in the Netherlands. In superb weather FFOP played against Gentlemen of Zami at Zypendaal Castle near Arnhem, thus replicating the matches of the late nineteenth century, when some major Dutch landowners made land available for cricket on their estates.

Then, in 2008, came a very unusual concept – an away match in the Vatican City. The match took place on 13 September 2008 in the beautiful Stadio dei Marmi in Rome. Built in 1932 the stadium had 60 9-ft (2.7-m) high marble statues around the ground. This was the first-ever cricket match in the stadium, a fact that might have been deduced from the state of the wicket.

The FFOP fellows flew in from around the world with the hope that they would be playing against an inexperienced Vatican XI put together especially for the occasion by Father Eamonn O'Higgins. But this was no ordinary scratch Vatican team. FFOP's opposition turned out to be a side of young and agile Indian priest students from the Pontifical International College Maria Mater Ecclesiae.

FFOP was formed by a group of cricketers who had all once played for the Haarlem-based Rood en Wit (Red and White) Cricket Club in Haarlem. By the time of the Vatican match, though, the Haarlem Old Boys really were old boys – their average age was just over 50. The FFOP players were also great traditionalists who weren't yet ready to switch to pyjama cricket. They refused to wear helmets while batting and wore white shirts and white trousers on the field. They could be seen in red-and-white striped blazers off the field. The Vatican XI dressed in sky blue.

During the preliminary ceremony FFOP's Dr Michel Bakker gave a speech in Latin while the flags of the Vatican, the Netherlands and Italy were raised. FFOP batted first in a 35-over match but were bowled out for only 58. The Vatican XI won comfortably with 14 overs to spare. Afterwards the FFOP officials presented the Vatican with a cheque for €1,000 for the Sagar Orphanage in India.

'OK, we lost,' said Erik Bouwmeester, a Lieutenant-colonel in the Grenadier Guards. 'It was semi-geriatrics versus lean and mean batting and bowling machines as well as a deadly pitch, but the whole thing was quite unique. Let's face it, we challenged a sovereign state into raising a national side and we were mere amateurs from the Netherlands playing in a Roman stadium.'

The FFOP players immediately began planning their next match – on an uninhabited island off the coast of the Netherlands. What really mattered to them was not the winning and losing but the playing of the game in strange places. The Fellowship of Fairly Odd Places CC has thus added to a fine tradition that has included matches on board ships, games on sandbanks such as Goodwin Sands and Bramble Bank, and ice cricket on frozen lakes, glaciers and ice-hockey rinks. The late Harry Thompson once played in a cricket match on the ice in Antarctica, an experience he recalled in his book *Penguins Stopped Play*. No prizes for guessing how Thompson's book got its title.

FELLOWSHIP OF FAIRLY ODD PLACES

M. Koch c Saiju b das Yesudasan	9
R. Snijder b Bastian	0
N. Meijer c Abilash b Ollikkara	1
R. Heikens run out	7
R. Kottman c das Yesudasan b Sacarias	13
E. Bouwmeester b Anoop	2
F. Oudshoorn Spaargaren b Ollikkara	5
J. Thon not out	4
M. Bakker b Saiju	0
A. de Vries b Saiju	0
A. de Bruin retired hurt	0
B.J. Henkes b Saiju	3
Extras	14
	<u>58</u>

Bowling: Ollikkara 9–4–14–1, Saiju 5–2–7–3, das Yesudasan 4–1–9–1, Anoop 3–0–6–1, Sacarias 1–0–1–1, Bastian 3.2–0–7–2.

VATICAN XI

R. Raphel not out	27
G. Abilash lbw Koch	4
J. Isac not out	17
Extra	11
	<u>59–1</u>

Bowling: Kottman 4–1–13–0, Koch 6.3–4–13–1, Snijder 1–0–12–0, Heikens 2–0–10–0.

CRICKETERS CONQUER EVEREST
MOUNT EVEREST BASE CAMP, APRIL 2009

When Richard Kirtley looked at a photograph of the Gorak Shep plateau in the Himalayas it reminded him of the Oval Cricket ground in London. Kirtley was surprised to discover that no one else had made the connection. Why had it never been used as a cricket pitch?

A 50-strong party, including 30 cricketers, groundstaff, doctors, spectators and photographers, set off to create a world record for a field sport played at high altitude. James Butler, a wicket-keeper/batsman from Harlow Cricket Club, trained for six months and lost 1st (6.4kg) in weight. At 33 he was the second oldest in the party.

The expedition began at Lord's cricket ground on 9 April and the match was played at the Mount Everest base camp on 21 April, birthday of Her Majesty the Queen. It took nine days of hard trekking through the Himalayas to reach base camp. Then they cleared stones, pebbles and rocks from an ice-covered crater so they could play competitive cricket at 16,945ft (5,165m). At that height it was like breathing through a straw.

In the Twenty20 match, Team Tenzing, captained by London lawyer Haydn Main, played Team Hillary, captained by Glen Lewis. The teams were named after the two men who, on 29 May 1953, were the first to stand on the mountain's peak – New Zealander Edmund Hillary and Nepalese Sherpa Tenzing Norgay.

With two overs to play Team Tenzing needed about 40 runs to win with the last pair at the wicket. That left them with a mountain to climb ... or, in this case, a mountain to descend. Team Hillary won by 36 runs and the party celebrated with champagne or cups of tea. They raised money for the Lord's Taverners and the Himalayan Trust UK.

UNDERGROUND CRICKET
HONISTER SLATE MINE, CUMBRIA, DECEMBER 2013

Threlkeld's cricket ground, one of the most beautiful in the United Kingdom, was seriously damaged by floods in June 2012. The estimated cost of the necessary repairs was £100,000. After the floods Threlkeld CC shared Braithwaite's ground for three years, by which time money for repairs had been raised and the ground was made ready for cricket.

The 2012 flooding was devastating. On the night of Friday, 22 June, the cricket club cancelled their annual summer dance because bad weather was forecast. Then hundreds of tons of rubble and sludge came down from the nearby Blencathra mountain and on to the cricket ground. A blocked culvert had made matters worse.

By the next morning the ground had been destroyed by the water and debris. It was a severe blow for the whole village because the cricket ground was used for school sports days and other local events such as the Threlkeld Olympics.

The Threlkeld club raised £60,000 by selling a calendar with photographs of cricketers in dramatic local settings. Photographer Stuart Holmes showed cricketers posing in places of natural beauty in the Lake District: underwater on the bed of the River Derwent (wearing wet-suits under cricket gear and using breathing equipment); on a frozen wicket at Sprinkling Tarn below Great End; on the back of a steam engine at Threlkeld Quarry; on the Lodore

Jetty at Derwentwater (with a wicket-keeper diving into the water); the rock-climbing venue of Shepherd's Crag (Borrowdale); on a disused railway line at Mosedale Viaduct (photographed from a gyrocopter); on the vertiginous Via Ferrata rope bridge above Honister Slate Mine, Keswick; at the ancient and mysterious Castlerigg Stone Circle at the top of Blencathra; on Rampsholme Island in the middle of Derwentwater; on stage at the Theatre by the Lake; near the summit of Blencathra Mountain; and in Market Square, Keswick. The last named needed an early morning call so that pictures could be taken before people arrived in the town centre.

Threlkeld's fund-raising also included the playing of cricket matches in unusual settings. They had a history of strange matches, including one against Braithwaite at the top of Latrigg on Boxing Day 2010. Then, on 5 December 2013, they raised awareness of the flood damage to their cricket ground by playing local rivals Caldbeck inside the Honister Slate Mine. The two teams made their way to 2,000ft (610m) underground and played a six-a-side, six-over match.

Honister was the last remaining working slate mine in England and had 11 miles (17.7km) of underground tunnels. The match rules meant that each cricketer bowled one over each and batsmen had to retire if they scored 24 runs. There were no boundary lines so batsmen had to run everything. Pieces of slate were used as bails. Caldbeck won with ten balls to spare.

CRICKETERS CONQUER KILIMANJARO

TANZANIA, SEPTEMBER 2014

Five years after the Everest cricket expedition, the record for the highest-ever cricket match was broken on Mount Kilimanjaro. This match was played near the 19,336ft (5,895m) summit.

The party took eight days to trek to the cricket pitch. Then they rolled out a plastic pitch over the ice and started a Twenty20 match. Gloves were needed by everybody during the match – not just the batsmen and wicket-keepers – and the cricketers had brought 24 spare balls in case too many ran away in the rarefied air.

On Kilimanjaro the Rhinos played the Gorillas. The Rhinos were captained by Ashley Giles, who had played 54 Test matches for England between 1998 and 2006, and the Gorillas were led by 23-year-old Heather Knight, a current England women's international. The party also included 37-year-old Makhaya Ntini, who had taken 390 Test wickets for South Africa in his international career, and Clare Connor, who had captained the England women's team from 2000–6.

One of the match sponsors was David Harper of Hotel Partners Africa. In an interview with *The Daily Telegraph*, Harper explained the rationale for his involvement: 'As I passed 40 it dawned on me the only way I was ever going to play cricket at the highest level was if I took the game to the top of a mountain.'

The cricket match raised money for three charities. Cancer Research UK was chosen because cancer had affected Clare Connor's family. Tusk Trust (an African wildlife conservation charity) was close to Ntini's heart. And the Rwanda Cricket Stadium Foundation, with Heather Knight as a patron, aimed to create a cricket pitch in Rwanda that was suitable for international cricket.

LIVINGSTONE'S INNINGS

NANTWICH, CHESHIRE, APRIL 2015

Nantwich played Caldy in a Dabbers' National Club Championship Knockout Cup tie. It was a 45-over match made remarkable for an amazing innings by 21-year-old Liam Livingstone.

'I think it was one of those days where everything I did came off,' Livingstone told Andrew McGlashan the day after the event. 'Every shot I tried to play came out of the middle, all my edges went past the fielders. I think it was just my day and luckily I cashed in when it was.' Livingstone didn't feel great when he went out to bat, and the third ball he received went through the gate and nearly bowled him. Then he hit the next ball for six and set the tone for a legendary innings.

Livingstone scored his first hundred from only 47 balls. After that he tried to whack every ball for six. He reached 150 from 67 balls and then his scoring rate became quicker and quicker. His parents hadn't originally planned to watch the match, but later they changed their minds so they were present for their son's innings.

When Livingstone reached 190 there was a break for fluid intake. A couple of his team-mates brought out drinks and told him that there were records to be broken. The team record was 499 and Livingstone wanted to beat that for the sake of his team.

The 21-year-old from Barrow, Cumbria, was considered an all-rounder as he was also a spin bowler. He had played for Cumberland before joining the Lancashire staff. In a match for Lancashire seconds, he had scored 204 from 242 balls against Yorkshire seconds. But his innings against Caldy was much more dramatic.

He reached 200 off 84 balls (21 fours and 15 sixes) and then 300 from 123 balls (31 fours and 22 sixes). Along the way he caused a bit of bother for the two scorers. The Caldy man was trying to keep up his scorebook with different coloured pens and the Nantwich scorer was being meticulous with his computer system.

Livingstone also caused trouble for his team-mates, who had to look for lost balls in the cemetery adjacent to Nantwich's Whitehouse Lane ground. It was estimated that Livingstone hit 16 balls into the cemetery during his innings. The Nantwich players spent a long time looking for them and the team's captain, Ray Doyle, jocularly threatened to charge the young man for losing them.

Eventually, Livingstone was caught by Nathaniel Alsop off the bowling of 17-year-old Harry Daniel-Jones. The Nantwich score was 493 for three, and Livingstone had made 350 from 138 balls. He had scored 298 in boundaries – 34 fours and 27 sixes – and in one over he hit four sixes and two fours. He went from 300 to 350 in only 14 balls.

Nantwich beat Caldy by exactly 500 runs. They scored 579 for seven from 45 overs and Caldy were 79 all out.

Livingstone received loads of congratulatory messages and he replied to them via Twitter: 'Had worse days ... Thanks for all the messages.'

Many people thought Livingstone's innings was a world record for a 45-over match but a more careful search showed that there were at least two other candidates. Shahzad Malik scored 403 in 137 balls (38 sixes) for Langleybury CC (Hertfordshire) against Middlesex Tamils in 2005, sharing a second-wicket partnership of 515 with P. Kerr; and United Cricket Club's Shabbir Mohammad hit an unbeaten 353 (25 sixes) in a 45-over match in California in 2006.

AFTERWORD

Three stories helped me sustain the momentum during the writing of this book. I didn't expect to find verification of the stories but I shall tell them anyway.

The first concerns a game in Lancashire which ended in stalemate. Two batsmen were trapped at the striker's end and the bowler held the ball over the stumps at the other end. One batsman set off towards the pavilion ... but the bowler wanted the other batsman out, so he waited in case the remaining batsman strayed out of his crease. Both teams then played for a draw.

Another story is a folk-tale about a single-wicket game of the 1800s. The details of the story vary between regions, but the essence is that two old men challenge each other to a game. One bats and scores ten or 20 runs over a long period. The other is so exhausted or injured by the unaccustomed bowling that he is incapable of batting. His opponent proceeds to bowl so many wides when aiming at the undefended stumps that victory goes to the man who never bats.

The final story is really a quiz question. In a limited-overs competition, the scores are level and there is one ball to come. The team batting first lost nine wickets, and the team now batting has lost only six wickets, thus looks certain to win as the team losing the least wickets will be the winner in the event of the scores remaining level. So how does the first team win without any of the batsmen being out in the same way? The answer is a bizarre assortment of strange events: one batsman is run out when backing up too far; another is out on the two-minute non-appearance law; a third backs up too far, the bowler shies at the stumps and the batsman, deliberately getting in the way, is given out for obstruction; the last is bowled. Please let me know if it ever really happens.

The selection of matches in this volume is probably affected by my personal biases, raised as I was in Yorkshire and Derbyshire in the 1950s and 1960s. The balance of games is almost certainly unfairly loaded towards the professional scene, which is better documented than the amateur game and which gives easier access to scorecards. I've been sure to include some local games but there must be many more and I would be interested to learn of worthy candidates.

There are some gaps I am very aware of. I have found no room for Married v Single, Left-hand v Right-hand, Slow bowlers v Fast bowlers, A to K against L to Z, Beardies v Shavers, Over-30 v Under-30 or even Over-32 v Under-32, all of which have taken place over the years.

The dominant source for the stories in this book has been local newspapers. *Wisden*, of course, has also been invaluable, as have Benny Green's *Wisden Anthologies*, *The Times*, *The Cricketer, Athletic News* and the *Illustrated Sporting & Dramatic News*. I am especially grateful to the staff of the Bodleian Library, Oxford, for allowing me easy access to the vast collection of cricket books.

I also acknowledge those people who pointed me towards some of the games – Ian Alister, Colin May, Tim Ward and David Watson. Special thanks are due to Keith Wright, who helped with the research for eight of the games, Karen MacDowell, vital to the Moreton-in-Marsh story, and David Kynaston, who generously gave his time and knowledge while also engaged on a book, *W.G.'s Birthday Party*. Any errors that remain, of course, are solely my own responsibility.

Andrew Ward